# Analytic
# Approaches to
# Twentieth-Century
# Music

# Analytic Approaches to Twentieth-Century Music

Joel Lester

Professor of Music, The City College of New York
and The Graduate Center, City University of New York

## W. W. NORTON & COMPANY

NEW YORK ▪ LONDON

## ACKNOWLEDGMENTS

Since this page cannot legibly accommodate all the copyright notices, page 304 constitutes an extension of the copyright page.

**Belmont Music Publishers**

Schoenberg, *Chamber Symphony No. 1*, op. 9. Used by permission of Belmont Music Publishers—pp. 160–61

Schoenberg, *Klavierstück*, op. 33a. Used by permission of Belmont Music Publishers—pp. 3, 10, 182–83

Schoenberg, *String Quartet No. 3*. Used by permission of Belmont Music Publishers—pp. 86, 204–5

Schoenberg, *Variations*, op. 31. Used by permission of Belmont Music Publishers—pp. 216–17

**Boelke-Bomart, Inc.**

Schoenberg, *Tot*, op. 48, no. 2 © Copyright 1952 by Bomart Music Publications, Inc.; assigned 1955 to Boelke-Bomart, Inc.; revised edition © 1979 by Boelke-Bomart, Inc. Used by permission—p. 132

**Boosey and Hawkes, Inc.**

Bartók, *Concerto for Orchestra* © Copyright 1946 by Hawkes & Son (London) Ltd. Copyright Renewed. Reprinted by permission of Boosey & Hawkes, Inc.—pp. 128–31

Bartók, *Contrasts* © Copyright 1942 by Hawkes & Son (London) Ltd. Copyright Renewed. Reprinted by permission of Boosey & Hawkes, Inc.—p. 21

Bartók, *Mikrokosmos* © Copyright 1940 by Hawkes & Son (London) Ltd. Copyright Renewed. Reprinted by permission of Boosey & Hawkes, Inc.—pp. 112, 116, 136

Bartók, *Music for Strings, Percussion, and Celesta* © 1937 by Universal Edition. © Renewed. All Rights Reserved. Copyright & Renewal assigned to Boosey & Hawkes, Inc., for USA. Reprinted by permission. Used for the territory of the world excluding the United States by permission of European American Music Distributors Corporation, sole U.S. and Canadian agent for Universal Edition—pp. 30, 48–50, 67–78

Bartók, *String Quartet No. 2* Copyright 1920 by Universal Edition. Copyright Renewed. All Rights Reserved. Copyright & Renewal assigned to Boosey & Hawkes, Inc., for USA. Reprinted by permission. Used for the territory of the world excluding the United States by permission of European American Music Distributors Corporation, sole U.S. and Canadian agent for Universal Edition—pp. 59–60

Bartók, *String Quartet No. 3* Copyright 1922 by Universal Edition. Copyright Renewed. All Rights Reserved. Copyright & Renewal assigned to Boosey & Hawkes, Inc., for USA. Reprinted by permission. Used for the territory of the world excluding the United States by permission of European American Music Distributors Corporation, sole U.S. and Canadian agent for Universal Edition—pp. 154–56

(Continued on p. 304)

#|18520606

Library of Congress Cataloging-in-Publication Data
Lester, Joel.
Analytic approaches to twentieth-century music.
Includes bibliographies and index.
1. Musical analysis.   2. Music—20th century—
History and criticism.   I. Title.
MT6.L365A5   1989      780'.904      88-28878

ISBN 0-393-95762-4

W. W. Norton & Company, Inc.,
500 Fifth Avenue, New York, N.Y. 10110

W. W. Norton & Company Ltd.,
Castle House, 75/76 Wells Street, London W1T 3QT

6 7 8 9 0

# Contents

Preface      ix

To the Student      xi

*UNIT ONE* **TONALITY AND TWENTIETH-CENTURY MUSIC**      1

     The Legacy of Tonality, 1

*Chapter 1* **Pitch in Tonal and Nontonal Music**      3

     Functional Harmony as Directed Motion, 4

     The Dissolution of Functional Tonality, 6

     Motives and Sets in Tonal and Nontonal Music, 7

     Pitch Names in Tonal and Nontonal Music, 12

     Points for Review, 13

     Exercises, 13

*Chapter 2* **Rhythm and Meter**      15

     Meter in Tonal Music, 16

     Meter in Twentieth-Century Music, 18

     Rhythmic Motives, 29

     Points for Review, 31

     Exercises, 31

     Suggestions for Further Study, 32

*Chapter 3* **Texture and Timbre**      33

     Texture, Phrasing, and Form, 34

     New Types of Textures, 40

     Timbre, 44

     Placement of Timbral Changes, 51

     Points for Review, 53

     Exercises, 54

     Suggestions for Further Study, 55

*Chapter 4* **Form**                                                                 56

    Forms Based on Tonal Models, 57

    New Formal Possibilities, 61

    Points for Review, 63

    Exercises, 63

*UNIT TWO* **PITCH STRUCTURES**                                                      65

*Chapter 5* **Pitches, Intervals, Melody**                                           66

    Pitches and Pitch-Classes, 66

    Intervals, 68

    Interval-Class, 72

    Model Analysis: Melody, 73

    Points for Review, 76

    Exercises, 76

*Chapter 6* **Pitch-Class Sets**                                                     81

    Pitch-Class Sets, 81

    A Single Name for Each Pitch-Class Set: Lowest Ordering, 84

    Locating Pitch-Class Sets, 88

    Points for Review, 90

    Exercises, 91

*Chapter 7* **Interval Content**                                                     97

    Interval Content, 97

    Compositional and Expressive Effects of Pitch-Class Sets, 101

    Points for Review, 105

    Exercises, 105

    Suggestions for Further Study, 107

*Chapter 8* **Using Different Pitch-Class Sets**                                     108

    Relations among Pitch-Class Sets, 108

    Unity and Variety Using Transpositions of a Set, 109

    Relationships among Inversions of a Set, 113

    Unity and Variety Using Different Sets, 114

    Some Other Relationships in Pieces and Sets, 132

    Points for Review, 134

    Exercises, 134

    Suggestions for Further Study, 143

*Chapter 9* **Pitch-Class Regions, Scales, Modes**              146

    The Diatonic Scale, 147

    The Whole-Tone Scale, 158

    The Octatonic Scale, 162

    Other Pitch-Class Regions, 168

    Summary to Unit Two, 169

    Points for Review, 169

    Exercises, 170

    Suggestions for Further Study, 171


*UNIT THREE* **SERIAL MUSIC**                                   173

  *Chapter 10* **Twelve-Tone Series**                  175

    The Twelve-Tone Series, 175

    Locating the Twelve-Tone Series in a Piece, 182

    Points for Review, 184

    Exercises, 184

  *Chapter 11* **Common Elements**                     189

    Hearing Twelve-Tone Series, 189

    Common Intervals and Subsets, 190

    Uncovering Common Elements, 203

    Points for Review, 203

    Exercises, 204

    Suggestions for Further Study, 207

  *Chapter 12* **Hexachordal Combinatoriality**         209

    Combinatoriality in the Works of Schoenberg, 211

    Hexachordal Compositions, 214

    Points for Review, 215

    Exercises, 215

    Suggestions for Further Study, 218

  *Chapter 13* **Derived Series**                       219

    Derived Series, 219

    Derived Series and Webern's Music, 221

    Multiple Derived Series in a Single
      Composition, 228

    Points for Review, 232

    Exercises, 232

    Suggestions for Further Study, 234

*Chapter 14* **Multiple Orderings of Twelve-Tone Series**     235

      In Schoenberg's Music, 235

      In Berg's Music, 237

      Stravinsky's Twelve-Tone Music, 242

      Points for Review, 252

      Exercises, 253

      Suggestions for Further Study, 253

*Chapter 15* **Other Aspects of Serialism**     256

      Series with Fewer than Twelve Pitch-Classes, 256

      Serialization of Rhythm, 264

      Serialization of Other Aspects, 269

      Points for Review, 271

      Exercises, 271

      Suggestions for Further Study, 273

*UNIT FOUR* **SINCE WORLD WAR II**     275

*Chapter 16* **More Recent Developments**     276

      A Century of Change, 276

      Serial Music, 277

      Freer Pitch Structures, 285

      Timbre, 288

      Improvisatory and Aleatoric Music, 295

      Simplification of the Musical Language:
         Tonality, Minimalism, 296

      A Codetta, 297

      Points for Review, 298

      Exercises, 298

Appendix: Combinatorial Hexachords     299

Glossary of Foreign Terms     302

Index     305

# *Preface*

The perception of twentieth-century music in the musical community has substantially changed during the last generation from awareness of "that dissonant mishmash" to recognition of a repertoire of expressive works taking their place alongside other musics of our heritage. This same generation has witnessed the development of several new theoretical approaches that treat the languages of twentieth-century music on their own terms, not as distortions of the rhetoric of earlier music, as some earlier approaches did. In addition to reflecting the way many musicians now perceive and react to this music, these new approaches are transforming the way we understand this music.

Unfortunately, most presentations of this new theory are replete with jargon, while containing little that assists novices in learning how to relate it to their perceptions and to an understanding of the music's expressive content. *Analytic Approaches to Twentieth-Century Music* introduces these theories with as little jargon as possible, emphasizing those aspects that lead to more informed hearing of this music's structure and content.

One problem in teaching analysis of twentieth-century music is the widespread ignorance of twentieth-century repertoire. *Analytic Approaches to Twentieth Century Music* addresses this problem by including numerous analyses of excerpts from the literature to demonstrate the audible and expressive effects of all the theoretical matters discussed. Excerpts from a wide range of repertoire are discussed in Units One, Two, and Three, but a small number of pieces by Babbitt, Bartók, Debussy, Messiaen, Schoenberg, Stravinsky, and Webern are the source for many discussions. As students come upon discussions of new aspects of these excerpts, they will add these new insights to what they have already learned, all the while gaining considerable familiarity with a number of works in contrasting styles. Most of these pieces are for solo piano or chamber ensemble. In many classes, the students themselves will be able to perform these works.

This book contains four separate units. Unit One focuses on aspects of musical structure other than pitch: including rhythm, texture, timbre, form, and the relationship of tonal music to the musics of the twentieth century. Units Two and Three deal with pitch structure: Unit Two with aspects of pitch-class sets and Unit Three with serial music. The single chapter in Unit Four surveys music of recent decades.

Throughout *Analytic Approaches to Twentieth-Century Music*, musical examples illustrate how each theoretical point affects the sound of a passage. In addition, most chapters contain analytic discussions of considerable length and depth, which serve a dual purpose: they demonstrate the effects of theoretical matters on structure and expression, focusing the student's attention on hearing the music, and they provide models for the student's own analytic work.

Each chapter concludes with Points for Review (a summary of essential factual material), Exercises (drills, definitions, analyses, and, in some chapters, structured composition exercises), as well as Suggestions for Further Study (references to readings and pieces for analysis).

This text is not a survey of twentieth-century music. Some composers of stature are not mentioned here, and many important works are omitted. Once students learn the approaches to analysis, they can study any piece or style.

Similarly, this is not a compendium of all theories of twentieth-century music. Nor does it offer any particular theory in full detail as presented by its original author. What is included are those aspects that I deem to be of the greatest relevance to a student beginning work in this field.

No book of this sort is possible without acknowledging the work of many theorists. The pioneering studies by Milton Babbitt, George Perle, and Allen Forte were invaluable guides, as were innumerable articles and books written during the past half-century. Suggestions and comments by readers of various drafts of the manuscript were particularly helpful, especially those from Professors Richmond Browne (University of Michigan), Douglass Green (University of Texas), Leo Kraft (Queens College), and Joseph Straus (Queens College). I am indebted to Claire Brook for her meticulous editing of the final draft, and to Juli Goldfein for attending to innumerable production details.

Joel Lester
Bronx, New York
October, 1988

# To the Student

The focus of this text is the analysis of twentieth-century music—the medium through which composers of our time address us. There is no single "correct" way to analyze or to listen to twentieth-century music, or to any music for that matter. Perception of a work of art is a personal matter. As a result, this book does not pretend to teach "the" way to listen to twentieth-century music. Rather, it introduces you to some approaches that can lead to more informed listening by giving you an idea of how musical materials are used and how sonic and expressive effects are achieved.

As you read this book, you will be assisted in gaining familiarity with its material by several aids. Under each chapter title you will find a list of important terms, and at the end of each chapter you will find *Points for Review*, both designed to help you locate the focal issues. Each chapter also contains a range of exercises designed to increase your facility in analysis and to introduce you to further applications of the material.

The music examples are an integral part of the text. It is important for you to *hear* the effects of an analysis in the music provided. Learn to hear these examples in any convenient way. Most of them are for solo piano or small chamber ensemble, so that you may be able to play them by yourself or with your classmates. If this is not possible, listen to the music on recordings. Since many of the excerpts are from the same compositions, as you familiarize yourself with the examples in one chapter you will be preparing to hear additional aspects of the same music in later chapters. Many chapters feature extended analyses that are intended to guide you in your own analytic work.

# Unit One

---

# Tonality and Twentieth-Century Music

## The Legacy of Tonality

Before the twentieth century, the word *music* generally meant *functional tonal music* in the Western world. Virtually all folk, popular, and concert music and most religious music was tonal and had been tonal for all living memory. Even today, the contemporary music world continues to include a great deal of tonal music. In the classical music world, a large portion of the repertoire in concerts, opera houses, and on the radio is tonal. In more popular and commercial styles, virtually all rock, jazz, country music, music in advertisements, in elevators, in department stores, in airports, in movies, and on television is tonal. All the nursery rhymes, children's songs, folk songs, hymns, and anthems that form our early musical experiences are tonal.

It is in this largely tonal environment that we experience nontonal music. And it is in this tonal environment that composers of our century create their music.

Because so much music we hear is tonal, and because most students come to the study of twentieth-century music from tonal music, it will help us to survey those elements of musical sound that are common to all music. In that way, we will have a point of reference in studying how those elements contribute to the sounds and sense of nontonal music.

For tonality is more than a way of organizing melody and harmony that projects a single central tone, and more than a relationship among harmonies or a particular way of handling voice leading. Tonality affects just about every aspect of music, including phrasing, form, the interaction of melody and harmony, texture, orchestration, dynamics, articulation, the structuring of time (rhythm, meter, and the sense of continuity and motion)—even the way we name pitches and intervals. If a piece is not tonal, then many of these musical aspects take on new characteristics.

The chapters in Unit One cover important elements that occur in all music: pitch, rhythm, texture, timbre, and form. These chapters survey these musical elements as they are used in tonal music and as they appear in a variety of twentieth-century musical styles.

# 1

# Pitch in Tonal and Nontonal Music

---

*functional harmony      motive      set*

---

Listen to the opening measures of the following two pieces:

EXAMPLE 1-1
*a:* J. S. Bach, *Two-Part Invention in C major*

*b:* Schoenberg, *Klavierstück*, op. 33a

Even before you have heard much of either piece, you know that Bach's *Invention* is tonal and that Schoenberg's *Klavierstück* is not. The former immediately establishes a tonic and the familiar sound of tonal voice leadings and harmonies, while the latter does not. The way the pitches interact with each other in these pieces is what makes this difference so apparent, for tonality is above all a language of pitch relationships.

Because the way in which pitches are used is such an important aspect of music, we will begin our survey of various elements in tonal and nontonal music by considering pitch. This chapter covers three aspects of pitch in tonal and nontonal music:

**1.** Tonal harmony or voice leading is a language of pitch relationships shared by all tonal pieces, a language that plays a major role in shaping the musical gestures and creating the sense of direction in tonal music. There is no comparable language of pitch relationships shared by nontonal pieces.

**2.** The motives of a tonal piece interact with the harmony and voice leading common to all tonal music. Since there is no pitch language shared by all nontonal pieces, motives in nontonal music play an essential role in determining the pitches of the piece.

**3.** There are such fundamental differences between the way tonal and nontonal music use pitches and intervals that in order to analyze nontonal music, we need new names for pitches and intervals.

## Functional Harmony as Directed Motion

What do we mean when we talk of harmony in tonal music? We may think first of groups of pitches called chords, of the voice leading that connects these chords to one another, and of the melodies that are supported by these chord progressions. When we study tonal harmony, these issues occupy our attention.

In a broader sense, tonal harmony also refers to the manner in which gestures are created and shaped in tonal music. As we will see, it is the very nature of tonal harmony that helps create these gestures and shapes. From this broader perspective, a progression or voice leading from one chord to another is more than just a succession of blocks of pitches, for that progression directs motion toward or away from important harmonic and melodic goals. The approach to, arrival on, and departure from these important harmonic goals and points of initiation are closely related to the creation of phrases and larger sections, thereby contributing to the sense of form and gesture in tonal music.

It is the absence of this organizing power of tonal harmony that we react to immediately when we hear nontonal music. Not only are familiar tonal chords absent, but in the absence of these familiar harmonies and progressions we may lose our bearings in terms of expected goals and gestures. Nontonal music does of course create its own gestures, but by a rather different sense of pitch, harmony, and voice leading.

*Tonal Harmony and the Flow of Time.*   The organizing power of tonal harmony lies in its ability to shape the flow of musical time. It does this by establishing different tonal harmonies as different locations in musical space and then channeling the direction of harmonic motion between these locations.

The tonic is clearly a different location from, say, the dominant; the supertonic is yet another location. When these harmonies move from one to another, they shape the motion between harmonic goals on several structural levels. The tonic, for instance, when approached by a strong dominant, is most often a goal of harmonic motion. Arrival at a tonic goal brings a span of motion to an end. Some harmonies in this span may have been extended for a time by neighboring or passing harmonies. For instance, a II chord, ultimately on its way to V, may be extended by a dominant of II, creating a digression from the main line of motion. Similarly, a deceptive resolution of V to VI signals a step backward to an earlier point in the directed motion toward a concluding tonic—VI will return to V, perhaps preceded by other harmonies, before completing the motion to I.

Also in tonal music, we hear similar harmonic motions both at local levels and in the large. A dominant, for instance, may elaborate a tonic locally (say, a first-inversion V between two tonic chords). The dominant may also be an important goal of its own at the phrase level. Chords other than the tonic may be elaborated by their own dominants. And the dominant as a key is a frequent large-scale goal leading eventually back to the tonic key. It is the interaction of all these factors that gives rise to the supple and expressive shaping of gestures in tonal music.

The tonal harmonic language is so powerful that it can even affect our perceptions in an abstract progression, such as:

EXAMPLE 1-2

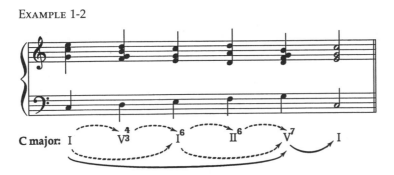

Arrows below the music illustrate various directions of harmonic motion in the phrase. The solid arrows indicate the essential, supporting I–V–I progression; the dotted arrows show subsidiary harmonic motions that lead in some cases to the chords immediately following, and in other cases to more distant goals. Listen to the progression while following the various directed motions indicated by the arrows.

Despite the apparent complexities of directed motions in this progression, the passage is actually far simpler than an excerpt from a real tonal composition. There are no nonharmonic tones here, the texture is entirely chordal, and only the simplest of harmonic interactions appear. There are no ambiguous chords, chromatic notes, deceptive resolutions, melodic motives over individual harmonies, and no variations in the harmonic rhythm. And the meter is ambiguous—that is, any of several meters would be plausible.

Although these factors are absent, we are aware of an intricate structuring of harmonic flow. This harmonic flow causes us to experience points of initiation and arrival, and to perceive motions to and from these points of initiation and arrival. We know which chords are goals, which are connections, which elaborate subsidiary goals, and so forth. In following these motions in a piece of music, we follow one aspect of the expression of the music.

*Functional Tonality.*    All of this is what is meant by the term *functional tonality*. Every tonal composition is unique in the way its gestures, motives, melodies, textures, phrasings, and the like are shaped. But in every tonal piece, the meaning of a given harmonic progression is similar. We may hear a tonal piece for the very first time, yet we still know that a V–I progression at the end of a phrase is a strong cadential motion (that is, the arrival on a goal), that V–VI is a deceptive resolution, and that II–VI is not the kind of progression that will articulate a strong cadence.

We know all this because all tonal compositions share this basic language of harmonies and voice leadings. We have been exposed to this language since birth, and have developed an extraordinary sensitivity to its expressive nuances.

Part of the reason that we have been able to learn this harmonic language is that the vocabulary of functional harmonies used in tonal music is so small, and the differentiation of intervals so clear-cut. Of all the possible ways that three pitches can be combined, only the major and minor triads are stable harmonies in tonal music. And these two types of chords contain the same intervals: major and minor thirds and sixths, and perfect fourths and fifths. The triads are the standard for consonance, an important criterion in defining a harmonic goal in tonal music.

# The Dissolution of Functional Tonality

Throughout the history of tonal music, composers expressed themselves within the tonal language of their time. What happened increasingly during the nineteenth century is that many composers sought new harmonic effects for individuality's sake. The long-term result of these new harmonic effects was a gradual loosening of the bonds of functional tonality. The principal features of this trend were:

**1.** The increasing use of chromaticism, which weakens the diatonic basis of functional tonality, the secure status of the key, and the secure status of goals within a key.

**2.** The increasing use of dissonance in the form of nonharmonic tones, dissonant chords, and altered chords, which weakens the consonance-dissonance distinction crucial to harmonic stability and resolution.

**3.** The increasing use of distant harmonic relationships between consecutive chords and key areas, which weakens the distinction between closely related and distantly related tonal areas, and blurs the status of harmonic goals.

**4.** The use of modal alterations and nondiatonic scales, often for exotic effects, which also weakens the clarity of harmonic and melodic goals.

**5.** The avoidance of direct statements of the basic functional harmonic progressions and voice leadings, since in this new harmonic and tonal environment, simple progressions sounded too old-fashioned and banal.

The first stages of this trend are perceptible in some music from the early nineteenth century. In works from the 1850s and later, most of these features are increasingly prevalent. By the beginning of the twentieth century, functional tonality ceased to be a controlling influence over harmony and voice leading in the music of some composers. Recognizable functional harmonies and progressions no longer appeared in their works.

This change in musical language took place at different times for different composers, arising from different sources and motivations for each of them. The music that was created in new pitch languages is the focus of most of this text.

Not all music after this transitional period is without a sense of tonic or without moments of functional tonality. Many composers continued to write music that is tonal in the traditional sense, although often with new types of harmonies and voice leadings not found in tonal music from before 1900. In addition, a great deal of nontonal music has focal pitches. But as we will see in later chapters, a focal pitch outside of functionally tonal music is not a tonic with all that that term connotes. Triads, seventh chords, ninth chords, and other chords that occur in tonal music also occur in quite a bit of nontonal music, but not necessarily as functionally tonal chords.

## Motives and Sets in Tonal and Nontonal Music

In most tonal pieces, the motives or thematic building blocks are so closely wedded to the harmonic-melodic structure of the work that we may think of the motivic and the harmonic/voice-leading structures as one. But even in these cases, the underlying harmonic-melodic structure may be identical to that of another tonal piece without these motives. We will study this feature in J. S. Bach's *Two-Part Invention in C major*. Listen to the opening of this piece:

EXAMPLE 1-3: J. S. Bach, *Two-Part Invention in C major*

The pattern announced by the first seven sixteenth-notes, labeled *x* in Example 1-3, is the motivic idea of the piece. Motive *x* appears alone, unaccompanied, at the very opening of the piece, and provides a basis for almost every pitch in the entire *Invention*. It is transposed, as in mm. 1 and 2; it is inverted, as in the right hand in m. 3. Parts of motive *x* occur separately, either in their original rhythm or with different durations. The four-note scale (*a*) that opens motive *x* recurs as eighth notes in the left hand in mm. 3 and 4. The arpeggiated thirds (*b*, the second half of motive *x*) recur in the right hand in beats 1 and 2 of m. 6. Finally, the voice-leading basis of motive *x* is the neighbor motion shown in Example 1-4. This neighbor pattern is the basis of the eighth-note counterpoint to motive *x* in mm. 1 and 2.

EXAMPLE 1-4

This invention, so typical of tonal music by the masters, allows all these appearances of motive *x* to fit into the harmonic plan and structural voice leading of the section with amazing ease. The opening three measures serve to establish the key, the principal registers, and the textures of the piece. The right hand, for instance, starts with C–E in m. 1 and opens up to E an octave higher by m. 3. In the process, the voice leading and harmonies announce the key and principal registers of the entire invention. Listen to the separate lines that converge on the right-hand E in m. 3 (the C–D–E and the G–F–E):

EXAMPLE 1-5

There are notes not a part of motive *x*, but important to the structural voice-leading, such as the D on the downbeat and third beat of m. 2. These notes frame *x* in the right hand. At other points, the content of *x* changes its import. The C–B–C eighth-note motion in the right hand in m. 1 forms a neighbor to C. But the G–F–G in the same position in m. 2 initiates the G–F–E motion leading to the E in m. 3 (see Example 1-5). This remarkable marriage between structure (the tonal language) and content (motives of a given piece) is a primary characteristic of all tonal music.

Yet the marriage is a fragile one. It does not take much change to retain the motivic structure of the *Invention* but destroy its harmonic and tonal structure. The motives could be transposed differently; the bass in m. 1, for instance, could answer on C♯ or F♯. Or the alternation of whole and half steps between adjacent notes in the motive could be retained in each transformation: the last seven right-hand notes in m. 3 could read F–E♭–D♭–C–E♭–D♭–F. The motivic structure of the invention would remain, but the piece would no longer be tonal.

This is precisely what happens in nontonal works of the twentieth century. Tonal voice leading and harmonies no longer provide a basis for the pitch structure of a piece. In their place, motivic relationships among groups of pitches generate melody and harmony. Analysis of this music entails locating these motives, and understanding the ways they are used. Listen to the opening of Schoenberg's *Klavierstück*, op. 33a:

EXAMPLE 1-6: Schoenberg, *Klavierstück*, op. 33a

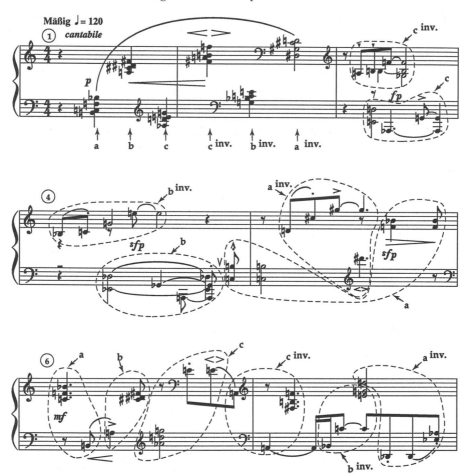

Like Bach's *C-Major Invention*, this piece announces its basic musical idea right at the beginning. The three four-note chords in m. 1 (labeled *a, b, c*) provide the pitch structures for the entire composition. Each chord occurs inverted in m. 2, as shown in Example 1-7. And in the measures that follow, the notes of *a, b,* and *c* in their original and inverted forms provide the basis for all the adjacent pitches. (See the circled groups of pitches in Example 1-6.)

EXAMPLE 1-7

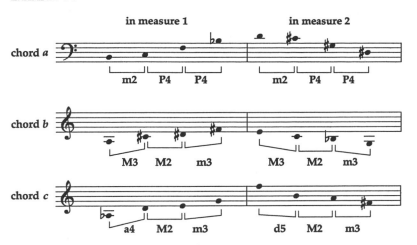

In that Schoenberg's *Klavierstück* opens with its basic motives, and derives every note in the passage from these motives, it resembles Bach's *Invention*. The difference between the pieces lies in how these motives function. The motives in the *Invention* exist along with the underlying voice leading and harmonies characteristic of all tonal music. By contrast, the *Klavierstück* contains no vestiges of functional tonality. To be sure, chord *b* is a seventh chord: a half-diminished seventh in m. 1, inverted to become a dominant seventh in m. 2. But these "seventh chords" are without any of the harmonic or voice-leading implications they would carry in a tonal composition. They do not resolve. The "C dominant-seventh chord" in m. 2 in no way implies the key of F major. And these seventh chords are no different in influence than the nontonal chords *a* and *c*. Rather, the pitch structure in this piece derives equally from the three chords *a*, *b*, and *c*.

The sense in which harmonies and melodies are motivic in the *Klavierstück* involves a more extended use of the term *motive* than is customary in tonal music. The motivic structure is the basis of all the melodies, all the harmonies, all the groupings of pitches, and even the voice leading (in the sense that the adjacent pitches come from the motives).

For this reason, we need a term different from *motive* to describe these pitch structures. This term is *set*, meaning a group of pitches. In this book we will continue to use *motive* for thematic patterns lying on the surface of the music, such as the motives in Bach's *Invention in C*. The term *set* will refer to the types of structural motives that underlie nontonal music. Unit Two discusses sets in general; Unit Three discusses special sets using all the twelve notes in the chromatic octave in a specific order.

# Pitch Names in Tonal and Nontonal Music

*Tonal Intervals and Pitches.*    The presence or absence of tonality affects the way we hear intervals and pitches. In tonal music, we determine the size of an interval according to the number of scale steps involved, not according to its absolute size. For a dramatic illustration, listen to the two intervals circled in Example 1-8. Each is eight semitones large, yet their effects differ dramatically. The first is a dissonant alteration of an interval (an augmented fifth), the second is a consonant interval (a minor sixth). As you listen to the example, note how little supporting evidence is needed to turn one form into the other. Our ears are so attuned to the subtleties of tonal harmony that a single preceding harmony can effect this change.

EXAMPLE 1-8

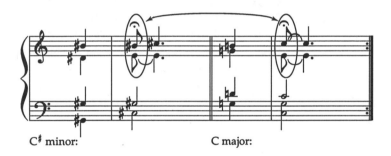

C♯ minor:                              C major:

Example 1-8 also demonstrates how pitch names are dependent upon tonal function. It would be wrong to notate the first circled interval as E–C, just as it would be wrong to notate the second as E–B♯, even though C and B♯ may be played on the same piano key.

In tonal music the very identity of a pitch or interval depends on its position in relation to a major or minor scale. This is part of the reason that we name the *twelve* pitches in the octave with *seven* letter-names according to the seven scale steps in a major or minor scale, using sharps or flats where necessary. Similarly, we recognize seven basic types of intervals: unisons (and octaves), seconds, thirds, fourths, fifths, sixths, and sevenths. We specify the exact size of an interval by its quality: major, minor, perfect, augmented, or diminished. As we have noted in Example 1-8, intervals that have the same number of semitones need not have the same number of scale steps. The sound and effect of such enharmonically equivalent intervals depends on the number of scale-steps they contain, not on their absolute size.

*Intervals and Pitches in Nontonal Music.*    Since much of the non-tonal music studied in this text is not based on a diatonic scale, there is no longer any basis for the classification of pitch names and interval names derived from seven scale-steps. Any change of a semitone is a change to a new type of pitch, rather than a mere change in the inflection of a scale step. E–B♯ and E–C, for instance, do not have a systematically different meaning outside of a diatonic scale.

Similarly, any change of an interval by a semitone results in a new interval, not merely a change in the quality of the interval. C–E♭ and C–E, for instance, are both types of thirds in tonal music, different in nature from C–F, which is a fourth. But in the absence of a diatonic scale, C–E♭, C–E, and C–F are simply three different types of intervals.

We need new names for intervals and pitches to reflect this new situation. The beginning of Unit Two discusses these new pitch and interval names. But before proceeding to that new terminology, we will pursue our survey of the effects of tonality on rhythm and meter (Chapter 2), texture and timbre (Chapter 3), and form (Chapter 4).

# Points for Review

**1.** Tonality is more than a system of harmony and voice leading. It affects all aspects of musical structure. Functional harmonies are a principal factor creating a sense of motion and shaping the gestures of tonal pieces.

**2.** Beginning in the nineteenth century, several factors contributed to the dissolution of tonality: increased chromaticism, increased levels of dissonance, increasingly distant harmonic relationships, use of modal and nondiatonic scales, avoidance of functional progressions, and the increased importance of motives as determinants of melody and harmony.

**3.** The language of functional tonality is common to all tonal pieces. In nontonal music, where there is no pitch language that is shared by all pieces, harmonic and melodic structures arise motivically. The term *sets* refers to the motives that underlie the pitch structure of nontonal pieces.

**4.** In tonal pieces, intervals and pitches are identified by their location in a major or minor scale. For nontonal music, we need new pitch and interval names that are not dependent upon a diatonic basis.

# Exercises for Chapter 1

## Suggestions for Further Study

1. Several composers around the turn of the twentieth century changed from tonal to nontonal styles, or flirted with a suspended sense of tonality. Listen for the stylistic evolutions in the following works by these six composers:

a) Arnold Schoenberg (1874–1951):
   *Verklärte Nacht*, op. 4 (1899)
   String Quartet No. 1, op. 7 (1905)
   *Chamber Symphony*, op. 9 (1906)
   String Quartet No. 2, op. 10 (1908)
   *Three Pieces for Piano*, op. 11 (1908)
   *Pierrot Lunaire*, op. 12 (1912)

b) Igor Stravinsky (1882–1971)
   *The Fire Bird* (1910)
   *Petrushka* (1911)
   *The Rite of Spring* (1913)

c) Béla Bartók (1881–1945)
   String Quartet No. 1 (1908)
   String Quartet No. 2 (1917)

d) Jean Sibelius (1865–1957)
   Symphony No. 2 (1901–02)
   Symphony No. 4 (1911)

e) Claude Debussy (1862–1918)
   *Rêverie for piano* (1890)
   String Quartet (1893)
   *La Mer* (1905)
   *Preludes for Piano* (1910–13)
   *Jeux* (1912)

f) Alexander Skryabin (1872–1915)
   *Preludes*, op. 37 (1903)
   *Poem of Ecstasy*, op. 54 (1905–08)
   *Prometheus*, op. 60 (1908–10)

2. Among the many articles written about the dissolution of tonality and its effects on musical structure, none is more important historically than Arnold Schoenberg's "Problems of Harmony," originally published in *Modern Music* 11 (1934): 167–86, and reprinted in *Style and Idea*, by Arnold Schoenberg, edited by Leonard Stein (New York: St. Martin's Press, 1975): 268–87. Another discussion by Schoenberg concerning the dissolution of tonality is found in the final chapter of his *Harmonielehre* (third edition, Vienna: Universal-Edition, 1922): 422–66; translated into English by Roy Carter (Berkeley: University of California Press, 1978): Chapters 19–22 (pp. 350–422).

# 2
# Rhythm and Meter

---

*rhythm*                        *polymeter*
*composite rhythm*              *ameter*
*meter*                         *tempo*
*irregular meter*               *metric modulation*
*added value*                   *rhythmic motives*
*changing meter*

---

The term *rhythm* denotes those aspects of music that deal with time and the organization of time. In its most common usage, rhythm refers to *durations:* of individual notes, of harmonies (the *harmonic rhythm),* of all the parts in a texture (the *composite rhythm),* of phrase lengths, of changes in dynamics, of changes in texture, and so forth. Rhythm also encompasses the qualities of *accentuation* that enliven these durational patterns: metric accents, accents caused by long notes, by high and low notes, by harmonic change, by dynamic stresses, and the like. And, finally, rhythm refers to the *continuity and flow* of musical gestures across all of these durations and accentuations.

Since rhythm arises from activity in other musical aspects, especially pitch, which we have not yet discussed, this survey of rhythm in twentieth-century music must remain somewhat superficial. Nonetheless, we can gain some perspective on this music and continue our survey of the similarities and differences between nontonal music and tonal music by examining some general rhythmic situations. When we proceed with a full discussion of pitch in Units Two and Three, we will have many opportunities to add to our understanding of rhythm in twentieth-century music.

An incredibly wide range of rhythmic situations may be found in twentieth-century music. Some of it features rhythm and meter much like that found in tonal music. Other works contain totally innovative rhythmic and metric effects. In yet other pieces, the composer leaves the choice of rhythmic values to the performer. Two performances of such a piece could offer rhythms entirely different from one another. Despite this extreme range, we can make some general remarks about rhythm in twentieth-century music.

# Meter in Tonal Music

In virtually all tonal music, regularly recurring pulses mark off the passage of time. These pulses fall into recurring patterns of strong and weak, a phenomenon we call *meter*. The *meter signature* indicates the notated value of the pulse and the number of pulses in the recurring patterns of strong and weak. In the case of a compound meter (such as $\frac{6}{8}$), additional notational conventions tell us how several pulses group into a larger pulse.

*Metric Regularity and Irregularity.*    In most tonal pieces, in addition to *metric regularity* (a continuous stream of stronger and weaker beats as indicated in the meter signature) on the level indicated in the meter signature, there is some metric regularity on faster and slower levels. For instance, in a piece in $\frac{2}{4}$ meter, the quarter-note beats are regularly divided into two eighths, with the eighths dividing regularly into sixteenths. And the two-beat measures may themselves be organized into pairs or groups of three.

Although metric regularity on several levels may continue for some time, hardly any tonal piece maintains metric regularity on *all* levels for very long. Changes may occur in the beat subdivisions (from eighths to triplets), in the number of measures in a group, and even in the number of beats in a measure (sometimes indicated by the meter signature, sometimes not). Two or more beat-divisions may occur simultaneously (such as triplets along with eighths). But at some levels, regularity is maintained through almost all tonal passages. For a particularly complex metric situation in a tonal passage, listen to mm. 23–27 from the slow movement of Mozart's *"Jupiter" Symphony*. (See facing page.) On the fastest level, the sixteenth sextuplets in the accompaniment conflict with the syncopated eighths in the melody. On a slower level, the quarters are grouped in pairs, conflicting with the previous triple meter. But throughout the passage the quarter-note units and the eighth-note units remain constant.

---

*Metric Regularity and Tonal Music.*    It is not coincidental that metric regularity is a feature of tonal music, for it is by this means that functional harmonies and voice leadings receive some of their strength. Regular metric levels in tonal music reinforce harmonic-melodic goals by providing specific points in time (namely beats, measures, and beat-subdivi-

EXAMPLE 2-1: Mozart, Symphony No. 41, K. 551, second movement

sions) at which goals (such as harmonic changes and cadences) and transitions between goals (such as nonharmonic tones and passing harmonies) will occur. For example, when we expect the tonic as a cadential goal, we await not merely a tonic harmony, but a tonic harmony on a particular beat of a particular measure. When harmonies change off the beats, the resulting instability is part of the expression of the piece.

Listen to the difference between the off-beat chords in the right hand (mm. 3–8) and the cadential progression (mm. 10–11) of the example on the following page. We know that the right-hand chords are anticipations because we know that their "proper" placement is on the following beats. The cadence would not be as emphatic if the right-hand chords continued to be syncopated, as in the recomposed cadence in Example 2-2b. In this passage by Beethoven and in tonal music in general, the arrival on harmonic-melodic goals at metrically strong points, and the clearly defined passage between those harmonic goals at metrically appropriate points is crucial to the shaping of phrases and to the expression of the music itself.

Just as regular meter supports the harmonic-melodic goals of functional tonality, the placement of harmonic-melodic motions helps to create our perception of meter. We perceive meter largely because chord changes, longer notes, melodic motives, accompaniment patterns, and other patterns tend to occur with certain periodicity. It is, therefore, no mere coincidence that regular meter became firmly entrenched in func-

EXAMPLE 2-2*a:* Beethoven, *Piano Sonata,* op. 31, no. 1, first movement

*b:* The same, recomposed

tional harmony, and that along with the gradual dissolution of tonality came the relaxation of regular meter in much of this music.

## Meter in Twentieth-Century Music

In many twentieth-century compositions, rhythm and meter function much as they do in tonal music. But other works expand rhythmic and metric situations beyond the norms of the earlier styles.

*Irregular Meters.* In a great deal of twentieth-century music, metric units are not of uniform length. Instead, they are of variable length, corresponding to expansions or contractions in melodic motives. Listen to the unaccompanied fanfare-like melody from the *Quartet for the End of Time* (1941) by Olivier Messiaen (born 1908). The excerpt seems to be in $\frac{4}{4}$ meter; but in each measure, the second beat expands to "make time" for a melodic expansion. In the first measure, the descending step F♯–E is echoed on the second beat as B♭–A♭. The interpolated C that elaborates this motive occupies an additional sixteenth within the beat. A similar expansion during the second beat of m. 2 adds a sixteenth to the beat.

EXAMPLE 2-3: Messiaen, *Quartet for the End of Time,* sixth movement

EXAMPLE 2-4: The same, recomposed

As a result, what might have been a pair of $\frac{4}{4}$ measures becomes a series of beats with *added values* (to use Messiaen's own term for the addition of durations to beats). Compare the recomposed version (Example 2-4) with the original (Example 2-3).

Note that Messiaen includes no meter signature here. A properly descriptive meter signature, like $4+5+4+4 \atop 16$, would be quite clumsy. With continually changing groupings, it is easier just to beam the notes according to their patterns.

The sixth movement of Messiaen's *Quartet for the End of Time* carries the subtitle *Dance of Fury for the Seven Trumpets [that announce the end of time],* referring to the Biblical description of the Apocalypse. The movement features unaccompanied melodies, doubled in unison and octaves throughout. The irregular metric groupings help impart the aura of an apocalyptic fanfare to the music.

A similar metric situation arises in *L'Histoire du Soldat* (1918) by Igor Stravinsky (1882–1971). The clarinet passage in $\frac{7}{16}$ (m. 75) contains too few notes to fill out the three beats of the previous seven measures. The resulting disruption of metric continuity is one of the characteristics of Stravinsky's style.

EXAMPLE 2-5: Stravinsky, *L'Histoire du Soldat,* music to Scene I

There are also instances in tonal music in which the elaboration of a motive or the working-out of a passage results in too many or too few notes to fill the beats in the prevailing rhythm. In such passages, either the motives or the beat-subdivisions were altered in order to maintain complete metric units, as in the following passages by Beethoven. As

EXAMPLE 2-6: Beethoven, *Piano Trio*, op. 70 no. 1

*a.* first movement

*b.* last movement

demonstrated by Examples 2-3 and 2-5, many twentieth-century composers preferred not to make such adjustments, and instead created irregular or changing meters.

Often the motivation for such irregular or changing meters arises from extramusical influences. Think of the busy market scene that opens Stravinsky's *Petrushka* (1911), the jaunty stroll of a soldier on leave reflected in so much of his *L'Histoire du Soldat* (1918), the pagan ferocity bursting forth from the final pages of his *Rite of Spring* (1913), and the just-mentioned apocalyptic fanfare from Messiaen's *Quartet for the End of Time* (1941).

In other music, the motivation for metric changes came from music outside the Western art-music tradition. In Messiaen's case, for instance, rhythmic influences came from Indian music and the *ragas* he studied extensively. The Hungarian composer Béla Bartók (1881–1945) spent many years investigating Eastern European and Near Eastern folk music. The following passage from his *Contrasts* (1938) reflects such influences. The meter signature indicates the groupings of the thirteen eighths in each measure. At ♪ = 330, the performer cannot be expected to count in eighths, and instead learns to count beats of different lengths. The result is similar to traditional East-European folk dances.

EXAMPLE 2-7: Bartók, *Contrasts*, third movement

***Different Meters Simultaneously: Polymeter.*** In some twentieth-century music, different parts in a musical texture are in different meters, an effect called *polymeter*. The following is an illustration. The accompaniment in the violin and bass maintains a regular $\frac{2}{4}$ meter under the changing groupings of the melody. The percussion section adds its own irregularities.

EXAMPLE 2-8: Stravinsky, *L'Histoire du Soldat*, Soldier's March

Listen also to the following passage by Messiaen in which the violin and cello play the same melody as in Example 2-3. Against the irregular beats of the melody, the clarinet pattern remains in $\frac{2}{4}$ throughout mm. 42–45. In the phrase that follows (mm. 46–50), the instruments reverse roles, with the clarinet playing the melody with irregular beats and the violin and cello accompanying, first in a $\frac{3}{16}$ pattern, then in $\frac{2}{16}$.

EXAMPLE 2-9: Messiaen, *Quartet for the End of Time,* fourth movement.

The noteheads above the violin part in mm. 42–45 and below the clarinet part in mm. 46–50 show the rhythmic notation of these parts as they occur in the sixth movement.

Polymeter is not entirely new to the twentieth century. There are occasional passages in the tonal repertoire that imply a polymeter, such as the following, in which the left hand implies a $\frac{3}{16}$ (or $\frac{12}{16}$ ?) meter temporarily.

EXAMPLE 2-10: Brahms, *Intermezzo,* Op. 119 no. 2

But the effect of polymeter in tonal music is quite different from that illustrated in Examples 2-8 and 2-9. As in similar tonal passages from the late nineteenth century, the implied polymeter in Example 2-10 enhances the unified sweep of the phrase. Brahms' left-hand part pulls at the beats, like an extreme rubato intensifying the lyricism of the passage. Here, as in virtually every tonal piece, all components of the texture participate in the same harmonic-melodic-metric plan.

In twentieth-century music, by contrast, the polymeter makes it seem as if the music is proceeding in two or more directions at once. The metrically separate strands conflict with each other. The texture of such passages is the combination of separate components. Many twentieth-century textures, in much music by Stravinsky and Messiaen, for example, maintain separate metric structures for their individual components.

*Metric Notation.*    Different composers have used different notations for passages with two or more simultaneous meters. Some have notated each part in its own meter. This can work for short passages, especially in chamber pieces, and where the conflicts are not too great between the meters. But in longer passages, or in passages where the interaction is particularly complex, such notations would hinder rather than help the performers. Imagine playing one part and following the others in the passage by Messiaen in Example 2-9 if it were notated as follows:

EXAMPLE 2-11:

Messiaen discusses this issue in his treatise *The Technique of My Musical Language*,[1] wherein he opts, in such situations, for writing all parts in a single unchanging meter, letting the nuances of each part emerge because of the shaping of that part. This type of notation occurs in many twentieth-century pieces.

---

1. Olivier Messiaen's treatise *The Technique of My Musical Language*, translated by John Satterfield (Paris: Leduc, 1956).

As a result, you cannot assume that metric notation is a reliable guide to the metric structure you hear. Although the melody in Example 2-9 *looks* syncopated against the notated beat, its structure is the same as when it appears unaccompanied in Example 2-3. (Compare the melody in Example 2-3 with the rhythmic notation above the staff in Example 2-9.) In these and many other passages, the notated meter may not accurately represent the meter of any line.

*Metric Modulation.* Some composers introduce metric changes by altering the metric grouping of a constant pulse, a technique called *metric modulation*. Although this technique was used by Alban Berg (1885–1935) early in this century, it is most often associated with later composers, such as Elliott Carter (born 1908). The passage from his *Sonata for Cello and Piano* serves as an illustration (see facing page).

In mm. 31–32 the septuplet eighths establish a new pulse against the preceding quarter-note beat. The septuplet eighth becomes the metric eighth in m. 33. When the grouping changes to sixes in mm. 37 and 38, a new beat arises in dotted quarters. This beat becomes the notated quarter-note beat in m. 39, preparing for the sixteenths and then the seven-note grouping of sixteenths. Similar procedures occur in all four movements of the sonata. The shifting metric groupings are one of the delights of the piece.

*Metric and Ametric Music.* We can discuss metric changes and simultaneous meters in a great deal of twentieth-century music because the music itself contains many of the features that give rise to our perception of meter. Thus, in Messiaen's *Quartet* (Examples 2-3 and 2-9), Stravinsky's *L'Histoire* (Examples 2-5 and 2-8), and Bartók's *Contrasts* (Example 2-7), various factors, including motivic patterning, harmonic changes, and long notes create the sense of meter in the individual parts, even though that meter may be continually changing, offset by conflicting accents and patterns, and contradicted by other meters within the texture. From this perspective, all these metric situations are merely variants of those found in tonal music.

But there are many other twentieth-century compositions in which we may question whether a meter in the traditional sense exists at all. If recurring patterns are not present, and if events are widely separated with no continuous pulse marking the time between them, we may not perceive a meter at all.

Listen, for instance, to the opening of Stravinsky's *Rite of Spring* (1913). The four sixteenths and the five triplet eighths in m. 1, and the six eighths in m. 2 create brief regularities of pulses on one level. But with the fermatas disrupting the continuity of any of these pulses, and with the

EXAMPLE 2-12: Carter, *Sonata for Cello and Piano,* fourth movement

changed disposition of the notes in relation to the notated beat when the melodic figure in m. 1 recurs, there is little sense of any larger metric units here. Meter and easily perceptible rhythms emerge only gradually during the opening section of the *Rite of Spring*, relating directly to the plot of the ballet: the Introduction leads into the highly rhythmic and metric music in the "Dance of the Adolescent Girls."

EXAMPLE 2-13: Stravinsky, *The Rite of Spring*

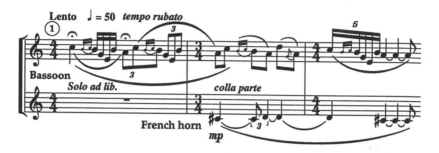

Listen also to the opening of the *Composition for Four Instruments* (1948) by Milton Babbitt (born 1916). The durations in m. 1 do not easily impart a sense of pulse. And the following longer durations do not fall into a clear metric pattern. The notated meter is more of a framework for the performer than a description of a metric structure that a listener might perceive.

EXAMPLE 2-14: Babbitt, *Composition for Four Instruments*

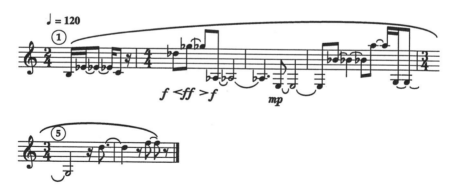

Finally, there are compositions in which precise rhythmic values are not notated. Listen to the passage from *Synchronisms No. 2* (1964) by Mario Davidovsky (born 1934). The unmeasured rhythms in the instrumental parts anticipate the types of rhythms that occur later in the piece in the part realized on tape.

EXAMPLE 2-15: Davidovsky, *Synchronisms No. 2*

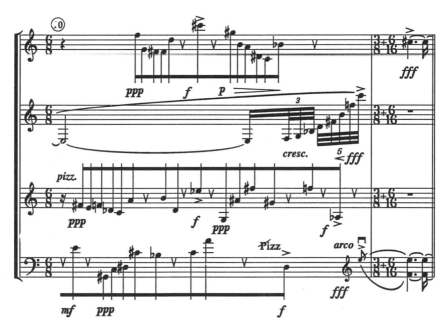

*Meter and Tempo.* Our perception of tempo is based more on the speed at which we perceive the basic beat of a passage than on the speed of notes in that passage. The basic beat in a passage results from the harmonic rhythm as well as the pacing of phrases. Slow movements, for instance, may contain rapid notes in accompaniment patterns or quick scales, yet still sound slow because the slow pace of harmonic rhythm and the slow unfolding of phrases produce a slow beat. And pieces can maintain a constant metronomic beat, yet can sound like they are in different tempos in different passages if changes in the harmonic rhythm and phrase rhythm shift the basic beat to a slower or faster rhythmic value.

Listen, for instance, to the following excerpt. There is no change in tempo marking for the second excerpt, and many performances maintain the same quarter-note duration for both passages. (Indeed, some performances actually use a faster quarter-note in the second passage.) Yet the famous love theme sounds much slower than the music around m. 111, because in the earlier passage the quarter note is perceived as the pulse, while in the love theme the half note, or even the whole note, performs the same function.

EXAMPLE 2-16: Tchaikovsky, *Romeo and Juliet Fantasy-Overture*

Since meter is such a strong determinant of tempo, we do not perceive any tempo strongly in music that projects meter only weakly. No matter what the speed of the notes, the music seems to be neither fast nor slow. This is particularly true of some pieces written since World War II. One that we have already encountered is Babbitt's *Composition for Four Instru-*

*ments*. Review the opening in Example 2-14; listen also to the entire opening clarinet solo section, and note how the lack of an easily perceived pulse affects both the sense of meter and of tempo.

# Rhythmic Motives

We think of a musical motive as a pattern that is both melodic and rhythmic. The opening motive of Beethoven's *"Eroica" Symphony*, for instance, is an arpeggiation in a specific rhythm. This is because we can recognize a recurring melodic motive more easily if the same rhythm characterizes all its appearances.

But there are also instances of rhythmic motives where the melodic content of the motive changes upon repetition. In Beethoven's *Fifth Symphony*, for instance, the famous short-short-short-long or upbeat-upbeat-upbeat-downbeat pattern underlies many different melodic figures:

EXAMPLE 2-17: Beethoven, Symphony No. 5, op. 67

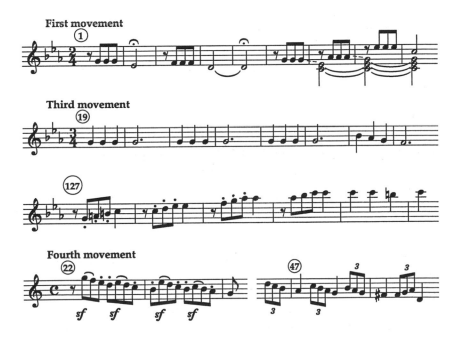

In twentieth-century music in which pitch structures are complex, we often hear rhythmic motives more clearly than pitch motives. A particularly striking instance of this occurs in the first movement of the *Lyric Suite* (1926) by Alban Berg. The identical rhythm of the melodies is obvious

EXAMPLE 2-18: Berg, *Lyric Suite*, first movement

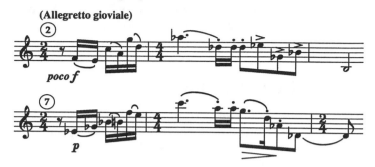

even on first hearing, despite the fact that the second melody is neither a repetition nor a sequence of the first. Much less obvious is the recurrence of the pitches from the first melody partway through the second melody (F–E–C–A–G–D–A♭–D♭).

In some twentieth-century compositions rhythmic motives become the sole content of a phrase or even an entire piece. The opening of the slow movement of Bartók's *Music for Strings, Percussion, and Celesta* (1936) arises from a rhythmic pattern, with only minimal pitch content:

Example 2-19: Bartók, *Music for Strings, Percussion, and Celesta,* third movement

**Xylophone**

In the remarkable composition *Ionisation* (1931), rhythmic motives replace pitch motives entirely as the essential ingredients of structure. Edgard Varèse (1883–1965) scored this piece for a percussion ensemble, with pitched instruments appearing only at the very end. To be sure, there are gross differences in pitch level between, say, the low bass drum and the higher wood blocks or snare drum, and these contrasts are exploited during the piece. But the recurring rhythmic motives are what function here as themes in the traditional sense.

# Points for Review

**1.** *Rhythm* refers to all aspects of music that deal with time. Its three primary subdivisions are *patterns of duration, accentuation* (including *meter*), and *continuity.*

**2.** *Meter* is the organization of pulses into groupings of strong and weak. In most tonal music, a single meter is continuous throughout the piece. Although some twentieth-century compositions feature meter resembling that in tonal music, many other works contain *changing meters, irregular meters* arising from *added values, polymeter* (two or more meters simultaneously), or little or no sense of meter *(ameter).*

**3.** Metric notation is not always a reliable guide to the perceived meter in many twentieth-century compositions.

**4.** A sense of *tempo* arises from the speed of the basic beat of a passage. The feeling of a fast or slow tempo is weak in twentieth-century music without a strong metric profile.

**5.** Rhythmic motives are essential building blocks in many twentieth-century pieces.

# Exercises for Chapter 2

## Terms and Concepts

Define the following terms:

| | | |
|---|---|---|
| *meter* | *polymeter* | *changing meter* |
| *composite rhythm* | *irregular meter* | *ameter* |
| *rhythmic motives* | *metric modulation* | *added value* |

## Analysis

**1.** Many of the musical examples in Units Two and Three are taken from the compositions listed below. Familiarize yourself with these pieces; listen to them; study their rhythmic characteristics. Which pieces are relatively traditional in rhythm and meter? Which use rhythmic devices associated specifically with twentieth-century music? Which use regular meter? Which use irregular meter? Study the uses of polymeter, the types of composite rhythms, and the relation between the rhythms and the types of rhythmic situations encountered in tonal music.

Milton Babbitt, *Composition for Four Instruments* (1948)
Béla Bartók, *Diminished Fifth*, No. 101 from *Mikrokosmos* (1926–37)
  String Quartet No. 3 (1927)
Claude Debussy, *La Mer* (1905)
Olivier Messiaen, *Quartet for the End of Time* (1941)
Arnold Schoenberg, String Quartet No. 4 (1937)
Igor Stravinsky, *Petrushka* (1911)
  *Symphony of Psalms* (1930)
Anton Webern, *Movement for String Quartet*, op. 5 no. 4 (1909)
  *Variations for Piano*, op. 27 (1936)

**2.** Listen to and study Edgard Varèse's *Ionisation* (1931). The snare drum rhythm at study number 1 is prominent in many passages of the piece. How is it set off from its surroundings? Is it developed? Or is it only restated? Are there any other prominent rhythmic motives?

**Composition**

Write a brief composition (or series of compositions) for three or four players, using rhythm only. Explore different possibilities of establishing a meter, changing meters, using polymeter, or using no meter at all. You may write for percussion instruments, or for objects found in your classroom (tapping on desks, music stands, piano soundboards [gently!], etc.). Have the class perform your piece(s).

# Suggestions for Further Study

**1.** Wallace Berry's *Structural Functions in Music* (Englewood Cliffs: Prentice-Hall, 1976) discusses rhythm extensively in Chapter 3 (pp. 301–424).

**2.** *The Rhythms of Tonal Music* (Carbondale: University of Southern Illinois Press, 1986), by the author of this text, contains a comprehensive discussion of various aspects of rhythm, especially accent, meter, and phrase rhythm.

**3.** The Finale to Act I of Mozart's *Don Giovanni* includes a ballroom scene with three orchestras simultaneously playing three dances in different meters and tempos. What features of this passage resemble twentieth-century polymetric passages? What other features make this passage sound like it belongs in an eighteenth-century opera?

# 3

# Texture and Timbre

---

*spacing*         *layered textures*
*register*        Klangfarbenmelodie
*ostinato*        Sprechstimme

---

*Texture* refers to the interaction of separate vocal or instrumental parts that sound along with one another. Textures have often been categorized as *monophonic* (a single sounding part), *polyphonic* (several parts of relatively equal importance sounding together), and *homophonic* (a primary part with accompaniment). But in actual music, the differentiation of these categories is often not so clear-cut. An unaccompanied part (monophonic texture) often contains in itself implications of polyphonic voice-leading. At any point in a polyphonic passage, one part may be primary with the remaining parts providing a background (a homophonic texture). And the separate parts that make up the accompaniment in a homophonic texture may interact polyphonically.

In fact, although texture is in part the result of the number and relative prominence of individual parts, additional factors also play crucial roles in determining the way we hear a texture. Among these factors are *spacing* (how close or far apart the parts are), *register* (whether the parts are predominantly low, medium, or high in range), *rhythm* (whether there are equal or unequal levels of activity throughout the texture, whether fast or slow values predominate, and whether changes in different parts of the texture are synchronized or unsynchronized), and even *timbre* or *tone color* (whether blended or contrasted). These aspects, separately and in combination, create a virtually infinite range of textural variety.

This chapter continues our survey of various musical aspects by focusing on many types of texture and timbre, observing how they function in various pieces. We begin our discussion by studying the role of texture in tonal music and the new possibilities of texture in twentieth-century nontonal music.

# Texture, Phrasing, and Form

*In Tonal Music.*    The types of textures that occur in tonal music, as well as the placement of changes in texture, are, like other aspects of that repertoire, coordinated with the complementary relationship between melody and harmony that we call functional harmony. Chapter 2 demonstrates how rhythm and meter in tonal music support that relationship. The shapes and gestures of tonal music are created and projected by texture working in concert with pitch and rhythm.

In most tonal textures, for instance, there is a clearly defined bass part supporting the voice leading of the upper parts. This is most obvious in homophonic textures. But it is even true in contrapuntal textures. Spacing is often arranged so that the main melody part is separate from the other parts, and the body of the accompaniment is in close position, emphasizing the blend of the supporting harmony. Register, both of individual parts and of the entire texture, often remains within clearly defined limits during a phrase or section. Changes of harmony most often occur with all or almost all voices moving together, so that we hear the harmonic changes clearly.

Finally, changes in texture, both obvious and subtle, most often reinforce harmonic and tonal goals on a variety of levels. A change in texture frequently heralds the beginning of a new phrase, and new textures differentiate new themes from their predecessors. Even within a phrase, a crucial harmony or melodic pitch may be reinforced by a change in texture. This is especially true at cadences.

For an illustration of many of these points, listen to Example 3-1. The opening measures are homophonic. We hear the melody clearly because it is doubled in octaves, with the first-violin part lying above any of the accompaniment. The inner voices, in the viola parts, are separated from the bass line in register. This nine-measure phrase-division is scored for strings, offering a blend of timbres. But the bass part, the viola accompaniment figure, and the violin melody all have different rhythms, so that we hear their sounds separately within the timbral blend.

The opening texture continues without change through m. 9—that is, until the return to the tonic that ends the first harmonic motion of the piece and the first phrase-division. The new phrase-division that continues the melody in mm. 10–13 is similar in texture to mm. 1–9 except for the sustained bass notes. Just as the opening phrase-division prolongs a root-position tonic, this second phrase-division marks off a new harmonic event: $I_6$. Further changes in texture signal both the motion to the half cadence in mm. 14–16 and the reiterated half cadence in mm. 17–20. The register expands and the relationship between the voices changes. The return to the opening texture in mm. 22–27 complements a return

EXAMPLE 3-1: Mozart, Symphony No. 40, K. 550, first movement, mm. 1–51

to the opening melody. The addition of the sustained wind parts complements the new harmonic function of this theme: the beginning of the modulation to the mediant. The new harmonic goal, B♭ in m. 28, is the occasion for the beginning of a new texture. Subsequent changes of texture in mm. 34 and 38 set off V of V and then V in this new key. The unification of the entire orchestra in the chords in m. 42 announces the end of the preceding section. After that point we hear the beginning of the second theme group of the sonata form. It differs from all the previous music in this movement by its chorale-type texture and by the total absence of any rhythmically activated accompaniment.

All these small-scale and large-scale changes in texture articulate the local and long-range tonal and thematic goals, allowing us to hear these goals more clearly. Yet throughout all these texture changes, the bass, middle voices, and soprano are each clearly projected by their register and often by their own rhythms. Although the textural details of every tonal piece differ, the principles underlying them are ubiquitous.

*In Twentieth-Century Music.* Many twentieth-century compositions feature textures similar to those in tonal music. Listen to Example 3-2. The opening fourteen measures feature a melody and accompaniment. The melody projects clearly as it passes from the first violin to the second and back to the first. The accompaniment differs from the melody in rhythm, and often in register. The texture remains melody-plus-accompaniment in mm. 17–20; but here the three upper instruments, though notated by Schoenberg as an accompaniment to the cello melody, vie with that melody for our attention. An imitative texture begins in m. 21.

EXAMPLE 3-2: Schoenberg, String Quartet No. 4, op. 37 (1937).

> Schoenberg used the symbols *H* and *N* to indicate the primary and subsidiary parts in a texture: *H* stands for *Hauptstimme* or Principal Voice; *N* stands for *Nebenstimme* or Subsidiary Voice.

Schoenberg's quartet and many other twentieth-century pieces share with tonal music not only the types of texture they employ, but also the manner in which changes in texture (such as changes in register, in levels of activity, or in spacing) support the articulation of goals. In fact, since nontonal pieces lack the clear-cut harmonic meanings common to many tonal pieces, texture may actually be more important than pitch in projecting a sense of cadence or another type of important goal.

Listen again to Example 3-2. The opening texture continues through m. 6, when all voices cut off abruptly at the same time. Following the brief silence, the second violin assumes the role of melody instrument, supported by new accompanimental figures and a change to a higher register for the ensemble as a whole. Clearly, this is a contrasting phrase. As we will see in Unit Three, the second-violin phrase emphasizes a different group of pitches than those emphasized in the opening phrase. The return in m. 10 to a texture similar to the opening signals a new phrase that resembles the first one. Finally, the unification of the entire ensemble in the three chords in mm. 15–16 marks the end of a larger section.

The first movement of this quartet is in sonata form. The melody-plus-accompaniment textures of mm. 1–16, the clear-cut phrases, and the cadential unification of the texture in mm. 15–16 help to articulate this music as the exposition of the first theme. The increasingly polyphonic music after m. 17 announces the beginning of the transition toward the second theme group.

Schoenberg's String Quartet No. 4 is reminiscent of tonal music in its phrasing and its approach to form. Not all twentieth-century music relates so closely to tonal music, but texture changes are almost always crucial indicators of phrasing, sectional divisions, and types of motion.

# New Types of Textures

We have already noted how the synchronization of various parts of a texture in tonal music supports the basis of functional harmony by emphasizing harmonic changes. In the absence of functional harmony, there is no need for synchronization of all parts of a texture. As a result, textures in which several components proceed in their individual ways are common to the music of many composers.

*Layered Textures.*    We have already discussed portions of Stravinsky's *L'Histoire du Soldat*. Review the excerpt from this piece on p. 21, in which there are three separate textural components, each with its own timbre, metric structure, and motives. Similarly unsynchronized components appear in the passage from Messiaen's *Quartet for the End of Time* on p. 22. An even more dramatic instance of unsynchronized components occurs in *The Unanswered Question* (1908), an astonishingly innovative work by Charles Ives (1874–1954). This piece features softly sustained string sonorities from beginning to end, joined from time to time by trumpet solos, and by woodwind phrases that are notated in a different tempo.

Such *layered textures* (that is, several independent layers of sound that produce the entire texture) are characteristic of much of the music of Stravinsky, Messiaen, and Ives, to name only a few composers. Often, one or more layers of these textures are *ostinatos* (repeated figures), such as the string parts in the passage from Stravinsky's *L'Histoire*, or the clarinet part at the opening of the Messiaen passage mentioned above.

Stravinsky's *Rite of Spring* (1913) provides numerous instances of layered textures. We have already discussed in Chapter 2 how the very opening of the ballet is ambiguous in terms of rhythm and meter (review Example 2-13), only gradually falling into more easily recognizable meters and rhythms. In texture too the work only gradually unfolds its resources. In this work for a huge orchestra, the opening is a single melody line, accompanied toward its end by single sustained tones. As more regular and easily recognizable rhythms and meters emerge during the introduction, more components begin to participate in the texture. The recurrences of the opening melody begin to function like an ostinato as other patterns join it and eventually supplant it. The introduction is built from a variety of short, recurring patterns that enter and dissolve as other ostinatos appear. The entire orchestra gradually accumulates in layered textures made up from such ostinatos.

The music of Debussy also features many instances of layered textures, as in these excerpts from *La Mer*. In the first passage (*a*), the strings establish the ostinato against which other music appears: first the woodwind figure, then the horn melody. The same horn melody occurs against a new string ostinato in the second passage (*b*). And in the third passage (*c*), the woodwind figure and a melody from earlier in the movement (in the trumpet) occur along with a new ostinato.

EXAMPLE 3-3: Debussy, *La Mer*, first movement

*a.* 3 mm. before study number 3

*b.* study number 5

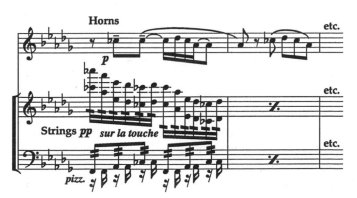

*c.* study number *8*

As you listen to layered textures, your ear travels among the various components. Although in some of the passages just cited there may be a principal melody, the accompanying layers are more than a mere background.

*New Concepts of a Single Part.* Another characteristic of many twentieth-century compositions is an expanded notion of what constitutes an individual part in a texture. Extreme registral shifts in individual parts, combined with changing timbres, dynamics, and articulations, give rise to wholly new textures unrelated to any tonal models. Study the analytic portion of the next example, which presents the pitch canon that is the basis for the passage.

The pitches in the canon are written within a single octave in open noteheads above and below the musical example. The second voice of the canon is a minor third below the first, and follows the first voice by six beats. In the music, there are numerous changes of register that move the notes of the canon to various octaves.

Then study the score itself. With the numerous changes in register, in instrumentation, and in dynamics, the resulting quartet texture hardly reflects the canon that underlies it.

In describing this texture, which aspects should we consider? The two-part canon, the instrumental parts (each of which contains notes from both voices of the canon), or registrally related notes (such as the first-violin B in m. 18 going to the second-violin A later in that measure)? That all these connections are possible gives rise to an intricate web of musical continuities. Clearly, the traditional sense of a part or a melody

EXAMPLE 3-4: Webern, String Quartet, op. 28, first movement

does not apply here, making the traditional terms homophonic and polyphonic somewhat irrelevant.

Similarly expanded possibilities of register and timbre in a single part occur in many twentieth-century musical styles. We react to the resulting new sounds even when the underlying melody is a familiar one. Below is Stravinsky's transformation of a familiar tune from the beginning of his *Greeting Prelude* (1955). With all the sudden changes of register and the instrumentation every few notes, is it proper to call this "melody" *Happy Birthday*?

EXAMPLE 3-5: Stravinsky, *Greeting Prelude*

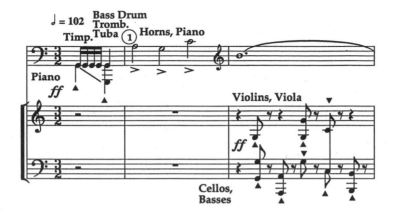

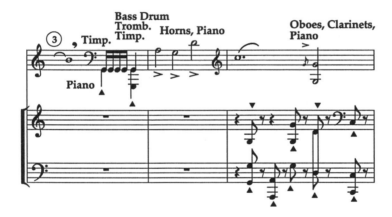

During the past two generations, composers have continued to create novel types of texture. We will discuss some of them in Unit Four.

# Timbre

*Timbre* (tone color) is another musical element that affects texture. Blended timbres (all strings, all woodwinds, and so forth) emphasize the textural unity of a passage, while contrasting timbres (say, solo oboe, solo French horn, and strings) help separate the lines in a texture. While many twentieth-century compositions feature timbres similar to those of tonal music, other compositions expand the range of usage.

***Blended versus Contrasting Timbres.*** In tonal music, a homogeneous blend of timbres often stresses the blend of parts that make up the functional harmonic structure. The string quartet, for instance, is the model for much chamber music. Similarly, the homogeneous string section of eighteenth- and nineteenth-century orchestral compositions is the foundation of most orchestral sonorities. Only in the mid and late nineteenth century does this begin to change. As the orchestra increased in size, composers sought new and striking timbral combinations—a trend already noticeable in the works of Berlioz early in the century.

A particularly expressive use of contrasted timbres opens Gustav Mahler's *Kindertotenlieder (Songs on the Death of a Child)* (1902). The

EXAMPLE 3-6: Mahler, *Kindertotenlieder*, No. 1: *Nun will die Sonn' so hell aufgehn*

text: Now will the sun rise so brightly,
      as if no misfortune had occurred during the night!

poignant contrast between the private grief of the narrator and the joy of the sun rising on a new day is underscored by the sharply etched timbral contrast of oboe and French horn versus the string blend in successive phrases. Mahler (1860–1911) is famous for innovative orchestrations that strongly influenced many twentieth-century composers, especially Schoenberg and his followers.

The composer who is perhaps most commonly associated with new timbres in early twentieth-century music is Stravinsky. Already in his early works, Stravinsky created striking timbral combinations and contrasts, whether within the huge orchestras of *Petrushka* (1911) and the *Rite of Spring* (1913), or in the chamber ensemble of *L'Histoire du Soldat* (1918), scored for a mixed ensemble of two woodwinds (clarinet and bassoon), two brasses (trumpet and trombone), two strings (violin and double bass), and a variety of percussion instruments. Stravinsky continued to emphasize striking and novel timbres and timbral combinations throughout his long creative life and through his many changes of style.

Other composers of the time also explored new timbres. Schoenberg scored his *Chamber Symphony*, op. 9 (1906), for an ensemble of fifteen solo instruments, mixing strings, brass, and woodwinds. *Pierrot Lunaire*, op. 21 (1912), also mixes instrumental families in a chamber setting. It is scored for violin/viola, cello, piano, flute/piccolo, clarinet/bass-clarinet, and voice. Each of the twenty-one movements of *Pierrot* is scored for a different combination of these instruments. The voice part requires a novel vocal production between speaking and singing, called *Sprechstimme* (a German term meaning "spoken singing"). The resulting combinations of clearly defined timbres in these works are far removed from the homogeneous blend common in most tonal music. The mixture of different families of instruments in Schoenberg's *Pierrot* and Stravinsky's *L'Histoire* served as a model for many twentieth-century chamber-music composers.

**Uses of Percussion.**    In tonal music, percussion instruments play a supportive role; the timpani solos at the opening of Beethoven's *Violin Concerto*, in the transition to the finale of Beethoven's *Fifth Symphony*, and in the transition to the *allegro giusto* in Tchaikovsky's *Romeo and Juliet*, or the anvils in Wagner's *Das Rheingold* are among the few notable exceptions. In many twentieth-century scores, percussion instruments play a leading role. This is as true of many chamber works as it is of orchestral compositions.

There are even compositions written entirely for percussion, like Edgard Varèse's *Ionisation* (1931), scored for thirteen percussionists, each playing a variety of instruments. Instruments that play specific pitches (piano, glockenspiel, chimes) appear only in the closing measures of the work. Prior to that, rhythmic motives, timbral characteristics (wooden instruments versus metal instruments versus drums, for instance), and gross registral differences (bass drums versus higher-pitched instruments) carry the musical activity.

**Solo Instruments.**    The more prominent role played by timbre in twentieth-century music has also given rise to compositions for many solo instruments that were rarely if ever used that way in the Classic and Romantic periods. Pieces for solo strings had antecedents by Bach and other Baroque composers, but works for solo woodwinds, solo brass, and even solo percussion are more recent innovations.

**New Instrumental Techniques.**    Like their counterparts in earlier eras, composers in the twentieth century have explored new registers, new timbres, and new playing techniques for all instruments. An historically famous instance is the opening of *The Rite of Spring* (1913), in which Stravinsky uses the bassoon as a solo instrument at the very upper limit of its register. Among timbral possibilities for string instruments, some of which were discovered well before the twentieth century, are *ponticello* (bowing near or on the bridge), *glissandos* (slides from one note to another), various types of *pizzicato* (plucked strings), and *col legno* (bowing with the wood of the bow). For woodwind and brass instruments, timbral possibilities include *flutter-tongue*, *multiphonics* (two or more notes at once), *pedal tones* (low-register fundamental notes) and *key clicks* for woodwinds. Various new piano techniques include playing inside the piano by plucking, strumming, or scraping the strings with fingers or various implements, hitting the bars and sounding boards, playing harmonics, and inserting objects on the strings (called *prepared piano*).

These new techniques, along with new combinations of instruments, create musical colors in many twentieth-century pieces that would have been unimaginable in earlier eras. Webern's *Movement for String Quartet*, op. 5 no. 4, which features a variety of timbral effects, is discussed extensively in Unit Two. Analysis Exercise 2 in Chapter 8 offers a score to the piece.

Listen also to the excerpts from the third movement of Bartók's *Music for Strings, Percussion, and Celesta* (1936) in Example 3-7. The solo xylophone and the timpani glissandos precede the entry of the strings. In the later passage (at m. 20), the violin trills cover all the notes within a perfect fifth in a shimmering background to the glissandos in the second violins. The piano here functions as a percussion instrument. This entire texture, reinforced by viola and cello tremolos, accompanies the melody that is doubled by the ethereal combination of solo violins and celesta.

EXAMPLE 3-7: Bartók, *Music for Strings, Percussion, and Celesta*, third movement

*a.*

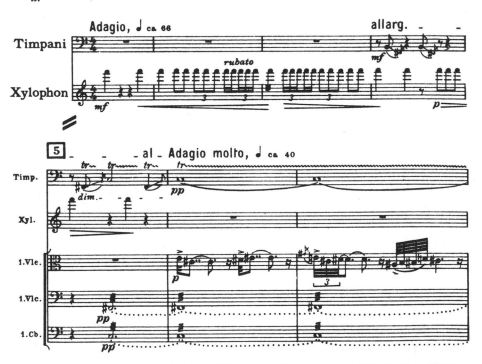

*b.*

In addition to all the timbral possibilities of traditional instruments, an increasing variety of electronically generated and electronically altered sounds have been used during the past two decades. This is obvious in music composed and performed on electronic instruments. But it is also characteristic of some music scored for traditional instruments. *Black Angels* (1970) by George Crumb (born 1929) is written for string quartet. But with the four instruments amplified, with added reverberation, and with a variety of gongs and musical glasses played by the quartet members, there is hardly a sound in the piece that is recognizable as that of a string

quartet in the traditional sense. Other works by Crumb that use unam-
plified traditional instruments also feature special timbral effects; among
them are his *Eleven Echoes of Autumn, 1965* (1966) and *Ancient Voices of
Children* (1970).

Even an instrument such as the player piano, on which musical sounds
can be produced only in the traditional manner, has been used in novel
ways in our time. The composer Conlon Nancarrow (born 1912) has
composed a large body of works for player piano in which notes at
superhuman speed, superhuman skips and stretches, and incredibly
precise control over rhythm are only some of the innovations. Several of
his *Studies for Player Piano* (composed since 1950) have been recorded.

All these innovations heighten the role played by timbre in music of
the twentieth century.

## Placement of Timbral Changes

In most tonal music through the middle of the nineteenth century, a
single instrument or a single combination of instruments presents an
entire melodic phrase or phrase subdivision. In a large ensemble piece,
different phrases or phrase subdivisions may well be set off from one
another by being played on different instruments. (Review the opening
measures of Mozart's Symphony No. 40 in Example 3-1.) Even in a solo
piece, say for piano, different registers or articulations may create the
effect of a range of timbres.

To be sure, there are many tonal passages in which a melody is shared
by several instruments, such as in the excerpt from Beethoven's "Eroica"
*Symphony* in Example 3-8. But even here, the change from one timbre to
another follows the motivic subdivisions of the melody.

EXAMPLE 3-8: Beethoven, Symphony No. 3, op. 55, first movement

Only after the middle of the nineteenth century, under the influence
of Richard Wagner, did persistent changes of timbre in midphrase become
a common feature of orchestrations. Listen to Example 3-9 from the first
movement of the Symphony No. 4 (1892) by Mahler.

There are continual changes in the instrumentation of the leading parts,

EXAMPLE 3-9: Mahler, *Symphony No. 4*, first movement

even within phrases. What starts in the lower strings in mm. 7–9 moves to bassoons and French horn on the last beat of m. 9, to solo French horn in m. 10, to French horn and bassoon on the downbeat to m. 11, to bassoon, cello, and basses in m. 11, and so forth.

This type of instrumentation appears in many twentieth-century compositions. To describe such continual changes in instrumentation in the third piece of his *Five Pieces for Orchestra,* op. 16 (1909), Schoenberg coined the term *Klangfarbenmelodie,* meaning a melody of tone colors (*Klang* = sonority or tone; *Farben* = colors; *Melodie* = melody). Much of that movement consists of sustained chords with subtle ever-changing orchestrations. For an instance of *Klangfarbenmelodie* in a single melody, listen to the leading part in Example 3-10, from Webern's *Concerto for Nine Instruments,* op. 24 (1934), in which nearly every note is in a different instrument.

EXAMPLE 3-10:  Webern, *Concerto for Nine Instruments,* op. 24, second movement

Webern used this orchestration technique even in his arrangements of older music. His orchestration of the six-part ricercare from Bach's *Musical Offering* uses eight instrumental changes during the twenty notes of the fugue subject. *Klangfarbenmelodie,* by requiring a highly refined sense of shaping and blending by several instruments to produce a single line, adds a chamber-music aura to many twentieth-century orchestral textures.

# Points for Review

**1.** *Texture* refers to the interaction of separate parts that sound with one another. Texture is the result of the number and relative prominence of the individual parts, spacing, rhythm, and *timbre* (tone color).

**2.** Textures in tonal music often feature a clearly defined bass part supporting a continuous melodic part, with changes of texture closely related to phrasing and form.

**3.** Twentieth-century music features a wide range of textures, including traditional tonal textures and *layered textures* (with relatively independent components). With individual parts that can include extreme registral shifts, changing timbres, dynamics, and articulations, many twentieth-century compositions contain textures wholly unrelated to any tonal models.

**4.** *Timbre* in tonal music often stresses ensemble blend and the coordination of timbral changes with motives, phrases, and formal divisions. This is characteristic of many twentieth-century compositions also. Other compositions, however, feature ensembles of diverse timbres, rapid changes of timbre in single parts (*Klangfarbenmelodie* = tone-color-melody), and new instrumental techniques.

# Exercises for Chapter 3

## Terms and Concepts

Define the following terms:

| | | |
|---|---|---|
| *texture* | *timbre* | *Klangfarbenmelodie* |
| *layered texture* | *ostinato* | *ponticello* |
| *key clicks* | *pizzicato* | *flutter-tongue* |
| *multiphonics* | *Sprechstimme* | *glissando* |
| *col legno* | *pedal tones* | |

## Analysis

**1.** Continue familiarizing yourself with the compositions that are the focus of Units Two and Three, concentrating on the types of textures, their relationship to themes and motives, to timbres, and to phrases and form.

Milton Babbitt, *Composition for Four Instruments* (1948)

Béla Bartók, *Diminished Fifth*, No. 101 from *Mikrokosmos* (1926–37)
  String Quartet No. 3 (1927)

Claude Debussy, *La Mer* (1905)

Olivier Messiaen, *Quartet for the End of Time* (1941)

Arnold Schoenberg, String Quartet No. 4 (1937)

Igor Stravinsky, *Petrushka* (1911)
  *Symphony of Psalms* (1930)

Anton Webern, *Movement for String Quartet,* op. 5 no. 4 (1909)
  *Variations for Piano,* op. 27 (1936)

**2.** Listen to the opening two sections of Stravinsky's *Rite of Spring* (1913)—the *Introduction* and *Dance of the Adolescents.* How are the textures in the introduction built?

The opening melody in the bassoon was considered revolutionary at the time of composition because of its use of a hitherto unexplored register of the bassoon, and for its use of the unaccompanied bassoon as the melodic instrument to open an orchestral piece. What other timbres, timbral combinations, and instrumental techniques differ from tonal usage?

**3.** Listen without a score to the opening section of *Black Angels* (1970) by George Crumb. How would you describe the textures and timbres? How do these textures and timbres create phrases and sections?

## Suggestions for Further Study

Wallace Berry's *Structural Functions in Music* (Englewood Cliffs: Prentice-Hall, 1976) contains an extensive discussion of texture in Chapter 2 (pp. 184–300).

# 4
# Form

The term *form*, as used by musicians, refers to the sections in a piece: their organization, the type(s) of music they contain, and their relationships to one another. In the Classical and Romantic eras, numerous compositions share similar orderings of themes and keys. These similarities led theorists and musicologists to develop standard names to refer to these commonly used forms: sonata form, rondo, song form, and so forth. These names remain in current usage.

But although these names have remained, attitudes of many musicians toward these forms have changed. In the nineteenth century, most musicians conceived of a musical form as an outline or mold to be filled in by the themes of a given piece. Nowadays, many musicians regard musical form in a more comprehensive manner. In this newer meaning, form refers to the unity that arises from the marriage of *all* aspects of a composition—the ordering of the themes, but also the harmonic-melodic structures, the voice leadings, the tonal motions, the phrasings, the textures, etc. The focus of attention is on the conceptual unity of each piece, not the degree to which that piece does or does not follow some abstract pattern. The themes participate in creating the form, but their presence is partly the result of other musical factors. In sonata form, for instance, the new theme that often occurs at the arrival in a new key cannot be divorced from the establishment of that new key, for the new theme is there in part to set off the new key. And the new theme may well be joined by a new texture, a new instrumentation, a new type of phrasing construction, new harmonic progressions, or new voice leadings.

This comprehensive perspective on musical form, stressing the participation of all aspects of structure, is particularly valuable when we turn our attention to twentieth-century music. For even where a nontonal twentieth-century piece may seem to be in a tonal form, the lack of a key creates a novel structure. Some twentieth-century composers have continued to organize their pieces in ways reminiscent of tonal forms, while other composers proceed in entirely novel ways. But in all these pieces, it is the interaction of all the aspects of a piece that creates its form.

Because we have not yet studied twentieth-century pitch structures in detail, the survey of twentieth-century forms in this chapter must remain somewhat superficial, dealing with some general principles, and providing an introduction to form in twentieth-century music. Only as we begin to study larger pitch structures in Units Three and Four will we be able to discuss form in more specific terms.

## Forms Based on Tonal Models

Many composers during the first half of the twentieth century continued to write in the genres and forms of the tonal period. They wrote sonatas, symphonies, string quartets, and sets of variations, using the thematic patterns of standard tonal forms in individual movements even as they abandoned functional tonality as the basis for their music. In many of these twentieth-century compositions, the forms take on new characteristics according to the goals of the individual composers.

Béla Bartók, for instance, was often concerned with creating various types of symmetries in his compositions. Many of his musical forms exhibit thematic orderings that are similar when read forward or backward. The term *arch form* or *Bogen form* refers to such symmetrical constructions. (*Bogen* is the German word for arch.)

In many of Bartók's movements in sonata form, for instance, the order of themes in the recapitulation is the reverse of that in the exposition, creating a symmetrical structure around the central development section:

| Exposition | theme group I ←┐ |
| | theme group II ←┐ |
| Development | ← |
| Recapitulation | theme group II ←┘ |
| | theme group I ←┘ |

On a larger scale, in some compositions Bartók organized the movements in a symmetrical pattern. His String Quartet No. 4 (1928) and String Quartet No. 5 (1934), for instance, have the following pattern:

```
      ┌──→ I     a fast movement in sonata form
      │ ┌─→ II    a scherzo and trio
      │ │ ─→ III  a slow movement in ABA form
      │ └─→ IV    a scherzo and trio
      └────→ V    a fast movement in sonata form
```

The entire string quartet is an arch form around the third movement, which is itself an arch form (ABA). The correspondences between movements 1 and 5 and between movements 2 and 4 arise from the use of similar or identical themes. As a result of these symmetries and thematic correspondences, these two string quartets are in five movements, not the three or four movements characteristic of eighteenth- and nineteenth-century string quartets.

Bartók's concern for formal symmetries and arch form affects his works in other constructions as well. His *Music for Strings, Percussion, and Celesta* (1936), for instance, opens with a fugal movement. The movement is constructed symmetrically around the climax of the piece (m. 56) that occurs about two-thirds of the way through the first movement. The climax itself is obvious from the loudest dynamic of the movement (*fff*), the widest registral span of the movement (one semitone short of five octaves), and the sudden reduction of the texture to bare octaves after a thick polyphony. Before the climax, the fugue subject appears only in its original form. Immediately after the climax, the subject appears inverted (turned upside down) several times. The remainder of the movement uses the subject in both forms.

The pitch structure of this movement is also symmetrical around the climax. The opening fugue statement begins and ends on A. Successive statements of the subject enter on pitches successively higher or lower by perfect fifths: [A]–E–B–F♯–C♯–G♯ and [A]–D–G–C–F–B♭. These two series then meet at the climax on the E♭ octave—E♭ is one fifth past the end of both series and is also the pitch furthest from A (a tritone away). Following the climax, the two series of fifths occur in reverse order, from E♭ back toward A, this time with the inversion of the subject.

Another feature of Bartók's music that is found in compositions by many other twentieth-century composers is the close relation of the themes to one another. The first movement of his String Quartet No. 2 (1917) is a case in point. Although each theme in this sonata-form movement is distinct from the others, the principal motives in each theme all share a rising and falling contour, as shown in Example 4-1. If Bartók had not called our attention to this relationship among the themes, listeners might never notice it. But in the recapitulation, this relationship comes to the fore as all four instruments join in a striking unison statement of the

EXAMPLE 4-1: Bartók, String Quartet No. 2, first movement

stepwise rise and fall on A–B–C–B–A. From this unison melody emerge all the principal motives of the movement, as shown in Example 4-2.

Interrelationships such as these are a legacy of tonal music. Sonata-form movements by Mozart or Beethoven, operas by Wagner, character pieces by Brahms, as well as other tonal works, often exhibit close underlying similarities among themes. Sometimes these similarities are obvious on first hearing; in other cases, it takes considerable familiarity with the work to notice the relationships. But in most tonal pieces, whatever the relationships among the themes, each theme retains an individual profile.

EXAMPLE 4-2: Bartók, String Quartet No. 2, first movement

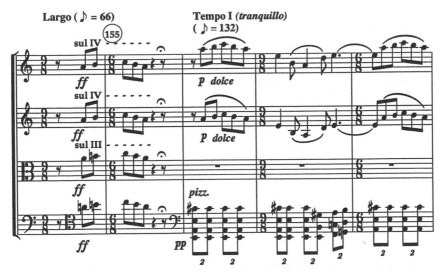

By contrast, in the works of some twentieth-century composers, themes are hardly ever restated in the same form; instead they are constantly evolving into new themes in a process called *continuous variation*. The music of Schoenberg and composers influenced by him is particularly rich in such continuous variations, giving entire movements the sense of being forever developmental.

***Transformations of Tonal Forms.*** In twentieth-century compositions based on a tonal form, the form is often compressed or expanded to such an extent that its nature is altered. Many pieces by Anton Webern, for instance, are so short by the standards of tonal music that what might be considered a bit of a phrase in another piece becomes a major formal unit.

Two examples of this are the *Movement for String Quartet,* op. 5 no. 4 (1909), which lasts just over one minute, and the second movement of the *Variations for Piano,* op. 27 (1936), which lasts a little more than half a minute, even with repeats of both halves of the movement. These and many other works by Webern are based on traditional forms: op. 5 no. 4 is in ABA' form; the second movement of op. 27 is in binary form. But given the miniature scale of these movements, both of which are discussed extensively in later chapters, what may seem at first to be part of a phrase may actually constitute an entire contrasting section.

At the other end of the spectrum are extremely long movements that arise from the expansion of very simple forms. The last movement of Olivier Messiaen's *Quartet for the End of Time* (1941), for instance, is over seven minutes long, yet contains only thirty-two measures of $\frac{4}{4}$ at $\flat = 36$. The movement is basically a single parallel period—two phrases of sixteen measures each that are the same in their first eight measures. But at the extremely slow tempo, the movement lasts many times longer than any comparable tonal composition. At the very beginning of the movement, for instance, one statement of a motive and its sequence (mm. 1–3, 4–6) last one minute and fifteen seconds. As with the extreme compression of material in Webern, this expansion of material changes the nature of the form. A single note can become a major event.

In summary, traditional tonal forms are the basis for many nontonal twentieth-century compositions. But the lack of a key, the addition of new aspects (such as formal symmetries and continuous variation), and the use of new time scales (extreme brevity or length) creates novel constructions in many of these works.

## New Formal Possibilities

In addition to adopting, adapting, or transforming tonal forms, twentieth-century composers have also developed totally new formal procedures. Many works of Claude Debussy, for instance, do not follow tonal formal models. Often in these works, traditional notions such as statement, variation, and development of themes seem to have been abandoned. One example, already cited in our study of texture in Chapter 3, is the orchestral work *La Mer* (1905). Themes enter and exit, recurring among other themes in new surroundings, but without the same sense of ordering as in tonal forms.

Many works by Igor Stravinsky also arise from new formal principles such as the juxtaposition of several contrasting elements (themes, textures, motives). The statement of one element may be interrupted by another element, followed by a recurrence or expansion of the first. The several different elements simply stand against one another. This juxtaposition of separate elements is similar to Stravinsky's layering of separate components to constitute his textures. The discussions of the opening of *Petrushka* (1911) and of the first movement of the *Symphony of Psalms* (1930) in Chapters 8 and 9 examine these constructive principles in more detail.

Another formal principle new to the twentieth-century arises from the use of continuous variation by Schoenberg and others. A theme or motive may appear only once, followed by a distant variant or totally new material, resulting in a continuous stream of new music. In the monodrama *Erwartung*, op. 17 (1909), the continuous introduction of new thematic materials parallels the text of the work, in which the soprano sings only fragments of sentences in a stream-of-consciousness fashion.

The years following World War II have seen a wide variety of approaches to musical form. As we will see in Unit Four, in many works of this period, themes and motives in the traditional sense are not present. Along with new textures and new notions of melody and harmony, new forms having little to do with traditional tonal constructions have emerged.

In Milton Babbitt's *Composition for Four Instruments* (1948), for instance, permutation, the basis of the pitches, is the conceptual underpinning of the overall organization of the work. The piece is written for flute, clarinet, violin, and cello. Every combination of these instruments occurs: one solo for each, all possible duos, all possible trios, and one quartet section. These sections are paired, with each instrument participating once in each pair of sections:

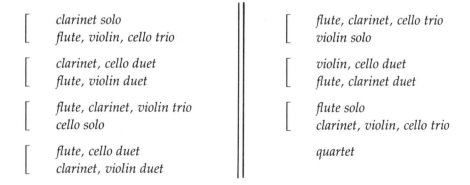

Each section features a different pair of harmonic intervals and a different group of underlying pitch motives, complementing the different instrumentations. (See Chapter 13 for a more extensive discussion of this piece.)

In other recent styles, the very notion of musical form and of a musical composition has come under attack. In Unit Four we will discuss pieces in which the performer decides the order of the sections, or even what notes to play. In pieces where two equally "correct" performances may differ entirely in pitch and sectional ordering, the notion of form as an inherent property of the work is irrelevant.

*Summary.* You should not regard the individual formal outlines surveyed in this chapter as typical of large numbers of twentieth-century compositions. As noted near the beginning of the chapter, there is a remarkably broad range of forms found in twentieth-century music. As we discuss specific pieces in Units Two, Three, and Four, we will explore their individual forms.

# Points for Review

**1.** Musical *form* is the unity that arises from the marriage of all aspects of a composition—the layout of the themes, the harmonic-melodic structures, the voice leadings, the tonal motions, the phrasings, the textures, and the like.

**2.** Traditional tonal forms are the basis for many nontonal twentieth-century compositions. But the lack of a key, the addition of new aspects (such as formal symmetries, perpetual variation), and the presentation of the forms in new time scales creates novel constructions in many of these works.

**3.** Other twentieth-century compositions are based on entirely novel constructions.

# Exercises for Chapter 4

### Analysis

**1.** Continue your study of the compositions used in Units Two and Three, concentrating on their approach to musical form. Do these pieces use themes and motives to build phrases and sections? Do any resulting layouts follow tonal models? With what differences?

Milton Babbitt, *Composition for Four Instruments* (1948)

Béla Bartók, *Diminished Fifth,* No. 101 from *Mikrokosmos* (1926–37)
    String Quartet No. 3 (1927)

Claude Debussy, *La Mer* (1905)

Olivier Messiaen, *Quartet for the End of Time* (1941)

Arnold Schoenberg, String Quartet No. 4 (1937)

Igor Stravinsky, *Petrushka* (1911)
*Symphony of Psalms* (1930)

Anton Webern, *Movement for String Quartet,* op. 5 no. 4 (1909)
*Variations for Piano,* op. 27 (1936)

**2.** Listen to the Introduction to Stravinsky's *Rite of Spring* (1913). How do the themes or motives contribute to the form of the section? Is this form based on a tonal model? Compare your study of the form here to your study of texture in Analysis Exercise 2 in Chapter 3.

**3.** Listen to Béla Bartók's String Quartet No. 4 (1928). Study the first movement's use of sonata form. How clear are the dividing lines between sections? What are the differences between the exposition and recapitulation?

Compare the second and fourth movements. What is the form of each? Which aspects of these movements are similar? Which differ?

**4.** Listen to Charles Ives's *The Unanswered Question* (1908). What formal processes underlie this piece? Is it based on a tonal model?

**5.** Listen to Edgard Varèse's *Ionisation* (1931). Some commentators hear sonata form as the basis of this piece. What aspects support such a contention? What aspects point in other ways?

**6.** The first movement of Bartók's *Music for Strings, Percussion, and Celesta* (1936) and the last movement of Igor Stravinsky's *Septet* (1953) begin as fugues. Study each of these movements as a fugue. What do they have in common? How do they differ? How do they relate to tonal fugues?

# Unit Two

---

# Pitch Structures

In Unit One, we have surveyed some differences between tonal and nontonal twentieth-century music in terms of tonality, pitch, rhythm, texture, timbre, and form. As mentioned earlier, the single most crucial difference between tonal and nontonal twentieth-century music lies in the area of pitch structure. For this reason, the focus of the chapters in Units Two and Three is on the ways that pitch structure is organized in twentieth-century nontonal music.

We will begin by introducing analytic methods with which to explore how pitches relate to one another in nontonal music, allowing us to understand the musical possibilities that reside in different combinations of pitches. The discussions of aspects other than pitch in Unit One bear witness to the wide range of styles in twentieth-century music. Yet almost all of them use pitches in such a way that their structure can be studied with these analytic methods.

# 5
# Pitches, Intervals, Melody

---

| | |
|---|---|
| *pitch* | *interval* |
| *pitch-class* | *interval-class* |
| *movable-zero notation* | *fixed-zero notation* |
| *complement* | *inversion* |

---

## Pitches and Pitch-Classes

There are twelve different notes in an octave. The term *pitch* refers to any single one of these notes in a single register, no matter what its spelling. Middle C, for instance, is the same pitch whether spelled as C, D♭♭, or B♯. The term *pitch-class* (that is, a *class* or a *category* of pitches) refers to all the pitches that are octave duplications of one another. Middle C, for instance, is a *pitch*. But all the notes named C, B♯, and D♭♭ belong to one *pitch-class*. Although there are many different *pitches* (eighty-eight on a piano keyboard), there are only twelve *pitch-classes*.

Because of our tonal heritage, we are used to naming these twelve pitch-classes with seven letter-names (A to G) plus sharps or flats. As we discussed in Chapter 1, this is cumbersome and often confusing for the analysis of nontonal twentieth-century music in which there is no systematic distinction between different spellings of the same pitch-class, such as C and B♯, or C♯ and D♭. And there is no systematic distinction between intervals that are enharmonically equivalent; C–E and C♯–F are four semitones large, despite the fact that on the staff one looks like a major third and the other like a diminished fourth.

To clarify the status of pitches in this music, many theorists now use a new system of note names when analyzing this music. Pitch-classes are named by numbers instead of letters. In this book, we will continue to use traditional letter-names when we refer to the notes in a score or on a staff. But we will use these new pitch-class names in most analyses.

*Numbering Pitch-Classes.* The numbers 0 to 11 refer to the twelve different pitch-classes in ascending semitones. Note that each pitch-class receives a single name, no matter how it is spelled: both the E♭ and D♯ in Example 5-1 are pitch number 6.

Example 5-1: Bartók, *Music for Strings, Percussion, and Celesta,* first movement

*Fixed- and Movable-Zero.* How do we know which pitch-class is number 0? There are two different ways of assigning the number 0 to a pitch-class. Sometimes it is advantageous to assign a 0 to whatever pitch-class is a convenient focal point in the piece or passage being analyzed. Often we will use 0 for the first pitch in the excerpt studied. This is *movable-zero notation,* as in Example 5-1. In movable-zero notation, we indicate pitch-class 0 by placing its letter name at the beginning of the example in square brackets: such as [A = 0] in Example 5-1.

Sometimes it is convenient to use 0 for the pitch-class C, regardless of whether C is particularly important in a given excerpt. This is *fixed-zero notation.*

Fixed-zero and movable-zero notations each have advantages. In fixed-zero notation, each pitch always has the same name, making it easier to remember. Movable-zero, which allows you to use 0 for any convenient pitch in a passage, often facilitates your analysis. We will generally use movable-zero notation in this text. But we will use fixed-zero where it seems more appropriate.

*An Analysis Using Pitch-Class Numbers.* In Example 5-2 (see p. 68), the pitches in a melody by Schoenberg are labeled according to both notations. The pitch numbers themselves illuminate various features of this melody. Note first that no pitch number is repeated in the course of the melody. This means that no pitch-class recurs after a new pitch-class appears. In addition, every number from 0 to 11 appears—all pitch-classes are present in this melody. Finally, there are quite a few adjacent num-

EXAMPLE 5-2: Schoenberg, String Quartet No. 4, op. 37, first movement

| fixed-0: | 2 | 1 | | 9 | 10 5 3 | 4 | 0 8 | 7 | 6 11 |
| [D=0] movable-0: | 0 | 11 | | 7 | 8 3 1 | 2 | 10 6 | 5 | 4 9 |

bers: 2–1, 9–10, 3–4, 8–7, and 7–6 in fixed-zero notation; 0–11, 7–8, 1–2, 6–5, and 5–4 in movable-zero notation. This tells us that if these adjacent pitch-classes appeared in the same octave, this melody could contain many semitones. All these potential semitones are in fact present as semitones in the melody since all the pitch-classes involved are in the same register.

This melody appears at the very opening of Schoenberg's String Quartet No. 4, op. 37 (1937). As happens in music from any historical era, this opening of the piece announces many of its important features. From this brief analysis of Example 5-2, you already know quite a bit about its use of pitches. That the melody contains all twelve pitch-classes in a single phrase tells you that the use of all the pitch-classes is a feature of the work. In fact, this quartet is composed in the twelve-tone system, a compositional method important to much twentieth-century music, and one that we will discuss in some detail in Unit Three. In twelve-tone music, all twelve pitch-classes are continually in circulation.

An additional feature of the melody in Example 5-2 is the abundance of semitones. Of the eleven intervals between consecutive notes, five are semitones. In fact, as we will see in later chapters when we study this movement in more detail, semitones are crucial intervals in the musical construction of the *Fourth Quartet*.

*Summary.* We now know the difference between *pitches* and *pitch-classes*. We have a new set of names for pitch-classes. And we have some idea of the musical insights we can get just from knowing the pitch-class names of the notes in a passage. As we will see in the next section of this chapter, these new pitch-class names help us to measure intervals easily.

## Intervals

How do we figure out the size and name of an interval in number notation? When we subtract the number of the lower pitch from that of the upper pitch, the resulting number is the size of the interval in semitones.

EXAMPLE 5-3                                    EXAMPLE: 5-4

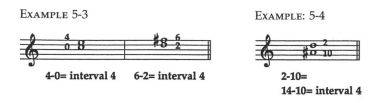

4-0= interval 4    6-2= interval 4             2-10=
                                               14-10= interval 4

What happens if the number of the lower pitch is larger than the number of the upper pitch? We would then end up with a negative number as the interval size. Such negative numbers are correct, but cumbersome to use. To avoid negative numbers, just add 12 (the number of semitones in an octave) to the number of the upper pitch when it is smaller than that of the lower pitch.

Example 5-4, which uses fixed-zero notation, demonstrates this. D (pitch-class 2) lies above A♯ (pitch-class 10). To show a D above A♯, we must add 12 to D ($2 + 12 = 14$).

***Interval Inversion.*** How do we invert intervals in numerical notation? Invert an interval by subtracting the number of the interval from 12. See Example 5-5. We call the inversion of an interval the *complement* of that interval.

EXAMPLE 5-5

[F=0]  4-0= interval 4   12-4= interval 8   0-4=
                                            12-4= interval 8

The reason that we subtract the number of the interval from 12 is that by definition a *simple interval* (an interval smaller than an octave) and its inversion add up to an octave. Since the octave contains twelve semitones, the inversion of an interval is the difference between the interval and 12.

***Compound Intervals.*** How do we deal with *compound intervals*—those that are larger than an octave and have a number larger than 12? In order to simplify many analyses, it is convenient to convert compound intervals into simple intervals by subtracting 12 or multiples of 12 (an octave or multiple octaves) until the interval size is a number between 0 and 11. Basically, this process changes an interval between pitches into the equivalent interval between pitch-classes.

EXAMPLE 5-6

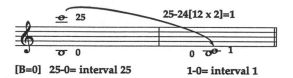

[B=0]   25-0= interval 25          1-0= interval 1

*Some Hints for Remembering Interval Sizes.*    As you begin using numbers to identify intervals, you may find it difficult to remember exactly which interval is referred to by which number. Table 5-1 lists all the intervals and their tonal equivalents.

TABLE 5-1

| Interval Number | Traditional Name(s) |
| :---: | :--- |
| 0 | Unison |
| 1 | Semitone, minor second, augmented unison |
| 2 | Whole tone, major second, diminished third |
| 3 | Minor third, augmented second |
| 4 | Major third, diminished fourth |
| 5 | Perfect fourth, augmented third |
| 6 | Tritone, augmented fourth, diminished fifth |
| 7 | Perfect fifth, diminished sixth |
| 8 | Minor sixth, augmented fifth |
| 9 | Major sixth, diminished seventh |
| 10 | Minor seventh, augmented sixth |
| 11 | Major seventh, diminished octave |
| 12 | Octave |

There are two mnemonic devices that may be helpful to you as you begin to relate these numbers to the interval names and sounds with which you are familiar. The first way is to remember a few basic intervals and learn the remaining intervals in terms of these:

*Intervals 1 and 2 are the semitone and whole tone. Therefore, the inversions of interval 1 and 2 are **intervals 11 and 10:** (12 − 1 = 11; 12 − 2 = 10)—the major and minor seventh.*

*Interval 6 is the tritone. It divides the octave into two equal halves. **Intervals 5 and 7** are, respectively, one semitone smaller and one semitone larger than the tritone—the perfect fourth and perfect fifth.*

*Intervals 3 and 4 are the minor and major third—one-and-one-half steps and two whole-steps. **Intervals 9 and 8** are their complements—the major and minor sixths.*

Another way to remember interval sizes is to think of dividing the octave into three or four parts. Since the octave has twelve semitones, and 12 is divisible by both 3 and 4, both divisions are easy:

*Dividing the octave into three parts (0,4,8,12) gives us the augmented triad, with all notes separated by four semitones (a major third). So interval 4 is a major third or diminished fourth and interval 8 is a minor sixth or augmented fifth.*

*Dividing the octave into four parts (0,3,6,9,12) gives us the diminished seventh chord, with all notes separated by three semitones (a minor third). So interval 3 is a minor third or augmented second, interval 6 is a tritone, and interval 9 is a major sixth or diminished seventh.*

*All intervals are either members of one of these divisions of the octave (0,3,4,6,8,9,12) or a semitone smaller or larger than one of these intervals (1,2,5,7,10,11).*

*Recommendations for Study.* Whichever way you learn to use number notation, you will soon be comfortable with these names. At this point, turn to Terms and Concepts Exercises 2 and 3 at the end of this chapter. Spending a few minutes with the drill exercises there will give you facility in using pitch and interval numbers, and will tell you what material in this section you should reread. Then proceed with the next part of this chapter.

# Interval-Class

Just as pitch-class is the grouping of all pitches of the same type (all C's, all C#–D♭'s, and so forth), *interval-class* is the grouping of all intervals of the same type. Each interval-class includes an interval, its complement, and all compounds of the interval and its complement. There are six different interval classes.

TABLE 5-2

| Interval Class | Members |
|---|---|
| 1,11 | Intervals 1, 11, 13, 23, etc. |
| 2,10 | Intervals 2, 10, 14, 22, etc. |
| 3,9 | Intervals 3, 9, 15, 21, etc. |
| 4,8 | Intervals 4, 8, 16, 20, etc. |
| 5,7 | Intervals 5, 7, 17, 19, etc. |
| 6 | Intervals 6, 18, etc. |

We will find interval-class an especially useful concept when we study the structure of groups of pitches in Chapter 7. At this point in our study, interval-class is useful in recognizing the similarity between ascending and descending forms of the same interval.

*Interval-Class and Ascending and Descending Intervals.* In measuring melodic intervals, figure out the interval by subtracting the first pitch number from the second. Thus, D to the E immediately above is interval 2 ($4-2=2$ in fixed-zero notation).

In the case of descending intervals, this process gives us negative interval numbers. For example, E to the D immediately below it is $-2$ ($2-4=-2$ in fixed-zero notation). This negative number is the correct size of the melodic interval between *pitch* E and *pitch* D. The minus sign tells us that it is a descending interval.

The negative number for a descending melodic interval can be converted into the positive numbers of the complement of the interval. Hence E to D, interval $-2$, becomes interval 10. This describes the interval size from *pitch-class* E to *pitch-class* D.

In our analyses, it is easiest to avoid negative numbers by measuring descending intervals between pitch-classes, not between pitches. The names of the ascending and descending forms of the same melodic interval are always those of a single interval-class. (See Example 5-7.)

EXAMPLE 5-7

pitch-classes: 0   4      4   0      1   3      3   1
[A=0]
intervals:     4         8         2         10

# Model Analysis: Melody

*Schoenberg,* **Serenade,** *op. 24, Variations theme.*     Example 5-8 presents the unaccompanied clarinet melody that is the theme for a set of variations in Schoenberg's *Serenade,* op. 24 (1920–23). Each pitch is labeled and all intervals are indicated below the melody. B♭ is labeled 0 in movable-zero notation; the melody begins and ends on B♭, which is, as we will see, an important pitch in this passage. Familiarize yourself with the melody by listening to it several times, playing it, and then singing it.

EXAMPLE 5-8: Schoenberg, *Serenade,* third movement

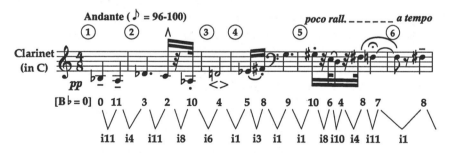

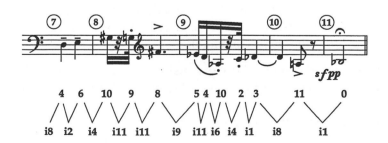

What strikes you about this melody? The following discussion begins with some of its general features and proceeds to details.

*Contour.*     Perhaps the most obvious aspect of this melody, even on first hearing, is how its contour expands both above and below its first pitch and then gradually closes back to that first pitch at the end.

EXAMPLE 5-9

Study of the pitch-class numbers reveals that this expansion from and contraction back to B♭ is part of a larger aspect of the melody. The entire second half of the melody (after the fermata in m. 5) is a reverse of the order of the pitches in the first half. Each pitch recurs in the second half in the same register as in the first half.

*Skips.*     The skips in the melody complement the expanding and contracting shape of the melody. Increasingly large skips appear as the melody encompasses an ever-larger register. Two skips of interval 4 (both rising and falling) in mm. 1–2 are followed by a skip of interval 6 in mm. 2–3 and a downward skip of eleven semitones in m. 4. The second half of the melody reverses this, of course, narrowing the size of the skips.

*B♭ as a Focal Pitch.*     Pitch 0 (B♭) is the point of origin and conclusion for this registral expansion and contraction. B♭ lies exactly at the center of range of the melody. Or, to put it another way, the melody radiates as far above B♭ as it does below. The highest pitches (pitch-class 8 in mm. 4 and 8) and lowest pitches (pitch-class 4 in mm. 5 and 7) are eight semitones distant from pitch-class 0.

*Interval-Class 4,8.*     The interval-class 4,8, therefore, plays an important role in this melody. It is the interval class that measures the distance from the opening and closing pitch to the highest and lowest pitch; interval 4 is also the interval between the lowest and highest pitches. Finally, there are more skips of intervals 4 and 8 during the melody than there are skips of any other interval-class: eight skips by 4 or 8 and only six skips by all other intervals combined.

*Rhythm and Phrasing.*     The expansion and contraction of this melody is not a property of pitch alone. Rhythmic activity plays a role, too. As the pitches open up the range and the skips increase in frequency and size, quicker rhythms appear.

Although the pitches of the second half of the melody are in reverse order, the second half of the melody does not sound like a mere reversal of the first half. Rather, it sounds more like a consequent or answer to the first half. Why is this so? Rhythm is a primary factor in creating this effect. The rhythms after the fermata are akin to those at the beginning of the piece, as shown in Example 5-10.

EXAMPLE 5-10

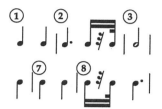

Just as the rhythm becomes more active as the melody expands in register, the rhythms toward the end slow down, creating a sense of cadence at the very end.

As a result, the entire melody sounds like a pair of phrases, an antecedent opening up from the beginning, and a consequent folding back and concluding. Within the antecedent phrase-division, increases in rhythmic activity support the registral expansion of the melody right up to the end of the phrase. In the consequent phrase, the peak of rhythmic activity comes earlier, allowing for the slow-down that prepares the cadence.

*Tonal Aspects.*    Although B♭ is a focal pitch as registral center of the diverging and converging registral limits, it is by no means a "tonic" in the tonal sense. The melody may be centered around B♭, but it is not in "B♭ major" or "B♭ minor." Eleven of the twelve pitch-classes are present (B, pitch-class 1, is absent), preventing the clear statement of any diatonic scale. Yet there is a tonal flavor at the opening and particularly at the closing of the phrase. The first four and last four pitch-classes do belong to a B♭-minor scale—an impression strengthened at the end by the melodic semitones leading to D♭ and B♭ in the last measures.

*Nontonal Melody Structure.*    As can be seen from the analysis above, the effect of a melody depends on many factors, including the overall contour, which pitch-classes are present and which are absent, the register in which the pitch-classes appear, what intervals and interval-classes are prominent both locally and long-range, how rhythm articulates these motions, the type of phrasing, and the presence or absence of tonal features. Each of the melodies for analysis in the exercises that conclude this chapter combines these factors in unique ways. In later chapters, we will add more detailed study of motivic cells and harmonic underpinnings to our study of melodies.

# Points for Review

**1.** The term *pitch* refers to any single note in a single register, no matter what its spelling. The term *pitch-class* (that is, a *class* or a *category* of pitches) refers to all the pitches that are octave duplications of one another.

**2.** The numbers 0 to 11 refer to the twelve different pitch-classes in ascending semitones.

**3.** 0 can be assigned to C in all cases (*fixed-zero notation*) or to any pitch (*movable-zero notation*).

**4.** Harmonic intervals are calculated by subtracting the number of the lower pitch from that of the upper pitch. If the number of the upper pitch is smaller than that of the lower pitch, add 12 (an octave) to the upper number before subtracting.

**5.** To invert an interval, subtract its number from 12. The *inversion* of an interval is its *complement*.

**6.** To reduce a *compound interval* (an interval larger than an octave) to a *simple interval* (an interval no larger than an octave), subtract 12 or multiples of 12 from the interval number until the result is between 0 and 11.

**7.** An *interval-class* contains an interval, its complement, and all compounds of the interval and of its inversion. There are six interval-classes: 1,11; 2,10; 3,9; 4,8; 5,7; and 6.

**8.** Measure melodic intervals by subtracting the first pitch from the second pitch. Descending melodic intervals will have negative numbers that can be converted into the positive numbers of the complement of the interval.

# Exercises for Chapter 5

## Terms and Concepts

**1.** Define the following terms:

| | | | |
|---|---|---|---|
| *pitch* | *movable-zero notation* | *interval-class* | *inversion* |
| *pitch-class* | *simple interval* | *complement* | |
| *interval* | *compound interval* | *fixed-zero notation* | |

**2.** Using numbers, label the following intervals. Reduce compound intervals to simple intervals. The first exercise has been completed.

**3.** Write the complement of the following intervals. The first exercise has been completed.

**a)** interval 2 ____i10____   **g)** interval 7 _____

**b)** interval 6 _____   **h)** interval 9 _____

**c)** interval 8 _____   **i)** interval 3 _____

**d)** interval 10 _____   **j)** interval 4 _____

**e)** interval 1 _____   **k)** interval 11 _____

**f)** interval 5 _____

**Analysis**

Familiarize yourself with each melody below. Listen to it several times. Play it, and, where the range is not excessive, sing it. Then label the pitches in each using number notation. (The first pitch has been labeled for you in each melody.)

Then answer the questions. For each melody, think also about how it is shaped. How many phrases does it have? How do you know? Where is the climax of each phrase?

Finally, consider that each melody occurs at the very opening of a piece or a movement. What kind of music might it foreshadow? What might its structure indicate about the intervals, pitches, contours, phrasings, and rhythms of the music that follows it? Listen to the piece of which it is the opening. Does the music that follows confirm your conclusions? Does it give you new insights into the opening melody?

For your study of each melody, use the model analysis of the melody of Schoenberg's *Serenade* (Example 5-8) as a guide.

**1.** Stravinsky, *Rite of Spring* (1913), Introduction. This opening melody begins without accompaniment. How many pitch-classes are used? Which are most prominent? Which are least prominent? Which pitch is a focal pitch for the melody? What factors lead you to this conclusion?

Chapter 3 discusses the layered textures characteristic of many Stravinsky works. This opening melody is one component of the layered texture that builds during the Introduction. What aspects make this melody ideal for its role in this type of texture? Study the remainder of the Introduction. Are other melodies similar in structure?

2. Bartók, *Music for Strings, Percussion, and Celesta* (1936), first movement. This is the unaccompanied fugue subject that opens the work. The dotted barlines indicate the subdivisions within each measure. How might you describe the pitch-classes under the first slur? Following the first phrasing slur, how are new pitch-classes introduced?

Label all intervals. What intervals are most prominent? Does any sequence of intervals recur? Describe the process of growth and contraction that shapes the melody. What role does meter play in this shaping?

Chapter 4 discusses some aspects of this fugal movement. Successive entries of the fugue subject follow one another up or down by interval 7. What role, if any, does interval 7 play in the construction of the fugue subject itself?

In addition, Chapter 4 noted that the climax of the movement is on interval 6 from the opening A. What role, if any, does interval 6 play in the fugue subject itself?

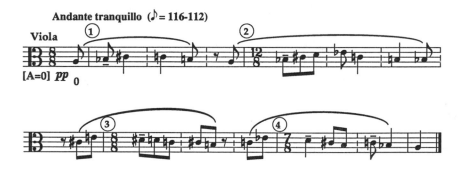

3. Schoenberg, String Quartet No. 4, op. 37 (1937), first movement. We have discussed the first phrase in Example 5-2. The excerpt here consists of the melody of the first three phrases. How many pitch-classes are in each phrase? As we discussed in Chapter 3, the texture in which

these three phrases are set projects an ABA' structure, with each phrase being one section. How do the rhythms and the registral contours support this effect?

/ = accented; like a strong beat.

ᵕ = unaccented, like a weak beat.

▼ = hard, heavy <u>martelé</u>

∧ = do not allow to weaken; used mostly for upbeats.

**4.** Babbitt, *Composition for Four Instruments* (1948). This unaccompanied melody opens the composition. How many pitch-classes are present? How many are absent? Label all intervals. How many different intervals occur in the melody? M. 1 contains a rising and falling contour. Where else does this contour occur? What other recurring contours can you hear?

**5.** Messiaen, *Quartet for the End of Time* (1941), sixth movement. The entire sixth movement of this quartet is monophonic, with single or multiple octave doublings providing reinforcement. Label all pitches and intervals in this opening melody. What pitches predominate? What pitch(es) seem(s) to be added to the basic pitch collection? On what pitches do phrase divisions end? By what interval is the approach to these final pitches made?

**6.** Webern, *Symphony*, op. 21 (1928), second movement. This melody, accompanied, is the theme for a set of variations. How many pitch-classes are present? How many are absent? Label all intervals. Where in this excerpt can you find intervals and their complements? What other aspects of this melody are also organized in the same way?

# 6
# Pitch-Class Sets

---

| | |
|---|---|
| *pitch-class set* | *tetrachord* |
| *transposition* | *pentachord* |
| *inversion* | *hexachord* |
| *lowest ordering* | *heptachord* |
| *prime form* | *octachord* |
| *trichord* | |

---

## Pitch-Class Sets

A *pitch-class set* is a group of pitch-classes, each different from the others. Pitch-class sets provide us with an analytic tool to study melodies, harmonies, and the interactions between melody and harmony in nontonal music.

*The Size of Pitch-Class Sets.* How many pitch-classes can there be in a pitch-class set? A pitch-class set may contain between one and twelve pitch-classes, but we will concern ourselves at first with those that contain between three and eight pitch-classes. The following terms tell us how many pitch-classes there are in these pitch-class sets:

> *a trichord* contains *three* pitch-classes
> *a tetrachord* contains *four* pitch-classes
> *a pentachord* contains *five* pitch-classes
> *a hexachord* contains *six* pitch-classes
> *a heptachord* contains *seven* pitch-classes
> *an octachord* contains *eight* pitch-classes

(We need not concern ourselves with pitch-class sets with one or two pitch-classes, because they are single notes or single intervals whose structure is self-evident. Similarly, the structure of pitch-class sets with twelve or eleven pitch-classes is self-evident: a complete chromatic scale, and a chromatic scale missing a single note. As for pitch-class sets with nine or ten pitch-classes, we will treat them in Chapter 9 under the heading of Pitch Regions.)

**Names of Pitch-Class Sets.** Every pitch-class set has a name that includes the number of all its pitch-classes notated in ascending order within a single octave. We write the name of the pitch-class set in square brackets, with a comma between each number, such as [0,2,4,7,9]. This pentachord is the source of all the notes in mm. 1–2 of *The Sunken Cathedral*, one of Debussy's *Preludes for Piano* published in 1910.

EXAMPLE 6-1: Debussy, *The Sunken Cathedral*, Prelude No. 10, Book I.

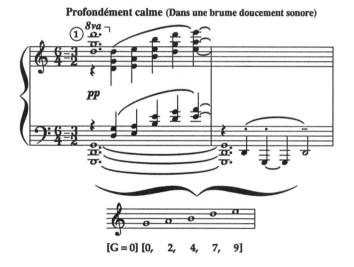

[G = 0] [0,   2,   4,   7,   9]

The members of the pitch-class set [0,2,4,7,9] (with G=0) appear on a separate staff below the example. We notate pitch-class sets with open noteheads in ascending order within a single octave. (Remember that we are notating pitch-classes, not pitches. So we can write the noteheads in any convenient register.) Accidentals affect only the notehead they precede.

A pitch-class set can occur in a piece in its original or *prime* form, transposed, or inverted.

**Transposition.** Transposition of a pitch-class set means moving it up by an interval. We transpose a pitch-class set by adding the interval of transposition to each pitch number, subtracting 12 from any pitch numbers over 11. For instance, to transpose the pitch-class set [0,2,4,7,9] in Example 6-1 four semitones higher, we add 4 to each pitch-class in the set:

| set: | 0 | 2 | 4 | 7 | | 9 |
|---|---|---|---|---|---|---|
| plus interval of transposition: | +4 | +4 | +4 | +4 | | +4 |
| equals transposed form: | 4 | 6 | 8 | 11 | (13 − 12 =) | 1 |

The transposition of [0,2,4,7,9] by four semitones gives us the set [4,6,8,11,1] or, to put the numbers in ascending order, [1,4,6,8,11].

Example 6-2 presents a later passage in Debussy's *The Sunken Cathedral*. The transposition of [0,2,4,7,8] up four semitones to [4,6,8,11,1] is the basis for this passage.

EXAMPLE 6-2: Debussy, *The Sunken Cathedral*, Prelude No. 10, Book I.

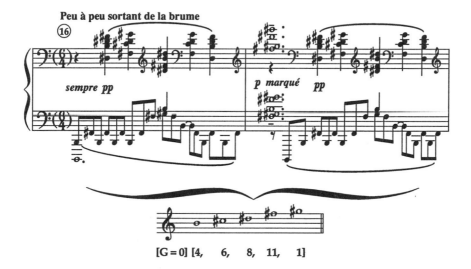

[G = 0] [4,   6,   8,   11,   1]

***Inversion.*** Inverting a pitch-class set means replacing every interval in the set with its complement. Example 6-3 presents a melody by Messiaen with which we are already familiar. The trichord that opens the

EXAMPLE 6-3: Messiaen, *Quartet for the End of Time*, sixth movement

first phrase (E–F♯–B♭ or [0,2,6]) recurs at the cadence to the second phrase in inverted form. Each interval in the prime form is replaced by its complement in the inversion: interval 2 (E–F♯) is replaced by interval 10 (C–B♭), and interval 4 (F♯–B♭) is replaced by interval 8 (B♭–F♯).

Invert a pitch-class set by following these two steps:

*Step 1: Write the name of the set beginning with 0.*

EXAMPLE 6-4

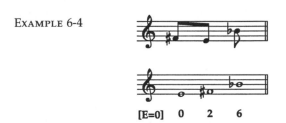

[E=0]  0  2  6

*Step 2: Subtract each number from 12, and reduce 12 to 0.*

EXAMPLE 6-5

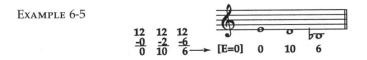

| 12 | 12 | 12 | | | | |
|---|---|---|---|---|---|---|
| -0 | -2 | -6 | | | | |
| 0 | 10 | 6 | → | [E=0] 0 | 10 | 6 |

An inverted set can then be transposed by any interval. The form of the inversion in Example 6-3 is transposed up eight semitones from the form in Example 6-5. The following example illustrates this.

EXAMPLE 6-6

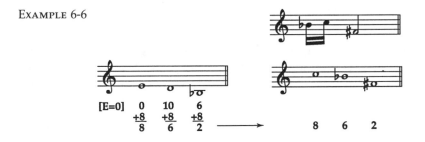

[E=0]  0    10   6
      +8   +8   +8           8    6    2
       8    6    2   ⟶

# A Single Name for Each Pitch-Class Set: Lowest Ordering

It should be clear by now that a single set can have many different names for its prime form, for its inversion, and for the transpositions of its prime form and inversion. The same set is the basis of Examples 6-1 and 6-2, even though the set is labeled [0,2,4,7,9], [4,6,8,11,1], and

[1,4,6,8,11] respectively. The trichord in Examples 6-3 through 6-6 has the names [0,2,6] and [0,6,8]. Furthermore, if we had used a different pitch-class as 0 in any of these examples, the sets would have had other names. You may well wonder at this point how you can tell if two sets are the same or different if any set can have so many names for its reorderings, transpositions, and inversions.

What we need, therefore, is a single name for any given pitch-class set, a name that stands for the set in all its forms. This single name is called the *lowest ordering* of that set. *The lowest ordering of a pitch-class set begins with 0 and contains the lowest possible numbering of that set.*

***Figuring Out the Lowest Ordering.*** You can figure out the lowest ordering of any pitch-class set by following the three steps given here. (In fact, for most sets, you need only carry out the first two steps.) The tetrachord in Example 6-7 will be our first example.

EXAMPLE 6-7

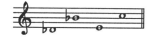

*Step 1: Notate all the pitch-classes in ascending order within an octave. You can start on any pitch-class. See Example 6-8.*

EXAMPLE 6-8

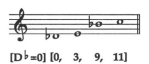

[D♭=0] [0, 3, 9, 11]

*Step 2: Find the largest interval between* consecutive *pitches. (Remember to consider the interval from the last note up to the first note in the next octave—from C up to D♭ in Example 6-8.) Reorder the pitches, beginning with the* upper *pitch of the largest interval. Number from 0. This gives you the lowest number between the first and last pitch-classes.*

*In Example 6-8, the largest interval is between E and B♭. By reordering the set beginning with B♭, we have the following result:*

EXAMPLE 6-9

[B♭=0] [0, 2, 3, 6]

*Step 3: If the last interval in your step 2 result is larger than the first interval, then you already have the lowest ordering. But if the last interval in step 2 is the same size or smaller than the first interval, rewrite the pitches from right to left, write the complement of each number, and transpose to begin on 0. Compare this new result to that of step 2 to find the lowest ordering.*

*The last interval in [0,2,3,6] is 3, which is larger than the first interval. So the lowest ordering of this tetrachord is [0,2,3,6].*

With [0,2,3,6], there is only one result to consider in steps 2 and 3. In some sets, there are several candidates for lowest ordering in steps 2 and 3. That makes the process of figuring out the lowest ordering a bit longer, but the steps remain the same. For a particularly complex example, consider the pentachord in violin II and viola at the opening of Schoenberg's String Quartet No. 3, op. 30 (1926):

EXAMPLE 6-10: Schoenberg, String Quartet No. 3, op. 30, first movement

*Step 1: Notate all the pitch-classes in ascending order within an octave.*

EXAMPLE 6-11

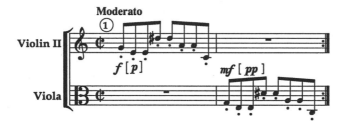

[G=0]  [0, 2, 5, 8, 9]

*Step 2: Find the largest interval between consecutive pitches. (Remember to consider the interval from the last note up to the first note in the next octave— from E up to G in Example 6-11.) Reorder the pitches, beginning with the upper pitch of the largest interval. Number from 0.*

*In the set above, the largest interval between consecutive pitch-classes is 3. It occurs three times: E–G, A–C, and C–D♯. In this case, therefore, we must write three versions, beginning on G, C, and D♯. Number each from 0.*

EXAMPLE 6-12

[G=0]  [0, 2, 5, 8, 9]    [C=0]  [0, 3, 4, 7, 9]    [D♯=0]  [0, 1, 4, 6, 9]

*Step 3: If the* last *interval in your step 2 result is* larger *than the* first *interval, then you already have the lowest ordering. But if the* last *interval in step 2 is the* same *size or* smaller *than the* first *interval, rewrite the pitches from right to left, write the complement of each number, and transpose to begin on 0. Compare this new result to the result(s) of step 2 to find the lowest ordering.*

*The third result to step 2 (beginning on D♯) begins with a semitone. Only the first ordering in Example 6-12 ends with a semitone. So we need to work out the inversion for only that first ordering:*

| | | |
|---|---|---|
| [0,2,5,8,9] | 9,8,5,2,0 | (reversed order) |
| | 3,4,7,10,0 | (the complement of each) |
| | [0,1,4,7,9] | (transposed to begin on 0) |

*In this case, the third ordering in Example 6-12, [0,1,4,6,9] and this inversion [0,1,4,7,9] agree in all but the fourth number. Since 6 is lower than 7, the third ordering in Example 6-12 is the lowest ordering: [0,1,4,6,9].*

Figuring out the lowest ordering of this pentachord is particularly complicated because there are three instances of interval 3 as the largest interval in step 1. It was included here to illustrate the most difficult possibility. In most instances, as we saw in Examples 6-7 through 6-9, there is only one set-form to consider in steps 2 and 3.

***Labeling Forms in Relation to the Lowest Ordering.*** Once we know the lowest ordering of a pitch-class set, we can give a single name to each transposition and inversion of that set. Consider this pitch-class set:

EXAMPLE 6-13

[F=0]   [0,   1,   4,   7]

We can label any transposition of this set with this name and T (for transposed) after the number of semitones up.

EXAMPLE 6-14

[F = 0]   [0, 1, 4, 7] T1     [0, 1, 4, 7] T4

Similarly, any inverted form can be labeled I (for inverted) followed by the interval of transposition between the first pitch-classes.

EXAMPLE 6-15

[F = 0]   [0, 1, 4, 7] I0     [0, 1, 4, 7] I7

# Locating Pitch-Class Sets

Now that we know how to name a pitch-class set, how to transpose it, how to invert it, and how to find the lowest ordering of that set, we can turn our attention to studying the use of pitch-class sets in pieces and to composing our own pieces.

*Pitch-Class Sets in Nontonal Music.*    When we listen to a piece of music, we become aware of the recurring patterns it contains: patterns in its melody, harmony, rhythm, dynamics, and so forth. We call these patterns motives. Motives help to make different parts of a phrase, a section, or a piece sound like they belong together. They are the thematic ideas of a piece that are points of reference or material for development. The first four notes of Beethoven's *Fifth Symphony*, for instance, comprise such a motive.

As we saw in Chapter 1, the motives in a tonal piece, no matter how closely they relate to the harmonic-melodic structures, exist on top of the functional tonal basis of the music. In nontonal music, where there is no harmonic language common to many or all pieces, every piece creates its own unique interaction of harmony and melody. It is the pitch-class sets that provide the raw material for harmony and melody in this music. In this sense, pitch-class sets in nontonal music are analogous to scales in tonal music. Like tonal scales, nontonal pitch-class sets provide the notes out of which melodies and harmonies arise.

In addition, the structure of a pitch-class set, like the structure of a tonal scale, sets limits for the resulting harmonies and melodies. For instance, a melody or a harmony using notes from a C-major scale will not contain augmented seconds because that interval does not occur in a major scale. Similarly, a pitch-class set that does not contain any tritones will not allow the presence of tritones in a passage based on that set.

But outside of these limits, the compositional possibilities are virtually infinite. The pitch-classes in a pitch-class set can appear in one register or in many. They can appear in any ordering. They can appear as a melody, as a harmony, doubled between melody and harmony, or divided between melody and harmony. They can appear in any rhythms, dynamics, textures, and timbres. They can appear once or recur any number of times. And so forth.

Earlier in this chapter, we saw a pitch-class set serve as the basis for two different textures in a single piece (Examples 6-1 and 6-2), and a pitch-class set serve as the basis for part of a melody (Example 6-3). Example 6-16 illustrates a variety of ways that a single pitch-class set appears within the opening five measures of Webern's *Movement for String*

*Quartet*, op. 5 no. 4. (See Analysis Exercise 2 in Chapter 8 for a score to the entire movement.)

EXAMPLE 6-16

[F = 0] [0, 1, 6, 7]          [0, 1, 6, 7] T11          [0, 1, 6, 7] T1

The pitch-class set appears as a tremolo chord, as a melody with all pitches in the same register, transposed as a melody, transposed differently as part of another chord, and as a result of the interaction between two different instruments. The recurrences of this pitch-class set as melodies, as harmonies, and as a structural relationship among parts help to unify the passage. The register, ordering, duration, and instrumentation of the pitch-classes may vary, but the relationships within the set remain the same.

*Locating Pitch-Class Sets.* Obviously, the results of a pitch-class set analysis depend to a large degree on which pitch-classes you select as members of the sets. In analyzing a given passage, there are no hard and fast rules for determining how many and which pitch-classes should be placed together in a pitch-class set. Context is all-important. The insight of the analyst focuses attention on crucial pitches. If this grouping of pitches is important to the sound of the passage, it becomes a candidate for designation as a pitch-class set in an analysis of that passage. It is up to the analyst to indicate as part of the analysis why these particular pitch-classes are being grouped into a set. In this sense, pitch-class set analysis is fundamentally different from tonal harmony, where the method of sorting out chord tones and nonharmonic tones varies little, if at all, from piece to piece.

Although there are no rules for identifying pitch-class sets, and there are a variety of ways of analyzing any given passage or piece, analytic decisions are not arbitrary. Remember that the purpose of pitch-class set analysis, if not of all musical analysis, is to supplement your hearing of the passage, helping you to understand the way it is organized and how it creates its effects. Any group of pitch-classes can theoretically be grouped into a pitch-class set. But when we analyze a passage or piece, we are not merely looking for pitch-class sets. We are looking for those sets that enhance our hearing and understanding of the piece.

Remember too that composers do not, as a rule, create incomprehensible auditory puzzles when they compose. The clues to the way their pieces are organized are usually apparent to a careful listener. Listening is thus an important part of identifying pitch-class sets.

With these considerations in mind, the following guidelines will help you as you begin your analyses. To be heard, and, therefore, to function as an organizing element, pitches in a pitch-class set must appear together, either consecutively as a melody, simultaneously as a harmony, associated texturally or timbrally as in the accompaniment to a melody, or related in some other way. You will find that after you have identified and learned to hear the set or sets that are prominent in a passage, and after finding these pitch-class sets as they occur in several ways in the passage, you can begin to listen for more subtle features.

Up to this point, we have discussed only the identification of pitch-class sets. During the next three chapters, we will study how the structure of a given pitch-class set and relationships among different forms of the same and among different pitch-class sets give rise to the compositional possibilities that come to life in nontonal music. But first you should do the exercises to this chapter to gain facility in naming, transposing, inverting, and recognizing pitch-class sets. The Analysis and Composition exercises at the end of this chapter provide excerpts to analyze and suggestions for composition.

# Points for Review

**1.** A *pitch-class set* is a group of pitch-classes, each different from the others. The types of pitch-class sets we will encounter most often are *trichords* (with three pitch-classes), *tetrachords* (with four), *pentachords* (with five), *hexachords* (with six), *heptachords* (with seven), and *octachords* (with eight).

**2.** The name of a pitch-class set includes all its members in ascending numerical order within a single octave. We write the name of the pitch-class set within square brackets, with a comma between each number, such as [0,2,4,7,9]. The *lowest ordering* of a pitch-class set is its formal name. Review Steps 1–3 on pp. 85–86 for a method of finding the lowest ordering of a set.

**3.** *Transposition* of a pitch-class set means moving it up by an interval. Transpose a pitch-class set by adding the interval of transposition to each pitch number, subtracting 12 from any pitch numbers over 11. Transpositions are labeled by T plus the interval of transposition following the lowest ordering of the set.

**4.** *Inverting* a pitch-class set means replacing every interval in the set with its complement. To invert a pitch-class set, write the name of the set beginning with 0. Subtract each number from 12, and reduce 12 to 0. An inverted set can then be transposed by any interval. Inversions are labeled with I plus the interval of transposition following the lowest ordering. The original form of the pitch-class set is called the *prime form*, distinguished from the *inversion*.

# Exercises for Chapter 6

## Terms and Concepts

1. Define the following terms:

| | |
|---|---|
| *pitch-class set* | *tetrachord* |
| *lowest ordering* | *pentachord* |
| *prime* | *hexachord* |
| *inversion* | *heptachord* |
| *transposition* | *octachord* |
| *trichord* | |

2. How do you transpose a pitch-class set?

3. How do you invert a pitch-class set?

4. List the steps necessary to figure out the lowest ordering of a pitch-class set.

5. Write the name of the following pitch-class sets, and transpose each by interval 1, interval 4, interval 5, and interval 9. The first is completed for you.

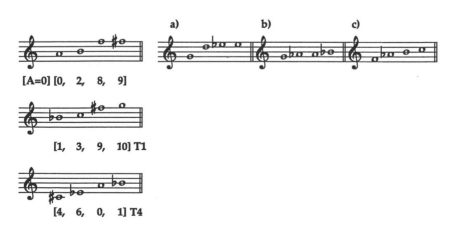

[A=0] [0, 2, 8, 9]

a)  b)  c)

[1, 3, 9, 10] T1

[4, 6, 0, 1] T4

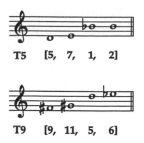

T5  [5, 7, 1, 2]

T9  [9, 11, 5, 6]

**6.** Write out the name of each of the following pitch-class sets, invert each, reorder each in ascending order, and transpose the name to begin with 0. The first has been completed.

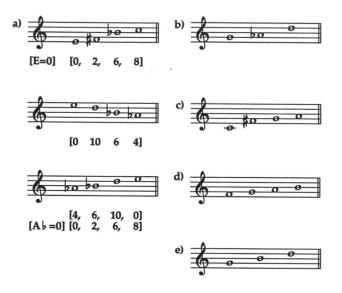

a)  [E=0]  [0, 2, 6, 8]

b)

c)

[0  10  6  4]

d)  [4, 6, 10, 0]
    [A♭=0] [0, 2, 6, 8]

e)

**7.** Place each of the following pitch-class sets in lowest order. The first has been completed.

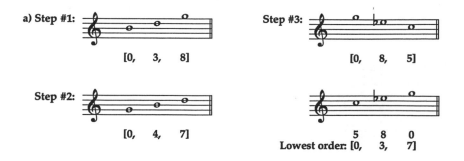

a) Step #1:  [0, 3, 8]

Step #2:  [0, 4, 7]

Step #3:  [0, 8, 5]

                5   8   0
Lowest order: [0,  3,  7]

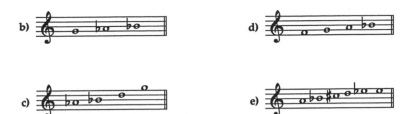

## Analysis

In each of the following passages, a single pitch-class set provides most of the pitch material. In what ways do the passages differ in how this takes place?

**1.** Stravinsky, *Petrushka*, First Tableau (1911). Identify the pitch-class set in the clarinets and horns. Write its name in lowest ordering. What is the relation between this set and the flute melody in mm. 1–5? When a new pitch-class (B) is added to the flute melody beginning in m. 9, what new form of a previously-stated pitch-class set is created?

**2.** Skryabin, *Etude,* op. 65 no. 3 (1911–12). What pitch-class set is formed on the first beat of m. 1? Where else does this pitch-class set occur in this passage?

**3.** Webern, *Concerto for Nine Instruments,* op. 24 (1934), second movement. Figure out the pitch-class sets formed by all simultaneously sounding pitches (that is, the B–B♭–G in m. 1, the D–F♯–D♯ in m. 2, and so forth). Does this pitch-class set also occur in the melodic instruments? In how many forms? Clarinet and trumpet are written at sounding pitch.

Webern, *Konzert*, Op. 24. Copyright 1948 by Universal Edition, Wien. Copyright renewed. All Rights Reserved. Used by permission of European American Music Distributors Corporation, sole U.S. and Canadian agent for Universal Edition, Wien.

**4.** Wagner, *Tristan und Isolde* (1859), Prelude to Act I. Wagner's *Tristan* is certainly a tonal piece. But its highly charged chromaticism caused a sensation throughout the latter part of the nineteenth century. Hearing the opening progression from the point of view of pitch-class sets imparts a new perspective on the passage. Identify the tetrachords formed by each of the chords in mm. 2–3. Which tetrachords are forms of the same pitch-class set? How does the rhythm of the phrase relate to the pitch-class sets you identified?

In this and in later sections of the *Prelude*, listen to the types of pitch-class sets formed by notes sounding together. How does this relate to the functional tonal harmonies in the piece?

## Composition

**1.** Use one of the following pitch-class sets as the basis for a melodic phrase or pair of phrases with the following features:

**a)** Every pitch in your melody should join with adjacent pitches to make a form of this set. Use different transpositions and inversions of the set.

**b)** Be free rhythmically. Expand or contract the metric units where appropriate (as in the Bartók melody in Analysis Exercise 2, Chapter 5), or be free within the meter (as in the flute melody from *Petrushka* in Analysis Exercise 1 in this chapter).

**c)** Write for an instrument you play or that is played by another student in your class. Make sure your melody is idiomatic for the instrument in terms of range and character. Notate the tempo. Add dynamics, articulations, and a word describing the character.

**d)** Make sure you can hear and play your melody.

[0, 1, 2, 5]  [0, 2, 5, 7]  [0, 1, 3, 6]

**2.** Add a second part or an accompaniment to the melody you composed. Try different textures and/or relationships between the parts:

**a)** Use as the basis for the second part the pitch-class set you used as the basis of your melody. Or use another pitch-class set from the list.

**b)** Try both a contrapuntal part and a repeating accompaniment (an ostinato).

**c)** Try a strictly metrical accompaniment as well as a free one.

**d)** Use an instrument other than the one used for your melody.

**3.** Write a contrasting melody to follow your original one, add a second part, and combine your two sections to form a piece in ABA form.

# 7
# Interval Content

The types of music that a given pitch-class set can produce depends in large part on the intervals present in that set. A tetrachord containing only one whole tone and no semitones, for instance, will not by itself be suitable for composing a lyrical, stepwise melody. Nor can a tetrachord containing only a dominant seventh chord create a jarring, highly angular and dissonant texture. Thus, the expressive possibilities of a given pitch-class set are related to the intervals it contains, called its *interval content*.

## Interval Content

The interval content of a set tells us the number of intervals present and their type.

*How Many Intervals Are There in a Set?*    The number of intervals in a pitch-class set depends entirely on the number of pitch-classes. There are three intervals in every trichord, six intervals in every tetrachord, ten in every pentachord, fifteen in every hexachord, and so forth. See Table 7-1 on p. 98.

*What Types of Intervals Are in a Set?*    For pitch-class sets with a small number of intervals, it is easy to see the interval structure at a glance. In Example 7-1, for instance, it is immediately obvious that the trichord [0,1,4] contains one instance each of intervals 1, 3, and 4.

EXAMPLE 7-1

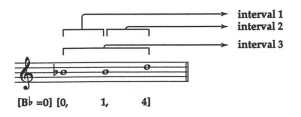

TABLE 7-1

| Numbers of Intervals in Pitch-Class Sets | | |
|---|---|---|
| **Pitch-Class Set** | **Number of Intervals** | **Explanation** |
| Trichord | 3 | From the first pitch-class to the second and to the third $\quad = 2$<br>From the second pitch-class to the third $\quad = \dfrac{1}{3}$ |
| Tetrachord | 6 | From the first pitch-class to the second, third, and fourth $\quad = 3$<br>Within the remaining trichord $\quad = \dfrac{3}{6}$ |
| Pentachord | 10 | From the first pitch-class to the second, third, fourth, fifth $\quad = 4$<br>Within the remaining tetrachord $\quad = \dfrac{6}{10}$ |
| Hexachord | 15 | From the first pitch-class to the second through sixth $\quad = 5$<br>Within the remaining hexachord $\quad = \dfrac{10}{15}$ |
| Heptachord | 21 | From the first pitch-class to the second through seventh $\quad = 6$<br>Within the remaining hexachord $\quad = \dfrac{15}{21}$ |
| Octachord | 28 | From the first pitch-class to the second through eighth $\quad = 7$<br>Within the remaining heptachord $\quad = \dfrac{21}{28}$ |

But for sets with a larger number of pitch-classes, we need a systematic way to figure out the interval content. We will use the pitch-class set [0,1,4] as an example.

To figure out the interval content of a pitch-class set:

*Step 1: Write the name of the pitch-class set, beginning with 0:*

$$[0,1,4]$$

*Step 2: Figure out the interval from the first pitch-class to each following pitch-class. Then figure out the interval from the second pitch-class to each following pitch-class, from the third pitch-class to each following, and so forth. If you arrange the set so that the first pitch-class is 0, the intervals from the first pitch-class are the remaining numbers in the name of the set. (Why?)*

*The intervals in [0,1,4] are:*

1 4—*intervals from the first pitch-class (pitch-class 0).*
    3—*interval from the second pitch-class (pitch-class 1): (4−1=3)*

*Step 3: Count up the number of instances of each interval-class and enter in the following format:[1]*

| Interval-class: | 1,11 | 2,10 | 3,9 | 4,8 | 5,7 | 6 |
|---|---|---|---|---|---|---|
| Number of Instances | 1 | 0 | 1 | 1 | 0 | 0 |

As noted in Example 7-1, there is a single instance each of interval-classes 1,11; 3,9; and 4,8.

Example 7-2 derives the interval content of the tetrachord [0,1,6,7].

EXAMPLE 7-2

[F=0]  [0,   1,   6,   7]

[0,1,6,7]      1  6  7—intervals from pitch-class 0
               5  6—intervals from pitch-class 1 (6−1=5; 7−1=6)
               1—interval from pitch-class 6 (7−6=1)

| Interval-class: | 1,11 | 2,10 | 3,9 | 4,8 | 5,7 | 6 |
|---|---|---|---|---|---|---|
| Number of Instances | 2 | 0 | 0 | 0 | 2 | 2 |

---

1. Allen Forte, in *The Structure of Atonal Music* (New Haven: Yale University Press, 1973), uses just the bottom row to list interval contents, calling the number display the *interval vector* of the set. Once you are familiar with the interval-classes in this order, you may do the same, but all listings of interval contents in this text use the complete table format.

***Does It Matter What Order the Set Is in When You Figure Out the Interval Content?*** No. Since the content is the total of all intervals between all pitch-classes, the result will always be the same no matter what order the pitch-classes are in. It is also unnecessary to number the first pitch-class 0. But to avoid having to deal with negative interval numbers, it is necessary that all pitch-class numbers be in ascending order.

***What Happens to the Interval Content When a Set Is Transposed?*** All transpositions of a pitch-class set have the same interval content. Moving a set up or down does not change its internal structure.

***What Happens to the Interval Content When a Set Is Inverted?*** The inversion of a pitch-class set has the same interval content as the prime form. Review the interval content of the trichord [0,1,4] in Example 7-1. The inversion of this trichord is [0,3,4], whose interval content is:

EXAMPLE 7-3

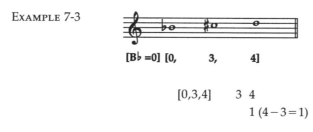

[B♭ =0] [0,  3,  4]

[0,3,4]  3 4
         1 (4−3=1)

| Interval-class: | 1,11 | 2,10 | 3,9 | 4,8 | 5,7 | 6 |
|---|---|---|---|---|---|---|
| Number of Instances | 1 | 0 | 1 | 1 | 0 | 0 |

Indeed, it is because pitch-class sets have the same interval content when inverted that we consider the prime and inverted forms a single pitch-class set and not two separate ones. It is true that the inversion of a pitch-class set contains the complement of each interval in the prime form. But in relation to different sets, the unity of sound of prime and inverted forms outweighs any differences. Take as an example a trichord with which we are all familiar: the triad. Major and minor forms of the triad are inversions of one another (the [0,3,7] trichord). In tonal music, we usually think of major and minor triads as opposites, not as two forms of the same structure. But in relation to other possible trichords, major and minor triads are certainly closely related, in that they are the only consonant trichords.

This situation is representative of all pitch-class sets. Inverted forms certainly sound different from one another (except of course for a number of sets whose inversions are identical with the prime form). But when contrasted to other types of sets, the inversionally related forms are similar to one another.

*Summary.* You now know how to figure out the interval contents of any pitch-class set. The remainder of this chapter discusses how the interval contents of a pitch-class set affects the music that uses that set. Before you begin this section, you should turn to the Exercises at the end of this chapter and do Terms and Concepts Exercises 1 and 2. Then proceed with the remainder of the chapter.

# Compositional and Expressive Effects of Pitch-Class Sets

Let us now return to several excerpts we have already studied (including examples and analysis exercises in Chapter 6) to see and hear how the interval contents of the sets that are used create the musical effects.

*Stravinsky,* **Petrushka,** *opening.* (See p. 93.) At the opening of *Petrushka,* a single tetrachord at a single level of transposition is the basis of both the melody and the accompaniment. This set, [0,2,5,7], has the following interval contents:

| Interval-class: | 1,11 | 2,10 | 3,9 | 4,8 | 5,7 | 6 |
|---|---|---|---|---|---|---|
| Number of Instances | 0 | 2 | 1 | 0 | 3 | 0 |

Interval-class 5,7 predominates, with interval-classes 2,10 and 3,9 represented to a lesser extent. There are no semitones, tritones, or instances of interval-class 4,8.

The predominant intervals clearly stand out in the music. The flute melody emphasizes interval-class 5,7 (A–D and E–A), while the stepwise tremolos in the accompaniment emphasize interval 2 (D–E and A–G) framed by interval 7 (D–A). Because of the way the tremolos are arranged, the second eighth of each beat presents all four pitch-classes as a harmony.

As we will see in many analyses in this text, the way a piece opens announces those features prominent in that piece. The [0,2,5,7] tetrachord, both for musical and extramusical reasons, is a brilliant choice to open *Petrushka.* In the first place, it suggests the eclectic musical surface of the ballet. *Petrushka* contains all sorts of music: folk tunes and composed melodies with simple tonic-dominant harmonizations, passages that are entirely nontonal, as well as others.[2] The opening tetrachord points to all these types of music. With the emphasis on D and A as important pitches in both the flute and the accompaniment, there is a D-as-tonic sound to the passage. But the static harmony and the absence of a third to the key (either F or F♯) precludes a clear sense of D major or D minor. This foreshadows the later presence of both simple diatonic tunes with tonal accompaniments and nontonal passages. Much of the remainder of the music through the raising of the curtain maintains these features, even though there is a wider range of pitches and motives.

Secondly, the perfect fourths in the flute (interval-class 5,7) add a fanfare quality to the opening. Thirdly, the presence of pitch-classes D, E, G, and A sounding together—the four open strings of a violin—suggest the familiar sound of orchestral tuning before the curtain rises.

***Webern*, Movement for String Quartet, *op. 5 no. 4, opening*.**    (See p. 89.) In Example 6-16 we saw several instances of the tetrachord [0,1,6,7] during the opening section of this piece. The interval content of this tetrachord is:

| Interval-class: | 1,11 | 2,10 | 3,9 | 4,8 | 5,7 | 6 |
|---|---|---|---|---|---|---|
| Number of Instances | 2 | 0 | 0 | 0 | 2 | 2 |

As in the tetrachord at the opening of *Petrushka*, only three interval-classes are present here, but the profile of this set is markedly different. Semitones, tritones, and interval-class 5,7 occur in equal numbers. There are no whole tones or thirds or sixths. And the set is not at all reminiscent of a tonal harmony or scale segment.

Each set statement in the piece emphasizes a different aspect of its structure. The tremolo chord in m. 2 contains intervals 5 and 7 in the separate instruments (C–F and B–F♯), whereas the chord on the downbeat of m. 4 places the two tritones in adjacent positions (F♯–C in viola-violin; G–C♯ in the cello). The viola and cello in m. 5 move in parallel tritones by semitone.

---

2. From the first reviews of the ballet to recent critiques, many writers have commented upon the eclectic surface of *Petrushka*. See the Norton Critical Scores edition of *Petrushka*, edited by Charles Hamm (New York: W. W. Norton & Co., 1967), for several early commentaries on the work.

In contrast to the large forms and eclectic combinations of elements Stravinsky was so fond of, Webern was always the miniaturist, composing compact pieces based on a few elements. In this excerpt the interval-classes 1,11; 5,7; and 6 are intensively developed. There are sets other than [0,1,6,7] that can be heard here—we will discuss these sets and their relationship to [0,1,6,7] in later chapters. But all pitch combinations in this passage emphasize the same interval classes.

The inventive timbres and articulations of phrases, melodies, chords, and interacting lines are part of the compactness of the music. These timbres isolate and highlight the groupings. Each musical statement is so complete in itself that it seems not to need repetition or further development. It is the unity of conception of all these elements, along with the wide range of timbres, articulations, melodic shapes, and registers in such a short time that gives the music much of its intensity.

***Webern,* Concerto for Nine Instruments,** *op. 24, second movement, opening.* (See p. 95). The trichord that is the basis of all simultaneously sounding pitches here is [0,1,4]. We worked out the interval content of this trichord in Examples 7-1 and 7-3. The trichord contains one instance each of interval-classes 1,11; 3,9; and 4,8. Two of these, 1,11 and 4,8, are the very essence of this passage. Each harmonic interval in the piano contains either 4 or 11 semitones. Every time a pitch in the melodic instruments sounds along with a piano interval, it creates some form of [0,1,4]. The melodic instruments form [0,1,4] in several ways, but only state interval-classes 1,11 or 4,8 in immediate succession (the same interval-classes as in the piano). Listen to Example 7-4.

EXAMPLE 7-4

Finally, when two intervals 4 or 11 follow each other in the piano part, the second interval is either interval-class 4,8 or 1,11 distant from the first. For instance, in mm. 2–3, the piano has D–F♯, then D♭–F—two instances of interval 4 separated by interval 11. Similarly, the intervals 11 in mm. 4–5 (A–A♭, A♭–G) are interval 1 apart. Intervals 3 or 9 do not sound in this passage as harmonies in the piano or as melodic intervals between adjacent pitches.

Webern composed the *Concerto for Nine Instruments,* op. 24, in 1934, twenty-five years after the op. 5 no. 4 *Movement for String Quartet* that we just discussed. We already noted how only a few intervals form the basis of so much of the earlier piece. The later work features an even greater concentration on even fewer intervals. This compressed intensity is reflected in other nonpitch aspects of the music. With the pitch structure so much more evident, a wider variety of tone colors pervades the single lines in this work. Thus, no single melodic instrument here plays an entire phrase: a characteristically Webernian instance of *Klangfarbenmelodie* (tone-color melody).

To a listener demanding grandiose effects and high drama, Webern's music can seem uneventful—just a series of similar and brief soundpatterns. But from another perspective, the concentration and economy of materials makes every single note, slur, timbral connection, and rest a crucial part of the music. In a fine performance, each event is a polished gem that radiates in its perfect setting. The effect is not unlike that of a simple line drawing by a great artist in which a few pen strokes evoke a vibrant picture.

**Debussy, The Sunken Cathedral, *from* Preludes, *Book I.*** Understanding pitch-class sets and their interval content can give insights into compositional relationships and processes that might not otherwise be obvious. Consider the two brief passages from Debussy's *Sunken Cathedral* in Examples 6-1 and 6-2. At first hearing, they might seem to be entirely different—the first offers bare fifths and octaves like organum, the second is lush, seeming to begin as a B-major triad with added sixth and ninth.

One might assume at first that Debussy simply composed these different passages to evoke in musical images the legend referred to by the title of the prelude: the sunken cathedral of Ys, buried beneath the waves, that rises from the sea. The organum is like church music of antiquity or the resonance of deep church bells, while the later passage suggests the surging sea.

But despite these differences, both passages are based on the same set: the pentachord [0,2,4,7,9], which is a pentatonic scale. The interval content of this set is:

| Interval-class: | 1,11 | 2,10 | 3,9 | 4,8 | 5,7 | 6 |
|---|---|---|---|---|---|---|
| Number of Instances | 0 | 3 | 2 | 1 | 4 | 0 |

Interval classes 5,7 and 2,10 predominate, and there are no semitones or tritones.

Just as we found with the sets that open *Petrushka* and the Webern works discussed earlier, the characteristics of this pentachord make it ideal for the varied expressive purposes of this piece. The many instances of interval-class 5,7 make possible the harmonic perfect fourths and fifths of mm. 1–2 (G–D, A–E, E–B); the many instances of interval-class 2,10 makes it likely that some of these perfect fourths and fifths can be connected to others by step. Finally, the triadic sonorities beginning in m. 16 are possible because of the predominance in the set of interval-classes found in tonal harmonies (5,7; 3,9; and 4,8). The section beginning in m. 16 belongs in the same piece as the opening measures because the overall sound of the pitch collections are similar. In addition, the melodic top pitches in mm. 16ff. are a transposition of the intervals in the upper part of mm. 1–2 (F♯–G♯–D♯ in m. 16 is a transposition of D–E–B in m. 1).

# Points for Review

**1.** The interval content of a pitch-class set is the total of all its intervals. Review p. 99 on how to figure out the interval content of a pitch-class set.

**2.** The interval content of a set determines many of the compositional and expressive features that can be drawn from that set.

# Exercises for Chapter 7

**Terms and Concepts**

**1.** Define interval content.

**2.** Write the name and figure out the interval content of each of the following pitch-class sets. The first has been completed.

a)

[0, 1, 4, 6]

```
1 4 6
  3 5
    2
```

This tetrachord is called an "all-interval tetrachord." Why?

| Interval-class: | 1,11 | 2,10 | 3,9 | 4,8 | 5,7 | 6 |
|---|---|---|---|---|---|---|
| Number of Instances | 1 | 1 | 1 | 1 | 1 | 1 |

**3.** Discuss how the interval content of a set relates to the melodic and harmonic possibilities of music using that set.

## Composition

Figure out the interval content of each of the following pitch-class sets. For each, compose several strongly contrasting melodies or textures, each emphasizing a different aspect of the set's interval content. Several compositional possibilities are illustrated for the first set, emphasizing intervals 5,7 connected by melodic semitones, emphasizing tritones with semitone connections, and emphasizing melodic semitones and tritones. Use only one form of the set in your excerpts. Keep the sections brief, but remember to notate a tempo, dynamics, articulation, and character. Think of the instrument that might best project your ideas, and write the excerpt for that instrument.

[0, 1, 2, 6, 7]

b)    [0, 1, 2, 5, 8]    c)    [0, 1, 4, 5, 8]

# Suggestions for Further Study

**1.** Listen to Webern's orchestration of the ricercare from J. S. Bach's *Musical Offering* (transcribed by Webern in 1935). Study Webern's use of instruments in bringing to the fore subtle aspects of pitch relationships in Bach's counterpoint. For a study of this transcription and others, see Joseph Straus, "Recompositions by Schoenberg, Stravinsky, and Webern," in *The Musical Quarterly* 72 (1986): 301–28.

**2.** For listings of all pitch-class sets containing from three to nine pitch-classes, along with the interval contents of each set, see Allen Forte, *The Structure of Atonal Music* (New Haven: Yale University Press, 1973), pp. 179–181, or John Rahn, *Basic Atonal Theory* (New York: Longman, 1980), pp. 140–143.

# 8
# Using Different Pitch-Class Sets

---

*subset*

---

## Relations among Pitch-Class Sets

For all the excerpts discussed in earlier chapters, we studied the presence and effects of only a single pitch-class set on that excerpt. Even when there were pitches present that were not members of that set, the discussion focused on a single set. Review the opening of Stravinsky's *Petrushka*, for instance. (See score on p. 93, and review the discussion of this passage on pp. 101–2 in Chapter 7.) We noted that both the flute melody and the accompanying tremolos use the same set. But we ignored the cello melody in mm. 6–9, which is based on a different set. Review also our discussion of Webern's *Movement for String Quartet*, op. 5 no. 4. (See score on p. 137, and pp. 102–3 in Chapter 7 for a discussion of the passage.) We saw the influence of [0,1,6,7] on the passage. But we did not discuss how the different transpositions of [0,1,6,7] relate to one another. Nor did we discuss the role of the other sets in this excerpt.

It is a rare or brief passage that uses only a single small set, and an even briefer passage that uses only a single form of one small pitch-class set. Usually the pitches can be grouped into more than one set which occur in more than one form. As a result, just knowing the interval content and other properties of an individual set is not sufficient for the analyst. It is also important to understand the relationships among pitch-class sets and among different forms of the same set, and how these relationships affect a passage.

***How Can Sets Relate to One Another?*** Sets can be related to one another by one or both of the following factors:

1. by the number of pitch-classes they share

2. by their interval contents

There are systematic methods for figuring out all the potential relationships between different forms of a set, and between different sets. But when analyzing a given passage, potential relationships are not important. What matters is how the relationships that are present in that passage affect *that* passage in *that* piece—how the relationships cause certain pitches or pitch-classes to become focal pitches, how they relate to texture, to motivic interplay, to processes of growth, and so forth. For this reason, we will adopt an informal approach to set relationships. Instead of presenting general principles of set relationships, we will study the relationships realized in specific examples and draw principles from them.

Our study of set relationships is divided into two parts. In this chapter we survey the relationships among comparatively small sets (trichords, tetrachords, pentachords, hexachords) in local contexts. In Chapter 9 we will survey larger contexts, including the way local sets add up to scales or pitch-class regions analogous to key areas in tonal music.

# Unity and Variety Using Transpositions of a Set

***Unity and Growth via Common Pitch-Classes.*** The beginning of most pieces announces the basic materials of that work. By focusing on these basic materials, the opening of the piece establishes an individual personality that colors all its later passages. Many works begin with only a few pitch-classes that emphasize certain crucial intervals. This allows the listener to hear immediately the pitch and interval structures basic to the piece. As new pitch-classes are gradually added, the listener is led to new material. One technique for doing this involves careful control of new transpositions of the opening pitch-class set.

Listen to the two excerpts from the opening flute fanfare of Stravinsky's *Petrushka* in Example 8-1 on p. 110. (Review score on p. 93.) Each excerpt is based on the set [0,2,5,7], first at T0, then at T7. But despite the transposition, there is an important similarity between these two forms of the set. T0 and T7 of this set share three out of the four pitch-classes (D, E, and A). Stravinsky emphasizes these pitch-classes by keeping them in the same register in the flute part. He also maintains the original tetrachord in the accompaniment throughout the passage.

EXAMPLE 8-1: Stravinsky, *Petrushka*

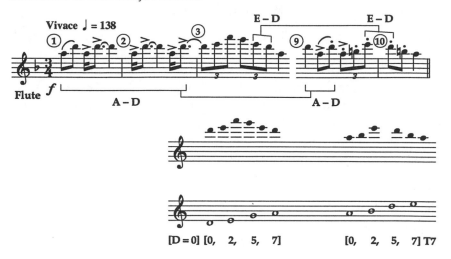

[D = 0] [0, 2, 5, 7]   [0, 2, 5, 7] T7

How does it happen that three out of four pitch-classes remain in common between T0 and T7? The general principle is the following:

*When a set is transposed by an interval other than 6, the number of instances of that interval-class in the set is the number of pitch-classes in common between the two transpositions.*

*When a set is transposed by interval 6, the number of common pitch-classes is double the number of instances of interval 6.*

*For example, if an interval other than 6 occurs twice in a set, transposing the set by that interval (or by its complement) will retain two pitch-classes.*

Consider the tetrachord [0,2,5,7] featured at the opening of Stravinsky's *Petrushka*:

EXAMPLE 8-2

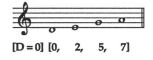

[D = 0] [0, 2, 5, 7]

| Interval-class: | 1,11 | 2,10 | 3,9 | 4,8 | 5,7 | 6 |
|---|---|---|---|---|---|---|
| Number of Instances | 0 | 2 | 1 | 0 | 3 | 0 |

There are three instances of interval-class 5,7. Thus, transposition by 5 or 7 semitones (as happens in the opening flute melody) gives rise to three pitch-classes in common with the original. See Example 8-3 and compare to Example 8-1.

EXAMPLE 8-3

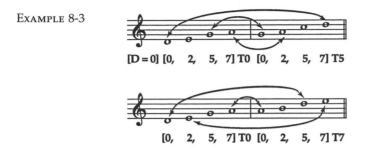

[D = 0] [0, 2, 5, 7] T0 [0, 2, 5, 7] T5

[0, 2, 5, 7] T0 [0, 2, 5, 7] T7

There are two instances of interval-class 2,10, and, therefore, two pitch-classes in common between T0 and T2 or T0 and T10.

EXAMPLE 8-4

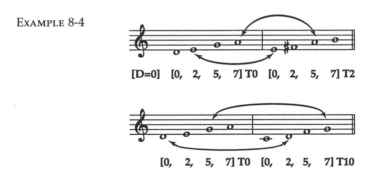

[D=0] [0, 2, 5, 7] T0 [0, 2, 5, 7] T2

[0, 2, 5, 7] T0 [0, 2, 5, 7] T10

Transposition by an interval that does not occur in the set gives rise to no common pitch-classes.

EXAMPLE 8-5

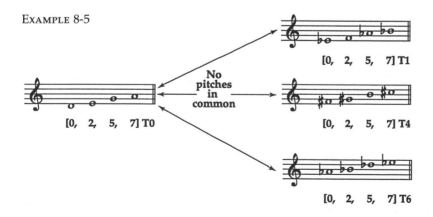

[0, 2, 5, 7] T1

No pitches in common

[0, 2, 5, 7] T0

[0, 2, 5, 7] T4

[0, 2, 5, 7] T6

The transposition at the beginning of *Petrushka* clearly emphasizes common tones so that only a single new pitch-class arises.

*Avoiding Common Pitch-Classes.* Other passages begin with a set transposed so as to avoid common pitch-classes. When the different transpositions are in different parts of the texture, the strong profile of pitch-classes within each part is clearly differentiated from the pitch-relations between parts.

For an instance of this, listen to the opening phrase from Bartók's *Diminished Fifth:*

EXAMPLE 8-6: Bartók, *Diminished Fifth (Mikrokosmos* No. 101)

| Interval-class: | 1,11 | 2,10 | 3,9 | 4,8 | 5,7 | 6 |
|---|---|---|---|---|---|---|
| Number of Instances | 1 | 2 | 2 | 0 | 1 | 0 |

The phrase features a freely imitative two-part texture. A single set, [0,2,3,5], is the basis of each part, transposed by a tritone from one to the other. Since there are no tritones in the set, transposition by a tritone gives rise to no pitch-classes in common between the parts.

In this piece, the set that is the basis of each part is a fragment of a diatonic scale. Since the four pitch-classes in each part occur conjunctly, there is a distinctly tonal or modal flavor to each part: A minor for the right-hand part, E♭ minor for the left. By using the tritone transposition with no pitch-classes in common, each part can retain its own tonal or modal flavor without making the entire texture sound tonal.

*Which Pitch-Classes and Intervals Are in Common Between Transpositions?* Knowing *how many* pitch-classes are in common between two transpositions of a set does not tell you *which* pitch-classes or intervals will be retained. In the flute melody that opens *Petrushka* (Example 8-1), what is important to the musical continuity of this passage is not only that there are three pitch-classes in common between T0 and T7 of [0,2,5,7], but also that the interval A–D, which reverberates throughout the melody, and whose pitch-classes frame the accompanying tremolos, is retained. And D–E, which elaborates D early in the phrase, is retained.

> *The general rule is: When an interval occurs at least twice in a set, there is a transposition that will retain the pitch-classes of at least one of these intervals.*

In [0,2,5,7] there are at least two instances each of interval 2 and interval 5. That means that there is a transposition that will retain interval 2 and a transposition that will retain interval 5. For this set, one and the same transposition retains both intervals. At T7, G–A becomes D–E, and D–G becomes A–D.

## Relationships among Inversions of a Set

*Intervals in Common Between Inversions of a Set.* We already know that the inversion of a set has the same interval content as the original or prime set. (Review Examples 7-1 and 7-3.) As a result:

> *The pair of pitch-classes that makes up any interval in a set may be retained when the set is inverted.*

In [0,1,3,7], for example, each interval-class occurs once. Example 8-7 demonstrates inversions that retain each interval.

EXAMPLE 8-7

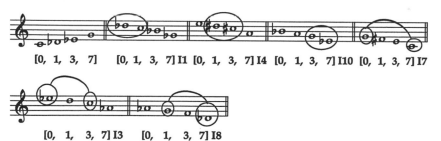

[0, 1, 3, 7]    [0, 1, 3, 7] I1   [0, 1, 3, 7] I4   [0, 1, 3, 7] I10   [0, 1, 3, 7] I7

[0, 1, 3, 7] I3    [0, 1, 3, 7] I8

| Interval-class: | 1,11 | 2,10 | 3,9 | 4,8 | 5,7 | 6 |
|---|---|---|---|---|---|---|
| Number of Instances | 1 | 1 | 1 | 1 | 1 | 1 |

Similarly, if an interval occurs twice in a set, both occurrences can be retained in a single inversion. [0,1,2,4], which contains two instances of interval 1, retains both at I 2. Both instances of interval 2 are retained at I 4.

EXAMPLE 8-8

[G=0] [0, 1, 2, 4] T0   [0, 1, 2, 4] I2

[0, 1, 2, 4] T0   [0, 1, 2, 4] I4

| Interval-class: | 1,11 | 2,10 | 3,9 | 4,8 | 5,7 | 6 |
|---|---|---|---|---|---|---|
| Number of Instances | 2 | 2 | 1 | 1 | 0 | 0 |

Using a set-form followed by an inversion that keeps a constant interval allows a composer to retain a pair of pitch-classes as focal pitches, while presenting them in a new but related setting.

*Sets That Are Their Own Inversions.* There are a number of sets that retain *all* their pitch-classes. Example 8-9 shows that T0 and I7 of [0,2,5,7] are identical.

EXAMPLE 8-9

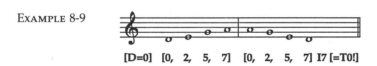

[D=0] [0, 2, 5, 7] [0, 2, 5, 7] I7 [=T0!]

For these sets, there is no need to cite an inverted form, since for every inverted form there is some equivalent prime form.

# Unity and Variety Using Different Sets

Thus far we have considered only transpositions and inversions of a single pitch-class set. Most passages feature more than one pitch-class set. The following discussion covers two fundamentally different ways in which different sets occur. First we will discuss *subsets*, smaller sets that are part of a larger set. Then we will discuss relationships among entirely different sets.

*Unity via Subsets.* Most subsets are quite close in interval content to their parent set since all the intervals in the subset must also be present in the parent set. (Why?) Subsets containing one or two pitch-classes fewer than the larger set usually emphasize the identical interval-classes.

Example 8-10 illustrates this point with the trichord [0,2,5], a subset in the tetrachord [0,2,3,5]. [0,2,5] contains three of the four interval-classes in [0,2,3,5], and is missing interval-classes 4,8 and 6, just like [0,2,3,5].

EXAMPLE 8-10

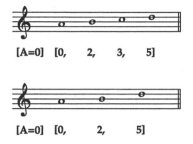

[A=0]  [0,  2,  3,  5]

[A=0]  [0,  2,  5]

| Interval-class: | 1,11 | 2,10 | 3,9 | 4,8 | 5,7 | 6 |
|---|---|---|---|---|---|---|
| Number of Instances | 1 | 2 | 2 | 0 | 1 | 0 |

| Interval-class: | 1,11 | 2,10 | 3,9 | 4,8 | 5,7 | 6 |
|---|---|---|---|---|---|---|
| Number of Instances | 0 | 1 | 1 | 0 | 1 | 0 |

Furthermore, [0,2,5] is a subset of [0,2,3,5] in its original form as well as in its inverted form:

EXAMPLE 8-11

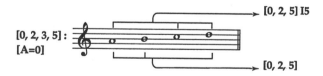

[0, 2, 3, 5] :
[A=0]

→ [0, 2, 5] I5

→ [0, 2, 5]

The close bond between [0,2,5] and [0,2,3,5] is a feature in Bartók's *Diminished Fifth*. As we already noted in our discussion of Example 8-6, the opening passage of this piece uses [0,2,3,5] as the basis of each melodic part. For a contrasting phrase in mm. 12–15, each melodic part uses the trichord [0,2,5]. (See Example 8-12.) As a result, mm. 12–15 contrast with the beginning of the piece because the underlying pitch-class set is different. (In addition, some of the pitch-classes are different in the two phrases.) Yet because of the similarity in structure between this subset and its parent tetrachord, the two sections are related as parts of a unified piece.

EXAMPLE 8-12: Bartók, *Diminished Fifth* (*Mikrokosmos*, No. 101)

Another piece that uses a subset related to a larger set is Debussy's *The Sunken Cathedral*. Like many of Debussy's compositions, this piano prelude is tonal. For much of the piece, a complete white-note diatonic scale is present, and the piece ends on a C-major triad; but the sense of tonality is quite extended. There are few functional harmonies, and many of the triads and seventh chords that do occur operate in a nonfunctional manner.

At the very opening, a pentachord subset of the diatonic scale establishes the unique sound of the prelude. Review Example 6–1 on p. 82, which illustrates the pentachord in mm. 1–2: [0,2,4,7,9]. The interval content of this pentachord, the pentatonic scale, emphasizes the two interval-classes that predominate in a complete diatonic scale: interval-classes 5,7 and 2,10:

The pentatonic scale [0,2,4,7,9] contains:

| Interval-class: | 1,11 | 2,10 | 3,9 | 4,8 | 5,7 | 6 |
|---|---|---|---|---|---|---|
| Number of Instances | 0 | 3 | 2 | 1 | 4 | 0 |

The diatonic scale [0,1,3,5,6,8,10] contains:

| Interval-class: | 1,11 | 2,10 | 3,9 | 4,8 | 5,7 | 6 |
|---|---|---|---|---|---|---|
| Number of Instances | 2 | 5 | 4 | 3 | 6 | 1 |

And as we saw in Example 6-1, interval-classes 5,7 and 2,10 are very strongly projected in mm. 1–2 of *The Sunken Cathedral*.

The very next measures of *The Sunken Cathedral* expand [0,2,4,7,9] into a complete diatonic scale by adding F and C. And the same procedure is followed with the contrasting music from mm. 16–18 (Review Example 6-2). The pentatonic scale in these measures again emphasizes interval-classes 5,7 and 2,10 in the bass triplets (B–F♯–G♯) and in the upper part (F♯–G♯–D♯). The following measures transpose this music up by interval 4 and add the pitch-classes necessary to complete a diatonic scale.

The result of all this is to allow the diatonic scale with its tonal heritage (including many triads and seventh chords) to be the basis of most of the piece, yet with a focus that is distinctly different from the diatonic music of any earlier composer. The triads and seventh chords that appear do not carry with them the obligations of tonal functions; nor do they fulfill these functions. From the passages early in the piece, we learn to hear the diatonicism of this piece as an expansion from the [0,2,4,7,9] pentachord with the special emphasis on interval-classes 5,7 and 2,10.

This is a procedure that occurs in many compositions by Debussy and other composers of the early twentieth century who wrote music with a strong tonal aura. By stressing interval structures that are not ordinarily used in this way in tonal music, these compositions suggest to us novel ways of hearing the diatonic heptachord and other aspects of tonal music, while at the same time we understand other effects arising from the tonal tradition.

Debussy's symphonic sketches *La Mer* (1905) similarly refocus our hearing through emphasis on subsets amid other materials. For instance, the first movement of *La Mer* ends with a D♭-major triad and contains much music focusing on D♭ major (especially in the *Modéré* passage beginning after study number 2). But the movement begins on B, suggesting B major, and offers a strong emphasis on the key of B♭ major in its second half (*Très rhythmé* beginning at study number 9). From a tonal point of view, the keys of B♭, B, and D♭ are not at all closely related to one another.

But a common core of pitch-classes exists in various guises during much of the first movement, acting as a subset to unite the music in these separate keys. The very opening of *La Mer* builds an ostinato containing B–C♯–F♯–G♯, the tetrachord [0,2,5,7]. These pitches form the core of a second tutti ostinato at study number 2, incorporating motives from the contrasting music that appeared in the interim. (See Example 8-13 on p. 118 for these two ostinatos.)

The music then takes an abrupt turn to D♭ major, establishing an ostinato with the pentatonic scale: D♭–E♭–F–A♭–B♭, or [0,2,4,7,9]. (See Example 3-3a on p. 41.) The tetrachord of the opening ostinato is a

EXAMPLE 8-13: Debussy, *La Mer*, first movement, opening and study number 2 (some octave doublings omitted)

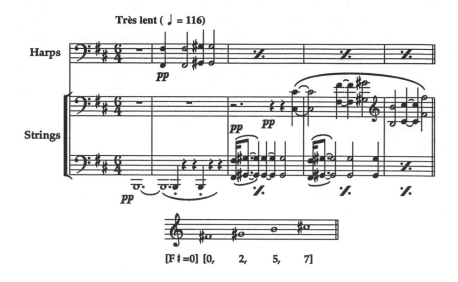

[F♯=0]  [0,    2,    5,    7]

[F♯=0] [0,  2,  (3),  5,  7]

subset of the pentatonic scale. So even though the ostinatos have only two pitch-classes in common (C♯ / D♭ and G♯ / A♭), the overall sound emphasizes the same intervals.

The D♭ ostinato accompanies a melody in the French horns, the beginning of which may be found in Example 3-3a. And the very opening of this horn melody stresses three of the four pitch-classes in the opening tetrachord of the piece: C♭ / B, D♭ / C♯, and A♭ / G♯. So the melody and the D♭ ostinato provide a strong link with the opening tetrachord. (See Example 8-14 for an illustration of the common pitch-classes.)

EXAMPLE 8-14: Debussy, *La Mer*, first movement

When the Db ostinato comes to an end at study number 4, the focus shifts to Bb, with the texture in Example 8-15. The three pitch-classes in common between the opening ostinato and the horn melody are the backbone of the melody: Ab/G♯, Cb/B, Db/C♯.

EXAMPLE 8-15: Debussy, *La Mer*, first movement

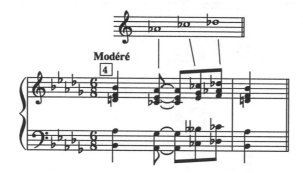

The remainder of the opening half of the movement brings a succession of ostinatos, blending new and old motives, and two returns of the horn melody, always at the same pitch-level. Example 3-3b (p. 41) illustrates the first of these thematic returns. At study number 8, yet another ostinato appears, in which elements of the Db ostinato recur, transposed to present the opening B–C♯–F♯–G♯ tetrachord. This ostinato then accompanies a theme from study number 1, now transposed to emphasize the same tetrachord. (See Example 3-3c on p. 42 for this passage.)

This leads directly into the *Retenu* and the dispersal of the ostinato. The opening tetrachord is the focus of attention once again.

EXAMPLE 8-16: Debussy, *La Mer*, first movement, five measures after study number 8

The music of the second half of the movement is in B♭ major—a key foreshadowed by the B♭ chords framing the passage in Example 8-15. In the opening of this section the pentatonic scale is displayed as a II₇ chord in B♭ major over a dominant pedal.

EXAMPLE 8-17: Debussy, *La Mer*, first movement, two measures before study number 9

In summary, a trichord subset (G♯–B–C♯) containing three of the four pitch-classes in the opening tetrachord (B–C♯–F♯–G♯) unites all the music in the keys of B and D♭, as well as hinting at B♭, the key of the contrasting second half of the movement (via the music in Example 8-15). And the entire [0,2,5,7] tetrachord is a subset of the pentatonic scale that underlies many of the ostinatos throughout all these sections, unifying the sound of the entire movement. All the themes emphasize the common trichord. These pitch structures provide many sounds familiar from tonal music, but the directions that *La Mer* takes are distinctly twentieth-century.

*Unity via Sets Similar in Structure.*   In addition to relationships between subsets, relationships among otherwise independent sets are the source for many musical contexts. The following analyses demonstrate the use of sets similar in structure in a variety of styles.

*Model Analysis: Webern's* **Movement for String Quartet,** *op. 5 no. 4.* The opening of this work uses two sets closely related to each other as the sole basis of the music.

EXAMPLE 8-18: Webern, *Movement for String Quartet*, op. 5 no. 4

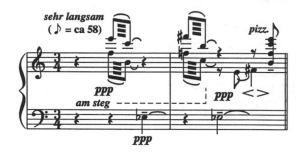

[B=0] [0,  1,  5,  6]     [0,  1,  6,  7]

[0,1,5,6]

| Interval-class: | 1,11 | 2,10 | 3,9 | 4,8 | 5,7 | 6 |
|---|---|---|---|---|---|---|
| Number of Instances | 2 | 0 | 0 | 1 | 2 | 1 |

[0,1,6,7]

| Interval-class: | 1,11 | 2,10 | 3,9 | 4,8 | 5,7 | 6 |
|---|---|---|---|---|---|---|
| Number of Instances | 2 | 0 | 0 | 0 | 2 | 2 |

Violin tremolos present the two tetrachords shown below the example. Several factors closely relate these tetrachords to one another: both contain two semitones and two instances of interval-class 5,7. Neither contains any whole tones or instances of interval-class 3,9. In addition, at the levels of transposition in Example 8-18, the tetrachords share three of their four pitch-classes. (See the black noteheads below Example 8-18.) Finally, the [0,1,6] trichord that is common to both tetrachords occurs twice as a subset in both [0,1,5,6] and [0,1,6,7]. Example 8-19 illustrates this.

EXAMPLE 8-19

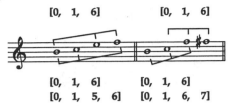

| Interval-class: | 1,11 | 2,10 | 3,9 | 4,8 | 5,7 | 6 |
|---|---|---|---|---|---|---|
| Number of Instances | 1 | 0 | 0 | 0 | 1 | 1 |

We have already noted in earlier chapters that Webern always derived a maximum of music from a minimum of structural elements. You can well imagine that with two closely related tetrachords and a common trichord, Webern creates a passage using these sets as much as possible. As Example 8-20 shows, this is indeed so. Melodies, harmonies, and counterpoint all are based on [0,1,5,6], [0,1,6,7], and [0,1,6].

You might describe Example 8-20 as being based on the two tetrachords and the trichord we have been discussing. Or you might describe it as being built from a semitone and two of its transpositions, creating

EXAMPLE 8-20: Webern, *Movement for String Quartet*, op. 5 no. 4

Dynamics, articulations, instrumentations, performance techniques, tempo nuances, and expressive descriptions have been omitted in the interest of clarity. See p. 137 for a full score to this passage. All sets are labeled in lowest ordering starting with 0.

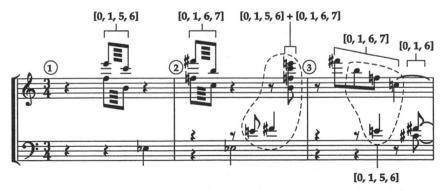

[0, 1, 5, 6]  [0, 1, 5, 6]

[0, 1, 6, 7]  [0, 1, 6, 7]  [0, 1, 5, 6]

[0, 1, 6]  [0, 1, 5]

④  ⑤  [0, 1, 5]  ⑥  [0, 1, 5]

[0, 1, 5, 6] + [0, 1, 6, 7]

[0, 1, 6, 7]  [0, 1, 6]  [0, 1, 6]

[0, 1, 6]  [0, 1, 6]

[0, 1, 5]  [0, 1, 6, 7]

the two analyzed tetrachords. Or you might hear the passage being built from the trichord [0,1,6] creating the same two tetrachords. But however you describe it, it is the sound of these intervals that you hear permeating every aspect of the section. Interval-classes 1,11; 5,7; and 6 are so prominent here that almost every melody and harmony is entirely based on these intervals as they form the two tetrachords and their subsets. And despite the brevity of the section (only six measures), so great is the structural concentration that it does truly seem a complete section.

Study of subsets and closely related sets helps us to get a grasp on the aural relationships between the intervals and pitch-class sets in this passage. See Analysis Exercise 2 in this chapter for a full score of the entire movement and questions that will lead to an understanding of the remainder of the movement.

*Model Analysis: Stravinsky's* **Petrushka.**     Listen again to the opening of *Petrushka* in Analysis Exercise 1 of Chapter 6 (p. 93). We have seen how the [0,2,5,7] tetrachord is the basis of the accompanying tremolos and the flute melody, and how the flute melody expands its pitch-field by transposing this tetrachord. (Review pp. 101–2.) But we have not yet discussed other motives present in the opening measures, or the way the first tetrachord and the other pitch-class sets of the opening gradually expand to create the tutti at study number 3.

The first new material added to the opening tetrachord is the cello melody at study number 1. As shown in Example 8-21, the cello melody is based on the tetrachord [0,2,3,5] at T9. The [0,2,3,5] tetrachord has an interval content similar to [0,2,5,7], and at the T9 level of transposition, it shares two pitch-classes with the opening [0,2,5,7] tetrachord, and three pitch-classes with the transposition of that tetrachord in the flute.

EXAMPLE 8-21: Stravinsky, *Petrushka*, opening

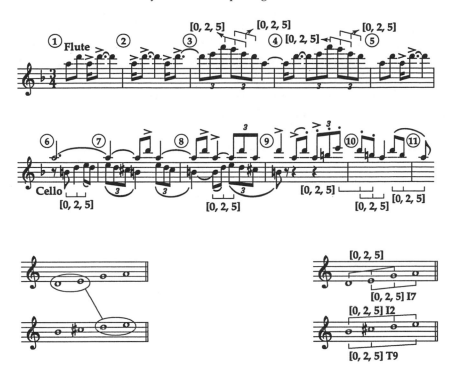

[0,2,3,5]

| Interval-class: | 1,11 | 2,10 | 3,9 | 4,8 | 5,7 | 6 |
|---|---|---|---|---|---|---|
| Number of Instances | 1 | 2 | 2 | 0 | 1 | 0 |

[0,2,5,7]

| Interval-class: | 1,11 | 2,10 | 3,9 | 4,8 | 5,7 | 6 |
|---|---|---|---|---|---|---|
| Number of Instances | 0 | 2 | 1 | 0 | 3 | 0 |

The trichord [0,2,5], a subset in both the [0,2,3,5] and the [0,2,5,7] tetra-chords, appears at numerous points in the flute fanfare and opens the cello melody.

We have already noted Stravinsky's predilection for beginning a piece with a small group of pitch-classes and gradually expanding to larger pitch-class collections. Let us trace this process at the opening of *Petrushka*. The piece opens with [0,2,5,7] at a single transposition (D,E,G,A)—used as fanfare and accompaniment in the winds. With the entry of the cello, B and C♯ are added.

In m. 12 a new instance of interval 2 (B♭–C) joins the original tremolo, expanding the tetrachord [0,2,5,7] to the hexachord [0,2,3,5,7,9] (six notes of a diatonic scale). The tune in the cellos that is accompanied by this new tremolo is, like the earlier cello melody, based on the [0,2,3,5] tetrachord. It appears in parallel sixths, creating the same hexachord as in the tremolos:

EXAMPLE 8-22: Stravinsky, *Petrushka*

At study number 3 (see facing page), the original texture returns more fully orchestrated. But now both the melodies and the accompaniment expand to include the entire D-minor diatonic scale.

The elements that started out as separate though related entities (the [0,2,5,7] tetrachord and the [0,2,3,5] tetrachord at T9) become a single unit as we hear each original tetrachord turning into a subset of larger and larger sets until they have blended into a single larger set. Corresponding to this expansion and merging of pitch-class sets comes an expansion and merging of timbres and register, leading from the sharply etched lines of the opening to the tutti. By the time the tutti arrives, we hear an entire diatonic scale. But because of the way the preceding music presents its elements, we hear this scale in a fresh manner. (Compare this to the discussion of Debussy's *The Sunken Cathedral*, on pp. 82–83.)

Stravinsky's predilection for repeated groups of pitches in his melodies aids in the immediate perception of these processes. Both the flute and cello melodies at the opening stick to their original four pitch-classes until several repetitions of the basic groups have been stated. Similarly repetitious figures occur at all later stages in the movement. Indeed,

EXAMPLE 8-23: Stravinsky, *Petrushka*

sometimes the melodies seem more like ostinatos than like developing lines.

*Model Analysis: Bartók's* **Concerto for Orchestra,** *first movement.* The surface of Bartók's music often seems quite varied. Melodies and harmonies arise from a wide range of pitch combinations, and there is often a blend of tonal elements alongside a range of nontonal ones. Symmetrical divisions of the octave (especially the tritone, which divides the octave into two equal parts) often coexist with nonsymmetrical features. (The combination of symmetrical and nonsymmetrical features characterizes even his use of forms, both of single-movements and of multi-movement pieces. Review the discussion of his forms in Chapter 4 on pp. 57ff.)

Despite these features, set analysis can illuminate many aspects of pitch structure in his music. The first movement of the *Concerto for Orchestra* (1943), for instance, contains a wide range of pitch structures unified at crucial points in the movement by a group of close relationships. The movement is in sonata form. Transitional and developmental sections contain a wide range of pitch-classes. But at crucial junctures in the form, the texture thins out to allow a few closely related structures to emerge. Listen, for instance, to the opening theme of the Allegro vivace:

EXAMPLE 8-24: Bartók, *Concerto for Orchestra*, first movement

[0,   3,   5,   8]

| Interval-class: | 1,11 | 2,10 | 3,9 | 4,8 | 5,7 | 6 |
|---|---|---|---|---|---|---|
| Number of Instances | 0 | 1 | 2 | 1 | 2 | 0 |

The main notes in the melody outline the tetrachord [0,3,5,8]. The melodic emphasis is on interval-class 5,7.

The continuation of this theme and its development use many additional pitch-classes and other pitch-class sets. But when the texture clears for the tranquillo second theme in m. 155, a trichord closely related to the opening tetrachord appears. The [0,2,7] trichord, like the [0,3,5,8] tetrachord of the opening theme, has a pronounced emphasis on interval-class 5,7.

EXAMPLE 8-25: Bartók, *Concerto for Orchestra*, first movement

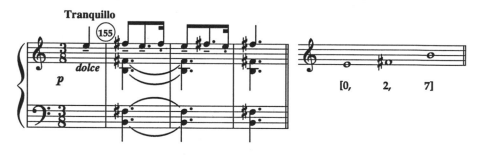

| Interval-class: | 1,11 | 2,10 | 3,9 | 4,8 | 5,7 | 6 |
|---|---|---|---|---|---|---|
| Number of Instances | 0 | 1 | 0 | 0 | 2 | 0 |

At the end of the development section a fugato appears, built on the following theme:

EXAMPLE 8-26: Bartók, *Concerto for Orchestra,* first movement

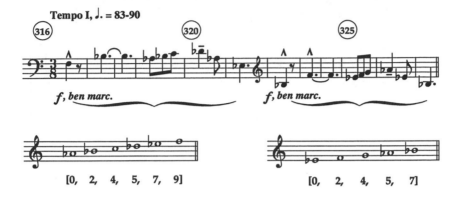

[0,2,4,5,7,9]

| Interval-class: | 1,11 | 2,10 | 3,9 | 4,8 | 5,7 | 6 |
|---|---|---|---|---|---|---|
| Number of Instances | 1 | 4 | 3 | 2 | 5 | 0 |

[0,2,3,5,7] (lowest ordering of [0,2,4,5,7])

| Interval-class: | 1,11 | 2,10 | 3,9 | 4,8 | 5,7 | 6 |
|---|---|---|---|---|---|---|
| Number of Instances | 1 | 3 | 2 | 1 | 3 | 0 |

The hexachord [0,2,4,5,7,9] is the basis of the fugato; its subset [0,2,4,5,7] is the basis of the tonal answer. Like the trichord and tetrachord of the first and second themes, there is a pronounced emphasis on interval-class 5,7. Entries of the subject are arranged so that repeated forms of [0,2,5,7] lead into and remain during an appearance of the first theme. (Listen to Example 8-27.) [0,2,5,7], like the tetrachord [0,3,5,8] that underlies the first theme, emphasizes interval classes 5,7.

EXAMPLE 8-27: Bartók, *Concerto for Orchestra*, first movement

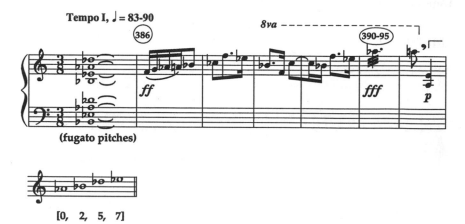

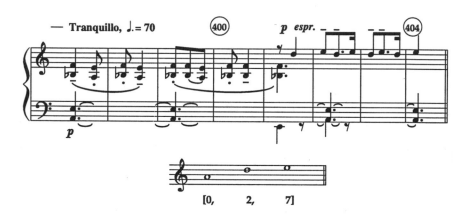

The recapitulation begins with the tranquillo theme, now based on an inverted form of [0,2,7]. (See mm. 401ff. in Example 8-27.) The movement ends with the fugato theme:

EXAMPLE 8-28: Bartók, *Concerto for Orchestra*, first movement

The pitch structures discussed here are embedded in a wide range of additional elements, but each section is set off by a thinning out of texture. Much as in tonal music, where keys are often most clearly defined at important junctures in the form, the beginnings of new sections in this movement are defined by clear relations with one another.

F is the focal pitch of the Allegro vivace at its beginning and end. Indeed, the first and last harmonies in the section are root-position F-minor triads (m. 77, see Example 8-24, and m. 521, see Example 8-28). But there is no sense of functional harmonies in this piece. The final F, for instance, is approached by interval 5 from above and below, as well as by a scalar motion leading to F.

With this orientation, listen to the entire movement. The Allegro vivace is in sonata form:

Exposition, mm. 76–230
        first theme begins in m. 76
        second theme begins in m. 155
Development, mm. 231–396
Recapitulation, mm. 396–521
        second theme begins in m. 402
first theme begins in m. 488

Analysis Exercise 3 at the end of this chapter offers suggestions for further study of this movement.

***The Same Sets in Different Pieces.***    You may have noticed in our analyses during the past two chapters that the same pitch-class sets occur in quite different pieces. For instance, Debussy's *The Sunken Cathedral*, *La Mer*, and Stravinsky's *Petrushka* (all discussed earlier in this chapter) feature the pentachord [0,2,4,7,9], a pentatonic scale. Similarly, the opening of Stravinsky's *Petrushka* and Bartók's *Diminished Fifth* (review the discussions earlier in this chapter) feature the tetrachord [0,2,3,5].

From one perspective, the quite diverse textures, tunes, and harmonies of these pieces vividly demonstrate how a single set can appear in many ways. But from another perspective all these pieces do indeed share common features. In all of them, there are links with tonal music. The two Debussy works exist on the borderline of tonality, while Stravinsky's *Petrushka* and Bartók's *Diminished Fifth* are clearly not functionally tonal pieces. But they all have melodies and/or harmonies and/or textures and/or aspects of phrasing and form reminiscent of tonality. Their pitch-class sets—tetrachords that are diatonic-scale segments, and the pentatonic scale—allow them to create their own sonic universes while imparting that tonal aura.

Perhaps their shared features are most dramatically highlighted when these Debussy, Stravinsky, and Bartók pieces stand in contrast to the two Webern compositions we have studied: the *Movement for String Quartet*, op. 5 no. 4, and *Concerto for Nine Instruments*, op. 24. Webern's pitch-class sets are not at all reminiscent of tonal structures, and his pieces share few melodies, harmonies, or phrasings with tonal music.

## Some Other Relationships in Pieces and Sets

*Similar Melodic Patterns from Different Sets.* Even when two sets are quite different from each other, a composer can arrange the sets compositionally to point out an unexpected similarity between them. A particularly imaginative instance occurs in Schoenberg's song *Tot* (Dead). In this case, the relationship Schoenberg reveals serves as a witty instance of tone-painting. Listen to the following two four-note phrases:

EXAMPLE 8-29: Schoenberg, *Tot,* op. 48 no. 2

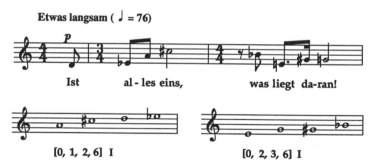

Text: It's all the same
What does it matter!

[0,1,2,6]

| Interval-class: | 1,11 | 2,10 | 3,9 | 4,8 | 5,7 | 6 |
|---|---|---|---|---|---|---|
| Number of Instances | 2 | 1 | 0 | 1 | 1 | 1 |

[0,2,3,6]

| Interval-class: | 1,11 | 2,10 | 3,9 | 4,8 | 5,7 | 6 |
|---|---|---|---|---|---|---|
| Number of Instances | 1 | 1 | 2 | 1 | 0 | 1 |

At first, it seems that the two tetrachords are quite different from each other. At the level of transposition used, they share no common pitch-classes, and their interval contents are quite different, what with [0,2,3,6] emphasizing interval-class 3,9, the only interval-class missing from [0,1,2,6].

Yet each phrase contains the same melodic intervals: one instance each of interval-classes 1,11; 4,8; and 6. This is possible because each tetrachord has a fairly even distribution of interval-classes. Each omits only a single interval-class—and the melody contains neither missing interval-class within a phrase. This feature, wherein two different tetrachords give rise to the same melodic intervals, is a laconic musical reflection of the textual meaning.

***Different Sets with Identical Interval Content.*** There are a number of sets that have identical interval contents even though they are different from one another (that is, they are not inversions of one another). Consider the pitch-class sets in Example 8-30. Of all pitch-class sets with between three and six pitch-classes, there are no trichords, one pair of tetrachords, three pairs of pentachords, and fifteen pairs of hexachords with this property.

EXAMPLE 8-30

[0,   1,   4,   6]

[0,   1,   3,   7]

[0,1,4,6] and [0,1,3,7]

| Interval-class: | 1,11 | 2,10 | 3,9 | 4,8 | 5,7 | 6 |
|---|---|---|---|---|---|---|
| Number of Instances | 1 | 1 | 1 | 1 | 1 | 1 |

When such sets are used in a composition, they can project a similar intervallic sound through different contents.

***Summary.*** This concludes our survey of relationships among different forms of a pitch-class set, among sets and subsets, and among different pitch-class sets. We have described various analytic tools and the application of these tools in analyses of several excerpts. The Exercises for Analysis and Suggestions for Further Study at the conclusion of this chapter present you with a number of pieces and analyses for you to explore. The next chapter continues our study of pitch-class sets by turning to the larger sets of a piece that form pitch-class regions.

# Points for Review

**1.** Pitch-class sets (whether transpositions or inversions of one set or different sets) can be related to one another by the number of pitches or the number of intervals they have in common.

**2.** When a set is transposed by an interval other than 6, the number of instances of that interval-class in the set is the number of pitch-classes in common between the two transpositions. When a set is transposed by interval 6, the number of common pitch-classes is double the number of instances of interval 6.

**3.** When an interval occurs more than once in a set, there is a transposition that will hold one form of the interval in common between the two transpositions.

**4.** Any interval in a set may be retained when the set is inverted.

**5.** If an interval occurs twice in a set, both occurrences can be retained in a single inversion.

**6.** A *subset* is a pitch-class set that is part of a larger set.

**7.** Some pitch-class sets have identical interval contents, even though they are not inversions of one another.

# Exercises for Chapter 8

**Terms and Concepts**

**1.** Define subset.

**2.** Find subsets that occur at least twice in each of the following pitch-class sets. The last example has been completed.

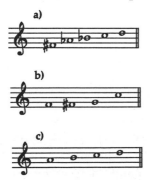

**[Terms and Concepts Exercise]**

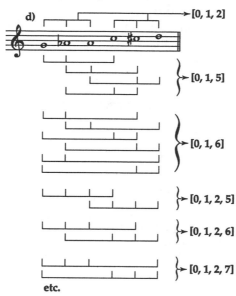

## Analysis

All of the pieces discussed below begin with a small number of pitch-classes, and then use the structuring of the opening cell(s) to expand the range of pitch-classes and intervals. In addition to answering the questions about each piece, consider how it develops from its opening. How do form, phrasing, texture, dynamics, register, and other aspects participate? Where are climactic moments and points of repose? How are they created? How does the composer assist the listener in perceiving the piece? Use the Model Analyses in this chapter as a guide.

**1.** Bartók, *Diminished Fifth* (*Mikrokosmos No. 101*). Some aspects of this piece were discussed on pp. 112 and 115–16. After familiarizing yourself with the work, answer the following questions:

  **a)** Identify the pitch-class sets used as the basis of the two parts in mm. 1–5. Identify the pitch-class set that results from the combination of right-hand and left-hand in mm. 1–5.

    (1) What interval is missing from each part taken separately, and is heavily emphasized by the combination of the two parts?

    (2) How many transpositions of the combined pitch-class set give rise to different pitches? Why are there so few transpositions that differ?

  **b)** What is the relationship between the pitch-class structure of mm. 1–5 and that of succeeding phrases? Which later phrases use the

original transposition of the basic pitch-class set, and which use a
different transposition?

c) What is the relationship between form and pitch-class sets in the
piece? How do dynamics and the pace of melodic development
relate to these aspects?

2. Webern, *Movement for String Quartet*, op. 5, no. 4. The opening portion of this movement has been partially analyzed on pp. 88–89, 102–3,
and 122–24. Comment on the following additional aspects:

a) What is the form of the piece? How are sections differentiated?
What aspects are changed when sections return?

**b)** What is the formal function of the passage in mm. 6, 10, and 13? How do the pitch-classes in these measures relate to those in preceding and / or following measures?

Webern, *Movements for String Quartet*, Op. 5, No. 4. © Copyright 1922 by Universal Edition, Wien. Copyright renewed. All Rights Reserved. Used by permission of European American Music Distributors Corporation, sole U.S. and Canadian agent for Universal Edition, Vienna.

**3.** Bartók, *Concerto for Orchestra,* first movement. Salient aspects of the form and the main themes were discussed earlier in this chapter. Continue with the analysis as follows:

**a)** In the Allegro vivace, study the way the individual phrases that make up each section begin and end. For instance, the first period in the first theme group extends from m. 76 to m. 93. How is the end of this period related to the beginning? The next period, containing several shorter phrases, extends from m. 95 through m. 133. What is the relation between the beginning and end of this phrase? How is it subdivided? What sets are emphasized at phrase-beginnings and phrase-endings?

**b)** What is the relation of the music in the Introduction to the structural bases of the themes during the Allegro vivace?

**4.** Edgard Varèse (1883–1965), *Octandre,* first movement (1924). Note that the score contains several transposing instruments: the Bb clarinet, which sounds a whole step lower than written; the French horn in F, which sounds a perfect fifth lower than written; and the string bass, which sounds an octave lower than written.

**a)** Listen first to the opening oboe solo. The first four pitches are under one slur, and followed by a breath. What is the structure of this tetrachord? What properties of this set are most prominent here? How is this set used in the following measures?

**b)** Transpositions and other related sets appear in mm. 4 and following. How are these transpositions and sets related to the opening?

**c)** As you proceed through the movement, note particularly those points where the textures change, such as study number 1, the ♩ = 56 after study number 2, the tempo primo before study number 3, and the concluding oboe solo. How do the harmonies and lines proceed from the opening?

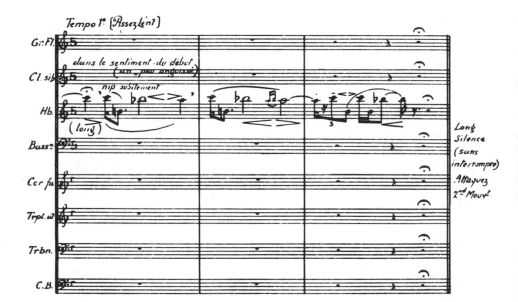

**Composition**

**1.** Compose a brief opening section of a work that begins with only four or five pitch-classes. Increase the number of pitches in circulation by introducing transpositions or inversions of the original set that add new pitches one or two at a time. Use a tetrachord or pentachord as the basis for your piece. Your composition should be under a minute in length, and scored for instruments available in your class.

**2.** Compose a short piece using two related pitch-class sets. Use two related tetrachords or a related tetrachord and pentachord. All pitches should come from these sets, including transpositions and inversions. You may wish to use some ideas you worked out in the Composition Exercise for Chapter 7.

# Suggestions for Further Study

**1.** Bartók, String Quartet No. 4, first movement (1928). Several writers have found two related tetrachords along with tonal and other elements to be the basis of much of the first movement: [0,1,2,3], [0,2,4,6]. See George Perle's article "Symmetrical Formations in the String Quartets of Béla Bartók," in *Music Review* 16 (1955): 300; Leo Treitler's "Harmonic Procedure in the *Fourth Quartet* of Béla Bartók, in *Journal of Music Theory*, 3 (1959): 292–298; and Elliot Antokoletz's *The Music of Béla Bartók* (Berkeley: University of California Press, 1984).

**2.** Bartók, *Music for Strings, Percussion, and Celesta* (1936). The fugue subject of the first movement is discussed in Analysis Exercise 2 of Chapter 5. As summarized in Chapter 4, the first statement of the fugue subject begins and ends on A, establishing this as the focal pitch for the movement. The climax of the movement occurs on the tritone E♭. Study how the transposition of fugue subject entries leads from the opening A to the climactic E♭.

This piece is often cited to demonstrate Bartók's interest in proportions derived from the Fibonacci series, a number sequence in which each number is the sum of the two preceding numbers: (0), 1, 1, 2, 3, 5, 8, 13, 21, 34, 55, and so forth. One characteristic of this series is that the ratios of pairs of numbers approaches .618 more and more closely as the series progresses. Thus $2 \div 3 = .666$; $3 \div 5 = .600$; $5 \div 8 = .625$; $8 \div 13 = .615$; $13 \div 21 = .619$; $21 \div 34 = .617$; $34 \div 55 = .61818$; $55 \div 89 = .6179$; and so forth. Many of the climaxes in this movement and within sections of this movement occur close to .618 of the way through the movement or through that section.

The second and third movements are good examples of Bartók's incorporation of folk elements in melody and rhythm. Note also the transformation of the first-movement's fugue subject when it returns in the finale, emphasizing the symmetrical relationship of movements 1 and 3. The second movement is replete with special timbral effects as well as symmetrical elements in pitch, rhythm, and form.

**3.** Stravinsky, *Three Pieces for String Quartet* (1914). All three pieces use a variety of small sets. Study in particular the second piece, which starts with a single tetrachord in two transpositions, and gradually introduces a much wider range of pitch structures.

**4.** Webern, *Five Movements for String Quartet*, op. 5. Study the remaining movements of this opus. You might begin with the first and third movements, which are closest in structure to the fourth movement in terms of their use of closely related sets.

Several studies discuss the fourth movement in detail. Among these are George Perle's *Serial Composition and Atonality* (Berkeley: University of California Press, four editions from 1963–1977), and Charles Burkhart's "The Symmetrical Source of Webern's Opus 5, No. 4," in *The Music Forum* 5 (1980): 317–334. For a detailed discussion of the first movement, see Stanley Persky, "A Discussion of Compositional Choices in Webern's *Fünf Sätze für Streichquartett*, op. 5, First movement," in *Current Musicology* 13 (1972): 68–74.

**5.** Schoenberg, *Pierrot Lunaire*, op. 21 (1912);
   *Three Piano Pieces*, op. 11 (1909).
   *Ich darf nicht dankend*, op. 14 no. 1 (1907). This song is an excellent example of the interaction of tonal elements and pitch-class sets in a work of Schoenberg's that was composed during the transition from tonal to nontonal writing. The harmonic and melodic motives in mm. 1–2 function as motives (subject to development) and pitch-class sets, while the voice leading of mm. 1–3 leads to the implied B triad at the end of m. 3. See the very end of the song for a condensation of this progression.

**6.** Maurice Ravel, *Sonate* for violin and cello (1922). The opening figure in the violin announces a motive (and pitch-class set) that is a musical source for all four movements. Study the way this set and other materials interact with each other in the various movements. For instance, when the cello melody at the opening returns in the recapitulation of the first movement, it has a new accompaniment.

**7.** Debussy, *Preludes For Piano* (volume 1 published 1910; volume 2 published 1913). Any of these pieces is ideal for studying the imaginative ways Debussy interweaves tonal reminiscences with newer usages.

Pursue a more detailed study of *The Sunken Cathedral* (No. 10 in Book I). What is the source of the middle section of the piece (with the four-sharp key signature)? How does this relate to the preceding and following music? How does the transition into and out of this section function? What tonal structures are created during this piece? Then turn to *Voiles* (No. 2 in Book I). What is the basis of the opening and closing sections? How does a focus on one pitch arise during these sections? What is the basis of the middle section of the piece?

8. George Crumb (born 1929), *Eleven Echoes of Autumn, 1965* (1966).
   a) Begin your study with Eco 1. What tetrachord is the basis of this section? In how many transpositions does it occur? What intervals are emphasized in this tetrachord? What intervals are added when the other transposition is included?
   b) How much of Eco 2 is based on the same material as Eco 1? Where are the new elements added? How distinct are they?
   c) Which elements in Eco 3 are continuations of previous material? Which are new?
   d) As you proceed through the piece, study the way old elements are combined in new ways to form new structures, and the ways in which these new structures are themselves transformed. The entire piece has a shape perhaps most immediately audible in the dynamics: growth to the loud passages in Eco 8 and tapering off to the end. Do any other structural aspects of the piece follow this pattern?

# 9

# Pitch-Class Regions,
# Scales, Modes

---

*pitch-class region*　　*octatonic scale*
*whole-tone scale*　　*fifth-series*
*altered scale*

---

The term *pitch-class region* refers to larger pitch-class sets containing all the pitch-classes in a given passage. In much nontonal music, pitch-class regions are similar to scales in tonal music. Just as tonal scales are the source for many of the harmonies and melodies in a passage, pitch-class regions are a resource for the more local pitch events in a passage.

In this sense, pitch-class regions point to the presence of larger levels of structure in much nontonal music akin to such larger levels in tonal music. In the latter, the harmonies, voice leading, and motives organize the local levels, while the changing keys provide new focal pitches and new pitch collections at larger levels. In the former, the interaction of pitch-class sets and the shifting of focus from one pitch-class to another organize the local levels, while changing pitch-class regions bring with them new focal pitches or changing pitch collections. Often changes in pitch-class regions occur in conjunction with changes of theme and the arrival in new sections, much as key changes in tonal music interact with and participate in creating the form of the composition.

Although we have not used the term to describe them, we have already encountered pitch-class regions. In Bartók's *Diminished Fifth*, for instance, we noted how two tetrachords that have no pitch-classes in common are the basis of each voice part. (Review Example 8-6 on p. 112.) In each phrase, these tetrachords join to form an octachord that functions as a pitch-class region, providing the pitch-classes for the tetrachords in each voice part, and also providing contrast as the octachord pitch-regions

146

change from one phrase to the next. Similarly, in the first movement of Debussy's *La Mer,* changes from one ostinato to another are changes in pitch-class regions.

In this chapter we will study these and other excerpts in more detail, examining the ways some commonly used larger pitch-class sets function as pitch-class regions in many twentieth-century compositions. Much of the chapter consists of analyses of representative excerpts.

# The Diatonic Scale

Much music composed in the twentieth century continues to use the diatonic scale of functional tonality (the major or natural-minor scale, or the heptachord [0,1,3,5,6,8,10]), even though the resources of this scale often appear in ways that would have been unimaginable during the tonal era. Part of the reason this scale has remained in use is historical. As listeners, we are familiar with diatonic scales and can perceive subtle changes in their content even when they are used in ways that are not traditional. We will not discuss here music that is largely based on functional tonality, but will stress other uses of this heptachord.

***The Diatonic Scale as a Harmony.*** One way of using an entire diatonic scale as a pitch-class region without implying functional tonal harmonies is to have the entire scale sound as a harmony. We have already encountered such passages in Stravinsky's *Petrushka* and Debussy's *La Mer.* Review the tutti texture from *Petrushka* in Example 8-23 (on p. 127) and the D♭ ostinato from *La Mer* in Example 3-3a (p. 41). The [0,1,3,5,6,8,10] heptachord is the basis of both passages. Yet because the ostinatos and melodies interact to keep all seven pitch-classes in constant circulation, the only harmony to emerge from the texture is the entire scale itself. In *La Mer,* the change from one pitch-class region to another provides larger harmonic regions, linked to one another by a common subset. (Review the discussion of Examples 8-13 through 8-15 on pp. 116–20.) In both excerpts, the various components of the texture are separated by means of register, timbre, and motives into the subsets characteristic of that piece.

***The Diatonic Scale as a Series of Fifths.*** In many pieces, the entrance of the diatonic scale is preceded by music that focuses attention on structures uncharacteristic of functional tonal music. This preparation strongly colors the way we hear the diatonic collection when it occurs. Even as we recognize the diatonic collection, we hear it as an expansion of the opening sonorities, and do not expect it to usher in functional tonal music.

In particular, these preparatory passages most often stress the most characteristic interval-class in [0,1,3,5,6,8,10]: 5,7.

| Interval-class: | 1,11 | 2,10 | 3,9 | 4,8 | 5,7 | 6 |
|---|---|---|---|---|---|---|
| Number of Instances | 2 | 5 | 4 | 3 | 6 | 1 |

With *seven* pitch-classes and *six* instances of interval-class 5,7, each member of [0,1,3,5,6,8,10] is a perfect fourth or fifth distant from one or two other members of the set. Indeed, all the pitch-classes in a major scale can be written as a single *fifth-series* (an uninterrupted series of perfect fifths):

EXAMPLE 9-1

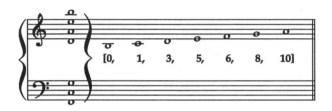

In pieces as diverse as Debussy's *Sunken Cathedral* and *La Mer*, and Stravinsky's *Petrushka*, the diatonic heptachord appears only after a sub-set has stressed interval-classes 5,7 and 2,10—a subset that is a smaller portion of the fifth-series. The pentatonic scale ([0,2,4,7,9]) that opens *The Sunken Cathedral* and the [0,2,5,7] tetrachord that opens *La Mer* and *Petrushka* are segments of the fifth-series. And the opening music to all three pieces stresses intervals 5 or 7: the parallel fifths in *The Sunken Cathedral*, the harmonic and melodic fifths and fourths in the B ostinatos in *La Mer*, and the fourths in the flute fanfare in *Petrushka*.

EXAMPLE 9-2

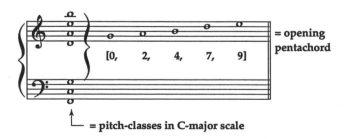

= opening pentachord

= pitch-classes in C-major scale

compare with Example 6-1 on p. 82. (Debussy, *The Sunken Cathedral*)

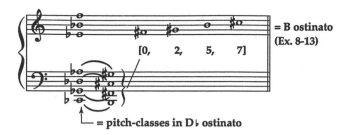

compare with Example 3-3a on p. 41 (Debussy, *La Mer*)

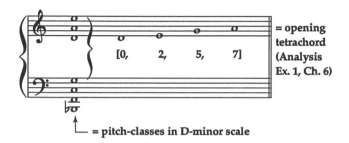

compare with Example 8-23 on p. 127 (Stravinsky, *Petrushka*)

*The Fifth-Series and Diatonic Subsets.*    Even where the entire diatonic fifth-series is not a prominent entity, segments of it often delineate
pitch-class regions. Because of the close relation between the fifth-series
and diatonic structures, such segments of the fifth-series easily establish
pitch-class regions.

*Bartók,* **Concerto for Orchestra,** *first movement.*    Review the discussion in Chapter 8. At several junctures in this sonata-form movement,
the pitch structure emphasizes small groups of pitch-classes. This happens primarily at the beginning of the first theme, the beginning of the
second theme, the end of the development section, and the end of the
movement. The [0,3,5,8] tetrachord that is the outline of the opening
theme of the *Allegro vivace* consists of four pitch-classes of the pentatonic
scale, a fifth-series. The [0,2,7] trichord that opens the second theme
group is a segment containing three pitch-classes of the fifth-series. And
the fugato theme that appears in the exposition and the end of the development outlines a segment of the fifth-series. Within and following these
sections, and throughout the movement, segments of the fifth-series
interact with other pitch-class sets that fill in the structural outlines. The
segments of the fifth-series provide focal pitch-classes for the remaining
materials.

EXAMPLE 9-3

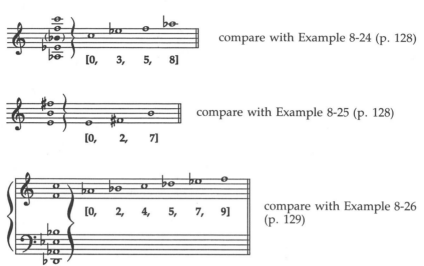

compare with Example 8-24 (p. 128)

compare with Example 8-25 (p. 128)

compare with Example 8-26 (p. 129)

*Diatonicism and "Wrong-Note" Harmony in Neo-Classic Music.* Beginning before 1920 and continuing at least into the 1950s, quite a few composers wrote music in which some aspects of pitch structure as well as of style in general seem to be functionally tonal and other aspects are clearly nontonal. The term *neo-Classic* refers to this music. Stravinsky was viewed by many as the chief exponent of this movement.

Listen to the following passage for solo piano from Stravinsky's *Concerto for Piano and Winds* (1924). Following the more chromatic, dissonant, intensely personal, and overtly expressive music of the late nineteenth and early twentieth centuries, neo-Classic passages such as this, with their obvious diatonicism, clean lines, and seemingly traditional sense of counterpoint and motivic play, certainly did seem like a return to an eighteenth-century style. But other aspects of neo-Classic music, among them the pitch language and the sense of continuity and form, are distinctly of the twentieth-century.

EXAMPLE 9-4: Stravinsky, *Concerto for Piano and Winds,* first movement

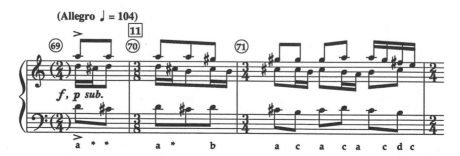

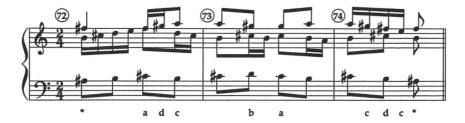

The harmonies are as follows:
\* = [0,1,5]
a = [0,5]
b = [0,1,6]
c = [0,2,5]
d = [0,2,7]
All sets are labeled in lowest ordering beginning with 0.

One key to understanding the delicate balance between the mimicking of eighteenth-century music and the piece's twentieth-century language may be found in a 1926 analysis of this excerpt by the theorist Heinrich Schenker.[1] Schenker, who was unsympathetic to post-tonal music, wrote his analysis to demonstrate that the passage was not acceptable because it was not tonal. Although his critique was motivated by a negative reaction to the music, it does illuminate crucial structural aspects of the music.

The crux of Schenker's argument is that there are tonal lines in the various voices and tonal-style elaborations of those lines (such as the many neighboring figures in both sixteenths and eighths), but that these lines are not coordinated to form tonal harmonies, as would happen in a tonal composition. Hence, for Schenker, Stravinsky's lines are essentially aimless. For instance, the top voice that begins on A in m. 69 descends via G♯ to the F♯ on the downbeat of m. 72. The completion of this descent, coupled with the pause on the quarter note, makes this F♯ sound like a tonal goal, and makes A–F♯ the span of motion. The middle voice also descends a third, from D to B, in the same measures. But the bass fails to support any of this, arriving on A♯ on the same downbeat in m. 72. Furthermore, all along the way the voices fail to form the triadic sonorities that would be expected in a tonal composition, and that are implied by stepwise diatonic lines spanning thirds and fourths. From Schenker's perspective, everything seems jumbled. If only the voices could somehow be realigned, all would be right.

Another perspective accepts the tonal features but recognizes that nontonal sonorities control the harmonies here. The [0,1,5] trichord (or one of its interval-classes: 5,7) that occurs on the downbeat of m. 72

---

1. Heinrich Schenker, *Das Meisterwerk in der Musik*, II (Munich: Drei Masken Verlag, 1926; reprinted Hildesheim: Georg Olms Verlag, 1974), pp. 37–40.

accounts for most of the harmonies in mm. 69 and 70 at the beginning of the phrase (as indicated by asterisks below Example 9-4). Most of the other harmonies are formed by the related [0,1,6] trichord (which shares interval-classes 1,11 and 5,7 with [0,1,5]) or other trichords stressing interval-class 5,7. These trichords are labeled by letters below Example 9-4.

As a result, this music features tonal but "wrong-note" harmonies and melodies in addition to its own nontonal organization. Those notes, such as that bass A♯ on the downbeat of m. 72, that are most "wrong" from the tonal perspective, are most "correct" in the nontonal structuring. It is the interaction of the "wrong-note" tonal aspects and the nontonal aspects that gives this passage, as well as so many others like it, its character.

Just as this music flirts with functional and nonfunctional usages of diatonic pitch collections, it also plays with the listener's expectations in the realm of meter. Whether notated in a strict meter or in changing meters, the effect is often of lines adding or subtracting beats or divisions of beats from the meter.

*Copland,* **Appalachian Spring** *(1943).* Another composition whose pitch structure combines tonal and nontonal aspects is *Appalachian Spring*

EXAMPLE 9-5: Copland, *Appalachian Spring*

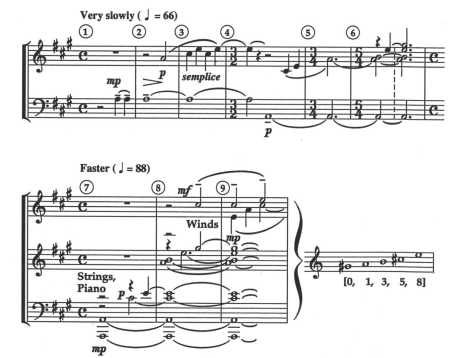

by Aaron Copland (born 1900). Much of the piece is entirely diatonic, and many sections are functionally tonal. But other passages treat familiar tonal elements more like pitch-class sets.

Quite a bit of the opening section, for instance, uses only the notes of the A-major scale, and the very opening outlines an A-major triad. But the characteristic pitch-collection of the piece is a combined A-major and E-major triad, forming the pentachord [0,1,3,5,8] that functions as a separate harmonic entity.

Functional harmonies appear in the piece in the recurring progression illustrated in Example 9-6.

EXAMPLE 9-6

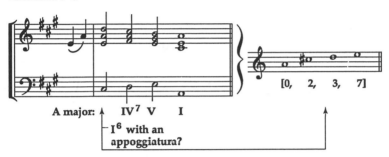

All but the first chord are functional harmonies. The opening harmony is [0,2,3,7], a subset of the characteristic pentachord [0,1,3,5,8]. But when this progression first appears, the first chord is the complete [0,1,3,5,8]. This ties together the functionally tonal harmonies with the nonfunctional union of triads from the opening.

EXAMPLE 9-7: Copland, *Appalachian Spring*

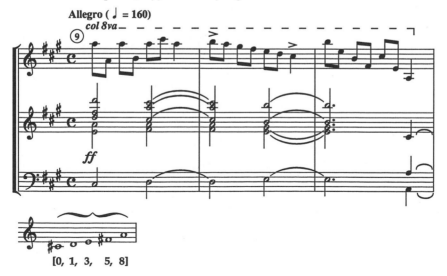

Elsewhere in this piece, major triads are used as both functional harmonies and as pitch-class sets without functional meanings.

*Several Diatonic Collections Simultaneously.* The simultaneous use of two or more diatonic scales is sometimes referred to as *bitonality* or *polytonality*. These terms are problematic if they denote two or more tonal centers, each supported by scales and harmonic progressions. For the establishment of a key in the traditional sense requires a special interaction of harmony and melody, an interaction not possible if there are conflicting lines and harmonies elsewhere in the texture. But whatever the merits of this term to describe the effects, many compositions use more than one diatonic collection simultaneously.

One such piece is Bartók's String Quartet No. 3 (1927), a work cast in a single movement. Example 9-8 illustrates the beginning of the *seconda*

EXAMPLE 9-8: Bartók: String Quartet No. 3, *seconda parte*

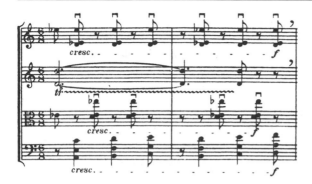

*parte,* in which a diatonic scale and its transposition up a semitone provide the pitch material for separate parts of the texture. Using two diatonic scales a semitone apart gives rise to all twelve pitch-classes.[2] But the twelve pitch-classes are clearly divided by texture, register, and timbre into two collections of seven pitch-classes each. The cello part uses the white-note collection with a strong emphasis on D, imparting a Dorian-mode sound to the passage. The first-violin melody uses pitches from the same scale built on the focal pitch E♭. D and E♭ are also emphasized as focal pitch-classes by the D–E♭ trill in the second violin and the D–E♭ pizzicatos in the viola.

This passage from the *Third Quartet* combines two divergent thematic ideas that are present throughout the work: sets emphasizing semitones and sets that are diatonic. The very opening of the quartet, shown in Example 9-9, builds two sets that are parts of a chromatic scale:

EXAMPLE 9-9: Bartók: String Quartet No. 3, *prima parte*

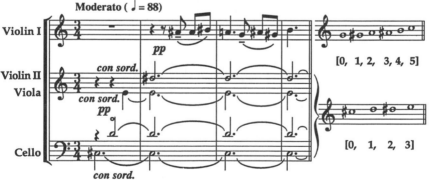

2. Since there are only two semitones in a diatonic collection, transposition by intervals 1 or 11 gives rise to only two common pitch-classes between the scales. Hence, there are seven pitch-classes in one scale plus seven pitch-classes in the other minus the two common pitch-classes: $7 + 7 - 2 = 12$.

In several later passages, diatonic scale segments combine at trans-positions that produce many semitones. One of these passages, illustrated in Example 9-10, juxtaposes the pentatonic scale in the viola and

EXAMPLE 9-10: Bartók, String Quartet No. 3, *prima parte*

| Interval-class: | 1,11 | 2,10 | 3,9 | 4,8 | 5,7 | 6 |
|---|---|---|---|---|---|---|
| Number of Instances | 6 | 4 | 4 | 5 | 6 | 3 |

first violin with a [0,2,7] trichord in the cello ostinato. Although there are no semitones in either set, the combination of the two sets gives rise to the octachord [0,1,2,3,4,7,8,9], in which no other interval-class outnumbers semitones. The second violin plays a measured trill alternating G and A♭—one pitch-class each from the two collections.

Through a gradual increase in texture, tempo, and the overall pacing of activity, the piece grows from the slow opening of the *prima parte* into the *Allegro* that begins the *seconda parte*. At that point, the passage in Example 9-8 appears as the climactic unification of the diatonic and semitonal sets: two complete diatonic collections that together produce all twelve pitch-classes.

The opening of Bartók's *Diminished Fifth* (Example 8-6 on p. 112) also combines segments of a diatonic scale that give rise to a larger pitch-class collection emphasizing an interval missing in the individual segments. In that piece the tritone transposition of the [0,2,3,5] tetrachord produces an emphasis on tritones in the larger collection—an interval-class not present in the tetrachord. The result is similar to the textures in the *Third Quartet*. The difference between the pieces lies in the complexity of presentation of set-material in the quartet, and the manner in which the preceding music leads up to the passage.

***Altered Diatonic Scales.*** Nineteenth-century composers such as Chopin, Saint-Saëns, and Bizet, seeking an ethnic or exotic flavor for some of their pieces, experimented with nondiatonic scales. But once having created such scales, they used them in the traditional tonal system.

In the twentieth century, several composers continued to explore influences from outside the main European traditions. Perhaps the most important among these was Bartók, who recorded many types of Eastern European and Near Eastern folk music, and who incorporated into his style many of the scalar and rhythmic patterns he discovered. The *Arabian Dance*, number 42 from his *Duets for Two Violins*, for instance, is based on a G harmonic-minor scale with a raised fourth step (see p. 158). But as Bartók uses it, F♯, not G, is the concluding pitch.

EXAMPLE 9-11: Bartók: *Arabian Dance*, No. 42 from *Duets for Two Violins*

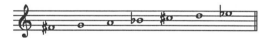

# The Whole-Tone Scale

The *whole-tone scale*, [0,2,4,6,8,10], is the basis for occasional passages in the music of many composers. But the resources of this scale are too limited for extensive use:

| Interval-class: | 1,11 | 2,10 | 3,9 | 4,8 | 5,7 | 6 |
|---|---|---|---|---|---|---|
| Number of Instances | 0 | 6 | 0 | 6 | 0 | 3 |

Only three interval-classes are present, two of them occurring the same number of times. The number of subsets is likewise extremely limited: there are only three different types of trichords ([0,2,4], [0,2,6], and [0,4,8]), three different types of tetrachords ([0,2,4,6], [0,2,4,8], and [0,2,6,8]), and one type of pentachord ([0,2,4,6,8]). Finally, since the scale is entirely uniform in structure, is its own inversion, and has another whole-tone scale as its complement, there are only two such scales. Any other transposition or inversion is a reordering of one of these two forms. With its uniform structure and limited resources, the scale or portions of it are often used in brief sections or along with other elements.

A notable exception is Debussy's *Voiles*, the second of his *Preludes for Piano*, I (1910). *Voiles* is in ternary form, with the outer sections based entirely on a single whole-tone scale. The middle section uses the pentachord [0,2,4,7,9]—the pentatonic scale made up of the black notes on the keyboard. This new pitch-class region allows contrasting sounds not found elsewhere in the piece (notably, perfect fourths and fifths and the absence of tritones).

In Messiaen's *Quartet for the End of Time,* the whole-tone scale exists along with traditional diatonic and other scales. The opening of the sixth movement is based on the whole-tone scale:

EXAMPLE 9-12: Messiaen, *Quartet for the End of Time,* sixth movement

Five notes of this scale (E–F♯–G♯–B♭–C) constitute the backbone of the melody, with occasional B's as additional notes, always neighboring or passing to adjacent whole-tone scale notes. In later sections of the movement, different scales alternate with this.

***Interaction of Diatonic and Whole-Tone Scales.*** The interaction of diatonic and whole-tone structures underlies an early work of Schoenberg's, the *Chamber Symphony*, op. 9 (1906). This is Schoenberg's last large work in a tonal language, however extended. It begins and ends "in E major." But functional progressions are avoided almost throughout and there are long sections with few recognizable harmonies characteristic of traditional tonal music.

Example 9-13 is the very opening of the work, the slow introduction and the beginning of the exposition. The progression from one harmony to the next in the introduction (mm. 1–4) sounds tonal. But the harmonic language is quite extended. The final F-major triad in m. 4 is preceded by its dominant seventh (C–E–G–B♭), but with the fifth of the chord split into an ascending and descending form: G in the melody is replaced by A♭ or G♯ leading to A, and G in the bass is replaced by G♭

leading to F. The opening chord is a series of perfect fourths creating the [0,2,4,5,7,9] hexachord, one fourth short of a complete diatonic scale. In an extended harmonic language, the progression sounds like $G^9_{sus4}$ to $C^{7\text{-with-a-split-fifth}}$ to $F^{maj}$, or some form of supertonic-to-dominant-to-tonic. But the sense in which this progression is tonal is weakened by the chromaticism (nine different pitch-classes appear in these chords) and the dissonance level (the first two chords contain six and five pitches). In addition, the retention of three notes between the first two chords works against hearing a harmonic progression between them.

EXAMPLE 9-13: Schoenberg, *Chamber Symphony*, op. 9

More important than these extended harmonic implications is the way in which the introduction announces the ideas contained in this piece. In turn, each chord of the slow introduction becomes the basis for melodic and harmonic structures in the opening of the *sehr rasch.*

The first chord of the introduction is built in six perfect fourths. In the first measure of the *sehr rasch,* this [0,2,4,5,7,9] hexacord appears as a melody.

The second chord of the introduction is a five-note segment of a whole-tone scale: [0,2,4,6,8]. Structures derived from a whole-tone scale predominate in mm. 6–8: the augmented triads moving to one another by whole steps. Since the rate of chord change in each part of the texture is different, up to five notes from a whole-tone scale sound together during mm. 6 and 7.

The third and final harmony of the introduction is a major triad. After the augmented triads in mm. 6–8 of the *sehr rasch,* a major triad appears in m. 10. The melody connects notes of this triad by a complete whole-tone scale: G#–A#–C–D–E–F#–G#.

There is some tonal basis to this progression, as notated on the lower staff-system in Example 9-13. The chords in mm. 6–9 emphasize dominants of E: the augmented V in m. 6 and following (B–D#–F×) and the VII₇ of E in mm. 8 and 9. These dominants resolve in mm. 10 and 11 to the E-major tonic chords. But the motivic relationships among harmonies within this passage and in relation to the introduction forms a more compelling determinant of the sounds and sense of the passage than the pre-existent harmonic language of tonality.

# The Octatonic Scale

An eight-note collection that has been particularly popular with many composers, the *octatonic scale,* features alternating whole tones and semitones.

EXAMPLE 9-14: The Octatonic Scale

[0, 1, 3, 4, 6, 7, 9, 10]

| Interval-class: | 1,11 | 2,10 | 3,9 | 4,8 | 5,7 | 6 |
|---|---|---|---|---|---|---|
| Number of Instances | 4 | 4 | 8 | 4 | 4 | 4 |

The popularity of the octatonic scale may be traced to the large number of tonal and nontonal elements it contains. Like traditional diatonic scales, it combines whole and half steps between consecutive scale degrees, allowing the creation of traditional-sounding melodies and arpeggiations. Because of the large number of thirds and perfect fifths, it contains eight major or minor triads (even more than in a major or minor scale).

Yet along with these features reminiscent of tonality, it has other features appropriate for use in nontonal twentieth-century music. The octatonic scale is based on a trichord cell [0,1,3] that recurs four times to create the entire scale (at T0, T3, T6, and T9, or at I0, I9, I6, and I3). Its simple repetitious structure (alternating half and whole steps) permits exact transpositions or inversions of any of its segments. Since it contains four tritones, its use suggests emphasis on even divisions of the octave (as well as on the uneven division into the perfect fourth and fifth characteristic of tonal music).

Finally, because of its modular and repeating structure, there are only three different forms of the scale. (See Example 9-15). Therefore, in a piece based on the octatonic scale, different regions of transposition akin to key changes in tonal music may be established.

EXAMPLE 9-15: The Three Transpositions of the Octatonic Scale

*Bartók.* **Diminished Fifth.**    We have already encountered one piece built almost entirely from the octatonic scale: Bartók's *Diminished Fifth*. See Analysis Exercise 1 (p. 136) in Chapter 8 for a complete score, and pp. 112, 115 and 116 for a discussion of local features. In this piece, two tritone-related transpositions of the tetrachord [0,2,3,5] create octatonic scales in every phrase. *Diminished Fifth* is a rondo:

$$
\begin{array}{ll}
A & mm.\ 1\text{--}11 \\
B & mm.\ 12\text{--}19 \\
A^1 & mm.\ 20\text{--}25 \\
C & mm.\ 26\text{--}34 \\
A^2 & mm.\ 35\text{--}44
\end{array}
$$

Each A section uses one transposition of the octatonic scale (*a* in Example 9-15). The B and C sections use different transpositions. The C section is the most developmental and harmonically mobile. It uses all three forms of the octatonic scale, returning to *a* for the concluding $A^2$ section. As a result, the piece has a form similar to a tonal composition in pitch structure as well as in thematic layout.

Other aspects of the music follow this thematic-pitch-region structure. The dynamics, for instance, relate directly to the use of octatonic scales: piano for the A section, mezzopiano for the B section, and mezzoforte for the mobile C section. The C section is the climax of the piece, being most varied harmonically (since it uses all three transpositions of the octatonic scales), having the loudest dynamics, and featuring the highest pitches in the piece. The following diagram summarizes these aspects of the form:

| Section: | measures: | scale:[3] | dynamics: |
|---|---|---|---|
| A | 1–11 | a | p |
| B | 12–19 | b | mp |
| A¹ | 20–25 | a | p |
| C | 26–34 | c, a, b | mf |
| A² | 35–44 | a | p |

*Messiaen,* **Quartet for the End of Time.**    The octatonic scale is used in connection with other types of scales (diatonic and whole-tone, among them) in several movements. Indeed, much of the exotic color of Messiaen's harmony arises from tonal elements within nontraditional sets such as the octatonic scale.

The opening of the *Intermède* is characteristic. The unaccompanied melody centers around E:

---

3. The letters refer to the forms of the octatonic scale in Example 9-15.

EXAMPLE 9-16: Messiaen, *Quartet for the End of Time,* fourth movement

Despite its octatonic basis, this melody works like a traditional tonal melody. If you play it in E major, it sounds rather tonal (and, also, rather banal):

EXAMPLE 9-17: The same, recomposed

The scale and melody in Example 9-16 interact with other types of scales. One recurrence of the tune, for instance, is accompanied by a line using the C-major scale:

EXAMPLE 9-18: Messiaen, *Quartet for the End of Time,* fourth movement

These different scales change along with new sections in the movement, delineating the form much like the changes in scale we noted in Bartók's *Diminished Fifth.*

But perhaps the octatonic scale's most intriguing appearance in the *Quartet* is in the fifth movement, the opening of which appears in Example 9-19.

EXAMPLE 9-19: Messiaen, *Quartet for the End of Time,* fifth movement

The key signature indicates E major and there are indeed E-major triads at the beginning and end of the first piano entry (as well as at the end of the entire movement). But the harmonic motion within the phrase, though entirely triadic, has little to do with E major, for the basis of the entire phrase is the octatonic, not the E-major scale. The triads, all major, occur in the ordering: E, B♭, G, B♭, and E. The tritone root relation between the first two and last two harmonies reinforces this crucial interval in the octatonic scale.

The melodic pitches interact in different ways with these harmonies. The G♯ on the downbeat of m. 4, for instance, could have been a member of the preceding E major triad. But we hear it change to an A♭ over the change in harmony. Similar reinterpretations of pitches and their interaction with the underlying harmony occur throughout the movement, imparting much of the intense expression of the movement. Throughout the movement, our hearing wavers between the tonal interpretation of local events and a nontonal perspective. The extremely slow tempo allows us to appreciate fully every one of these interactions.

The G-major-triad-plus-C♯ in m. 5 is a characterisic harmony for this scale and for much of Messiaen's music. It is an all-interval tetrachord [0,1,3,7]—containing one instance each of every interval-class. Messiaen often voices it as a ⁶₄-chord with an added note, emphasizing its tonal element, but with a tritone over the root. (The first chord in the measure is the same tetrachord voiced similarly.)

***Stravinsky*, Symphony of Psalms.** Much of Stravinsky's music through the 1940s includes the octatonic scale among its resources. In the first movement of the *Symphony of Psalms* (1930), a single form of the octatonic scale interacts with the white-note diatonic collection for much of the movement. E is established as a focal center by several factors, among them the strikingly individual voicing of the E-minor triads that punctuate the opening and one later passage in the movement and the insistence on E with an upper neighbor of F as the principal line in the chorus parts for much of the movement.

Textures based on the octatonic scale beginning E–F and on the white-note scale (the Phrygian mode) alternate for the first portion of the movement:

EXAMPLE 9-20: Stravinsky: *Symphony of Psalms*, first movement

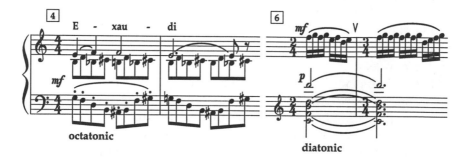

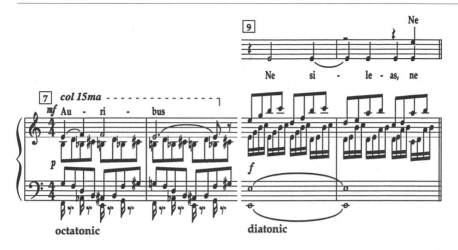

Various characteristically octatonic constructions appear, among them the minor thirds related by semitones so important throughout the *Symphony* (see study numbers 4 and 7).

After a brief passage featuring the octatonic scale in the orchestra and white-note writing in the chorus, the movement ends on a G–D fifth. The tonal motion from E to G is already foreshadowed in the very opening E-minor harmony with its quadruply doubled G.

The octatonic scale beginning E–F and the Phrygian mode on E share five pitch-classes, including the first three scale degrees (E–F–G), allowing smooth transitions from one to the other. There are other pitch-classes in the course of the movement. But the strong profiles of these two scales and the recurring passages based on them are the referential collections of the movement.

Changes among these collections function like key changes in tonal music. E remains the focal pitch-class for much of the first movement of the *Symphony of Psalms,* even while the scale changes from Phrygian to octatonic. This is similar to what happens in tonal music when a dominant chord (say, a G-major chord in C major) changes from V in the original key to I in its own key—the chord remains unchanged, but its new context gives it a new meaning. The difference, of course, between this type of situation in tonal and nontonal music is that in tonal music the meanings of these shifts are always the same, and, hence, we have developed names for them (such as *on* the dominant chord or *in* the dominant key). In a case like the *Symphony of Psalms* we can refer to the change, but not draw from it such universal meanings. Yet we hear the effects of the change as we listen to the piece.

In the first movement of the *Symphony of Psalms,* several separate textures, each with a strongly individual profile, alternate with each other.

Such alternation, which often accompanies and articulates pitch changes, is a characteristic of much of Stravinsky's music, as we noted in Chapter 4. Instead of stressing continuity and gradual development, these often abrupt textural articulations set off sections from one another, creating dramatic contrasts. This is a broad parallel to Stravinsky's characteristic ostinato-like melodies and harmonies that we noted in connection with *Petrushka* (review the discussion of Examples 8-21 through 8-23). Even the excerpt from the *Concerto for Piano and Winds* (Example 9-4) features a melody of small range with repeating pitches. As we will see again when we study Stravinsky's idiosyncratic use of the twelve-tone system in his late works, certain underlying characteristics of his style remained relatively unchanged despite the several dramatic changes in surface style that took place during a creative life that spanned more than six decades.

# Other Pitch-Class Regions

Changes from one pitch-class region to another are most obvious in styles where the pitch-class collection serves as a resource from which melodies and harmonies are drawn, much as melodies and harmonies arise from the scale of the prevailing key in tonal music. But even where there is little sense of a prevailing scale, the total pitch-class content of a nontonal passage is often a factor in the music. Review Webern's *Movement for String Quartet*, op. 5 no. 4 (score on p. 137). At several points in the movement, harmonies or melodies sum up most of the pitch-classes in use. The chord at the end of m. 2, for instance, contains all six pitch-classes in mm. 1–2. Mm. 3–6 use nine pitch-classes, seven of which are in the second-violin figure that concludes the measure. The same figure, when it recurs transposed in the viola in m. 10, contains among its seven pitches all six pitch-classes in the opening phrase of the movement (mm. 1–2), thereby announcing the return to a recomposed opening section of the ABA[1] form. As we have seen earlier with Webern, every note in his pieces serves an important function.

In the music of other composers, a completed pitch-class region of a certain size often marks the end of a section. Varèse, for instance, will often come to a formal juncture upon completion of the entire chromatic scale. Review the score to the first movement of *Octandre* on pp. 138–42. The oboe solo is the principal line for the first nine measures of the movement. The opening tetrachord [0,1,2,3] provides all the pitch-classes in mm. 1–3. Transposition of this tetrachord down four semitones in m. 4 expands the number of pitch-classes to eight. This tetrachord as well as other pitch-class sets expand the pitch-class region to eleven by the downbeat of m. 6. The only missing pitch-class is G, which enters at the very end of the solo in the extreme high register of the oboe, accented and *ffff*.

## Summary to Unit Two

This concludes our exposition of some principles underlying nontonal music of the twentieth century. The principles laid out here will continue to be used in our study of twelve-tone music in Unit Three, as well as in Unit Four, which surveys some aspects of music of the past generation or two.

It was for some time traditional to draw clear dividing lines between tonal music, the nontonal music of this century, and twelve-tone music. Tonal music was based on tonal principles and analyzed accordingly; nontonal music that preceded the development of the twelve-tone system was called free atonal or contextual atonal music and analyzed according to its motivic or pitch-class structures; twelve-tone music had its own principles.

But as the discussions in this Unit have demonstrated, these sharp distinctions are not borne out by study of the music. Many nontonal twentieth-century compositions retain tonal features. In addition, we have used pitch-class sets to illuminate features of compositions by Wagner and Debussy that are at least partially tonal. Finally, some excerpts used in this Unit are from twelve-tone compositions (Webern's *Concerto for Nine Instruments* and Schoenberg's *Tot*).

As a result, the focus of many studies of twentieth-century music in recent years is turning toward those principles that underlie all music of our era. The study of pitch-class sets (the properties of the pitch-class collections of a piece, and how they relate to each other) gives analysts one set of tools with which to work. For these pitch-class sets of all sizes determine many of the sound limits within which a piece exists. But it is up to the analyst to determine which pitch-classes to include in sets, which to relate to one another, how to explain the varieties of contrast and unity that exist in a piece, how to relate these features to the organic nature of the piece, and how to relate these features to the other elements that exist in a piece, be they tonal, twelve-tone, or other. In short, a well-done pitch-class set analysis is not a mechanical processing of the piece, but an interpretive study.

## Points for Review

**1.** *Pitch-class regions* (larger pitch-class sets) serve as sources for local harmonies and melodies in many twentieth-century compositions, much as scales and keys organize the larger pitch aspects of tonal compositions.

**2.** The *diatonic scale*—the [0,1,3,5,6,8,10] heptachord—and its subsets appear in many twentieth-century compositions in ways that combine reminiscences of tonal features with aspects characteristic of twentieth-century music. Many usages stress the diatonic scale as a *fifth-series*.

**3.** *Altered scales* and the *whole-tone scale* function as pitch-class regions in some compositions.

**4.** The *octatonic scale*, with alternating whole and half steps, contains features reminiscent of tonality (step-related scale degrees and eight major or minor triads) and nontonal features. It is used in a wide range of twentieth-century compositions.

# Exercises for Chapter 9

## Terms and Concepts

Define the following terms:

> *pitch-class region*     *octatonic scale*
> *altered scale*          *whole-tone scale*
> *fifth-series*

## Analysis

Any of the following pieces are suitable for study using the concepts discussed in this chapter.

**1.** Bartók, String Quartet No. 3. What is the form of the entire quartet? Study the ways pitch structures help project this form.

**2.** Debussy, *Voiles*, from *Preludes for Piano*, I. Study the use of the whole-tone scale in the outer sections. Is there a focal pitch-class? How is it established? What happens to this focal pitch-class in the B section of the piece?

*Images* for piano, third movement. The movement begins with the open fifth C–G. How does this interval influence the order in which pitch-classes appear during the opening section of the piece? What is the form of the piece? How do pitch-class regions help establish that form?

**3.** Ives, *The Unanswered Question* (1908). Read Ives's program for this piece as you familiarize yourself with it. This piece contains three separate ideas: the string background, the trumpet "question," and the woodwind "answer." Study each separately. Then study their interaction. Is there any synthesis of these separate ideas in the piece? Is the "question" ever "answered?"

**4.** Messiaen, *Quartet for the End of Time*. Movements 4, 5, and 6 are suitable for studying the interaction of different scales and pitch-class regions and the interaction of tonal and nontonal features.

**5.** Stravinsky, *Rite of Spring* (1913). The Introduction and *Dance of the Adolescents* provide numerous instances of small sets intensively used and placed in juxtaposition with different and often contrasting sets. What pitch-class regions arise in these sections? How do they relate to the form? See the *Jeu du rapt* for several different large pitch-class regions, including the octatonic scale.

*Symphony of Psalms.* Continue with an analysis of the first movement. Stravinsky has described the motive basic to this piece as two minor thirds linked by a semitone. For one instance, see the bass part and the "alto" part at study number 7 in Example 9-22. How does this motive shape the fugue subject that opens the second movement? Study the interaction of tonal and nontonal elements in this movement.

### Composition

**1.** Invent an altered diatonic scale by adding two or three accidentals to a diatonic scale so that the result is not another diatonic scale. Use your altered scale to compose several melodic phrases. Make each different from the others in tempo, rhythm, meter, range, and character. Write for instruments available in your class.

**2.** Compose several contrasting textures using a single diatonic scale. Avoid any references to functional tonal harmony in some of your textures—introduce tonal features in others. Use changing meters or different meters simultaneously.

**3.** Use one form of the octatonic scale as the basis for two or more contrasting phrases. Emphasize aspects reminiscent of tonality (such as triads) in one phrase. Avoid such references in the other.

**4.** Select what you consider to be your most successful phrase from Exercises 1, 2, and 3. Use it as the basis of a short piece scored for instruments in your class.

## Suggestions for Further Study

**1.** Studies of Stravinsky's music that amplify aspects discussed in this chapter include Arthur Berger's "Problems of Pitch Organization in Stravinsky," and Edward T. Cone's "Stravinsky: The Progress of a Method."

Both articles originally appeared in *Perspectives of New Music* in 1962 and 1963, and are reprinted in *Perspectives on Schoenberg and Stravinsky*, edited by Benjamin Boretz and Edward T. Cone (New York: W. W. Norton & Co., 1972). A book-length study is Pieter C. van den Toorn's *The Music of Igor Stravinsky* (New Haven: Yale, 1983). A recent article surveys the origins of the octatonic scale in nineteenth-century music, especially in Russian music preceding the turn of the century. It was the popularity of Stravinsky's music that called attention to this scale outside of eastern Europe. See Richard Taruskin, "Chernomor to Kashchei: Harmonic Sorcery; or, Stravinsky's 'Angle'," in *Journal of the American Musicological Society* 38 (1985): 73–142.

**2.** Olivier Messiaen's treatise *The Technique of My Musical Language*, translated by John Satterfield (Paris: Leduc, 1956), presents Messiaen's own views on melody, harmony, and modes in his music.

**3.** Elliott Antokoletz's study on Bartók, *The Music of Béla Bartók* (Berkeley: University of California Press, 1984) analyzes a number of the composer's works in detail.

# Unit Three

# Serial Music

In the early 1920s Schoenberg began composing music built on a specific ordering of the twelve pitch-classes. He used such an ordering, known as a *twelve-tone series*, as the source for all the pitch-classes in a given piece.

Music featuring ordered series is known as *serial music*; that is, music based on a series of pitch-classes. *Twelve-tone music* is serial music that uses a series of twelve pitch-classes.

Composers who wrote serial music did so with their own individual aims. Schoenberg developed twelve-tone composition in order to get away from what he regarded as the overly contextual structuring of pitch in his earlier atonal compositions written after 1908. He argued that by keeping all twelve pitch-classes in continual circulation, and by providing a sort of master-motive for the entire composition, the twelve-tone series would ensure consistency in a composition—a consistency that he achieved only with some difficulty in his earlier atonal music. Once he developed the twelve-tone method of composition, the only nontonal music that Schoenberg wrote was twelve-tone music. He believed that twelve-tone music would one day become as universal a musical language as functional tonality had once been.

Schoenberg's close associates, especially Berg and Webern, immediately adopted the twelve-tone method. In the ensuing years many other composers have adopted this method as well, some permanently, others temporarily, some rigorously, others freely, and some exclusively, others in combination with other techniques. Even Stravinsky, whose neo-Classic style and approach to composition had seemed antithetical to serial music, adopted the twelve-tone method in the 1950s, adapting it to his own compositional ends.

Twelve-tone music has not become the universal musical language that Schoenberg and others envisioned. Nor does it seem likely to do so in the foreseeable future. Nevertheless, there is a substantial and growing body of major serial works. This music is the concern of Unit Three.

Twelve-tone series differ from the pitch-class sets we studied in Unit Two in that a twelve-tone series is an ordered entity; that is, its structure depends on its ordering as well as its content. The material on pitch-class sets in Unit Two is applicable to serial music, as we have noted already in Unit Two. Pitch-class set analysis helps us to understand the sounds of nontonal music and the relations among pitch-class sets, motives, and harmonies. Indeed, as we noted in Unit Two, some examples in Unit Two are taken from twelve-tone compositions. But the twelve-tone and serial theory discussed in Unit Three is applicable only to serial music.

The first chapter in this unit (Chapter 10) surveys some aspects of twelve-tone series and how they appear in compositions. The remaining chapters explore the compositional uses and effects of twelve-tone series.

# 10

# Twelve-Tone Series

---

| | |
|---|---|
| *twelve-tone series* | *prime* |
| *series-form* | *retrograde* |
| *aggregate* | *inversion* |
| *pitch-class number* | *retrograde inversion* |
| *order number* | *P, R, I, RI* |
| | *matrix* |

---

## The Twelve-Tone Series

***What Is a Twelve-Tone Series?*** A *twelve-tone series* is an ordering of the twelve pitch-classes, each of which occurs once.[1]

***How Do Twelve-Tone Series Occur in a Piece?*** The ordered pitch-classes of a twelve-tone series can appear either in a single part or divided between two or more parts of a texture.

Example 10-1 (see p. 176) illustrates the series of Schoenberg's String Quartet No. 4, op. 37 (1937), as it appears in a melodic part, as it appears divided between two voices, and as it appears in two chords. At the opening of the first movement, the first-violin melody states the series, with each pitch-class occurring in turn. In m. 27, the first and second violin share the same series; some pitch-classes occur one at a time, while others occur along with the following pitch-class. In m. 280, the series occurs as two six-note chords.

***What Are the Forms of a Twelve-Tone Series?*** A twelve-tone series can occur in any of four *series-forms:*

**1.** The *prime* (P) is the form as first stated.

---

1. The terms *row, twelve-tone row, tone-row,* and *twelve-tone set* are synonymous with *twelve-tone series* as defined here.

2. The *retrograde* (R) is the prime in reverse order.

3. The *inversion* (I) replaces each interval of the prime with its complement.

4. The *retrograde inversion* (RI) is the inversion in reverse order.

EXAMPLE 10-1: Schoenberg, String Quartet No. 4, op. 37, first movement

Example 10-2 presents the series from Schoenberg's String Quartet No. 4 in all four forms.

EXAMPLE 10-2

P0 Prime

R0 Retrograde

I0 Inversion

RI0 Retrograde inversion

Any form of the series could be called the prime form. The prime form, after all, is the inversion of the I form, the retrograde of the R form, and the retrograde inversion of the RI form. As a rule, we label as P the first series-form stated in a given composition, with the other forms named accordingly.

***Transposition of Series-Forms.*** Each of the four forms of the series can begin on any pitch-class. A number from 0 to 11 following the letter designation indicates the level of transposition of the series-form. The first note of P0 is pitch-class 0 for all series-forms. For example, P2 refers to the prime form transposed to begin on pitch-class 2, and I8 refers to the inversion transposed to begin on pitch-class 8. Example 10-3 illustrates some transposed forms of the series in Examples 10-1 and 10-2.

EXAMPLE 10-3

P1 Prime transposed up a semitone

I5 Inversion transposed up five semitones

Note that in R and RI forms, it is the *last* note of the series that determines the level of transposition. Thus, R0 is the retrograde of P0, and RI0 the retrograde of I0. Review the R0 and RI0 forms in Example 10-2.

With four forms of each series, and twelve transpositions of each form, there are forty-eight forms of each series (four forms times twelve transpositions of each). In some series, two forms may be identical (say, an inversion may equal a retrograde form), halving the number of series-forms that are different from one another.

**Series and Series-Form.** The term *series* refers to an ordering of the twelve pitch-classes and to all forty-eight forms of that series. The term *series-form* refers to any one form of the given series. Thus, all the illustrations in Examples 10-1 through 10-3 feature a single series. The examples feature different forms of that series.

**What Are the Names of the Pitch-Classes in a Series?** Once we decide on a series-form to call P0, we know that pitch-class 0 is the first pitch-class in series-form P0. From that pitch-class, we can figure out the pitch-class number of all the members in a series the same way we figured out pitch-class numbers in Unit Two.

**Order Numbers.** *Order numbers* from 0 to 11 indicate the position of every pitch-class in a series-form (that is, whether a given pitch-class is first, second, third, and so forth).

**Aggregates and Series.** The term *aggregate* refers to all twelve pitch-classes in any collection or ordering. Strictly speaking, every twelve-tone series is an aggregate, and vice versa. But the terms are not fully interchangeable. We will use the term *series* to refer to the ordered series on which a given passage or work is built. We will reserve the term *aggregate* for twelve-tone collections other than those stated in the ordering of the series of that passage or work.

Example 10-4 and the discussion following illustrate the difference between a series and an aggregate. Following the statement of P0 in the first violin in mm. 1–6 (already identified in Example 10-1), the second violin enters with a melody based on I5. (See series-form I5 below the score.) These are statements of series-forms.

The chords accompanying these two phrases also arise from the series, as indicated by the order numbers next to each note. For each three pitch-classes in the first-violin melody (mm. 1–6), there are three chords containing the remaining nine pitch-classes. Along with the first-violin D–C♯–A (order numbers 0–1–2) are chords presenting order numbers 3–4–5, 6–7–8, and 9–10–11. Along with the next three pitch-classes in the first violin, B♭–F–E♭ (order numbers 3–4–5), are chords presenting order numbers 6–7–8, 9–10–11, and 0–1–2. This procedure is the same

EXAMPLE 10-4: Schoenberg, String Quartet No. 4, op. 37, first movement

for each group of three melodic pitch-classes. During the second violin melody in mm. 6–9, chords made up of three consecutive order numbers accompany the principal melody.

Although the pitch-classes in these accompanying chords are derivable from the series of the piece, there is no way that the pitch-classes of melody and accompaniment together could be derived from the series in the order in which they occur. Already in m. 1, the first violin C♯ (order number 1) occurs after order numbers 3, 4, and 5. The first violin A in m. 2, order number 2, occurs after order numbers 3 through 11.

Hence, the first violin melody in mm. 1–6 and the second violin melody in mm. 6–9 present series-forms. But the remaining pitch-classes here, though derivable from the series-forms, form aggregates.

*Convenient Ways of Listing All Series-Forms.* When analyzing a piece, it is most cumbersome to have to continually refer back to P0 to figure out any given series-form. It is far more convenient to have a listing of all the forms of the series. There are two convenient ways of making such a list:

**1.** If you prefer seeing the series-forms in music notation, take a piece of twelve-staff paper, and draw a line down the middle from top to bottom. Write P0 in the upper left and I0 in the upper right. Then simply transpose up by semitones on each succeeding line: the first line will have P0 and I0, the second line P1 and I1, the third line P2 and I2, and so on. Reading from right to left gives the R and RI forms. In Example 10-5 you will find the series from the opening of Schoenberg's String Quartet No. 4.

EXAMPLE 10-5

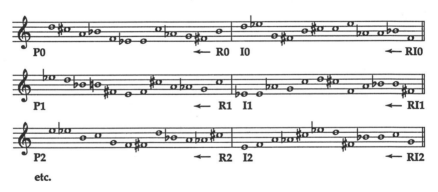

etc.

It is not necessary to notate all series-forms before you begin your analysis. Just lay out the paper as described, and enter the series-forms in the proper place as they appear in the music.

**2.** Another way of listing all series-forms is to construct a matrix. A matrix is a grid upon which all forty-eight forms of a series are listed. (Yet you need write only thirteen forms to end up with all forty-eight.) Begin by writing the P0 form of the series in letter names. The series from Schoenberg's String Quartet No. 4 serves us again as an example:

P0 → D  C♯  A  B♭  F  E♭  E  C  A♭  G  F♯  B  ← R0

Reading from right to left gives the R0 form.

Then write the I0 form down the left-hand margin. Reading from bottom to top gives the RI0 form:

```
        I0
        ↓
P0 →  D  C♯  A  B♭  F  E♭  E  C  A♭  G  F♯  B  ← R0
      E♭
      G
      F#
      B
      C#
      C
      E
      A♭
      A
      B♭
      F
      ↑
      RI0
```

Taking each pitch in the left-hand margin, write the P form beginning on that pitch:

|     |    | I | I | I | I | I | I | I | I | I | I | I | I |     |
|-----|----|---|---|---|---|---|---|---|---|---|---|---|---|-----|
|     |    | 0 | 11 | 7 | 8 | 3 | 1 | 2 | 10 | 6 | 5 | 4 | 9 |     |
|     |    | ↓ | ↓ | ↓ | ↓ | ↓ | ↓ | ↓ | ↓ | ↓ | ↓ | ↓ | ↓ |     |
| P0  | →  | D | C♯ | A | B♭ | F | E♭ | E | C | A♭ | G | F♯ | B | ← R0 |
| P1  | →  | E♭ | D | B♭ | B | F♯ | E | F | C♯ | A | A♭ | G | C | ← R1 |
| P5  | →  | G | F♯ | D | E♭ | B♭ | A♭ | A | F | C♯ | C | B | E | ← R5 |
| P4  | →  | F♯ | F | C♯ | D | A | G | A♭ | E | C | B | B♭ | E♭ | ← R4 |
| P9  | →  | B | B♭ | F♯ | G | D | C | C♯ | A | F | E | E♭ | A♭ | ← R9 |
| P11 | →  | C♯ | C | A♭ | A | E | D | E♭ | B | G | F♯ | F | B♭ | ← R11 |
| P10 | →  | C | B | G | A♭ | E♭ | C♯ | D | B♭ | F♯ | F | E | A | ← R10 |
| P2  | →  | E | E♭ | B | C | G | F | F♯ | D | B♭ | A | A♭ | C♯ | ← R2 |
| P6  | →  | A♭ | G | E♭ | E | B | A | B♭ | F♯ | D | C♯ | C | F | ← R6 |
| P7  | →  | A | A♭ | E | F | C | B♭ | B | G | E♭ | D | C♯ | F♯ | ← R7 |
| P8  | →  | B♭ | A | F | F♯ | C♯ | B | C | A♭ | E | E♭ | D | G | ← R8 |
| P3  | →  | F | E | C | C♯ | A♭ | F♯ | G | E♭ | B | B♭ | A | D | ← R3 |
|     |    | ↑ | ↑ | ↑ | ↑ | ↑ | ↑ | ↑ | ↑ | ↑ | ↑ | ↑ | ↑ |     |
|     |    | RI | RI | RI | RI | RI | RI | RI | RI | RI | RI | RI | RI |     |
|     |    | 0 | 11 | 7 | 8 | 3 | 1 | 2 | 10 | 6 | 5 | 4 | 9 |     |

When completed, all forty-eight forms of the series appear: the P forms from left to right, the R forms from right to left, the I forms from top to bottom, and the RI forms from bottom to top. To check your work, remember that the first pitch of P0 always appears in a diagonal line from upper left to lower right.

## Locating the Twelve-Tone Series in a Piece

*How Do You Find the Series of the Piece?*    Clearly, one of the first tasks confronting the analyst of a twelve-tone composition is figuring out the series. In many pieces, such as Schoenberg's String Quartet No. 4, finding the series is easy. Review the opening of the piece on p. 179. In this piece, recognizing an ordering of all twelve pitch-classes in the first-violin melody in mm. 1–6 provides an unmistakable clue. When the analyst recognizes that the next melody (that in the second violin in mm. 6–9) is another form of the same series (namely, I5), he or she can be sure that that is the series.

Finding the series in many other twelve-tone pieces is just as easy. But in some others, this task may be more difficult. Two or more series-forms may begin simultaneously in m. 1. Or the ordering within the series may be obscured by a chordal texture. Or the piece may not begin with a statement of a complete series-form—the complete series may emerge gradually during the opening section of a piece. Or there may be more than one series used in the piece.

Consider the opening of Schoenberg's *Klavierstück*, op. 33a. Finding the series in mm. 1–2 is not possible because the chordal texture obscures any ordering from one pitch-class to the next. But since the three tetrachords in m. 1 as well as those in m. 2 form aggregates, we can begin by assuming that each measure states a series-form.

EXAMPLE 10-6: Schoenberg, *Klavierstück*, op. 33a

To find the ordering within these series-forms, look ahead in the piece for a passage where pitch-classes enter one at a time. Such a passage occurs in mm. 3–5. The treble notes in these measures follow the ordering of the chords in m. 2. Hence the ordering of the series-form in m. 2 and the right-hand in mm. 3–5 is that listed below Example 10-7.

EXAMPLE 10-7: Schoenberg, *Klavierstück*, op. 33a

When you are looking for the series in a new piece, knowing something about the composer's practices is helpful. For instance, in the twelve-tone music of Schoenberg and Berg, melodies and accompaniments often form aggregates from which the ordering of the series may not be determined (as in Example 10-4). The twelve-tone music of Webern, on the other hand, always follows the ordering of the series strictly. In the works of Webern and most of those of Schoenberg, a single series is the basis for an entire composition. In the works of Berg and some other twelve-tone composers, different series often appear in the course of a single composition.

*How Do You Recognize a Given Series-Form in a Piece?*   With a complete listing of series-forms it is quite easy to identify any series-form in the music. Often, it is necessary to locate just two or three pitch-classes and then check your results. The reason you need locate only a few pitch-classes to identify a complete series-form is that each series-form often begins with a different interval. Once you recognize that interval, you can make an educated guess about the series-form.

Let us use the series of Schoenberg's *Fourth Quartet* as a model. Study the opening intervals of the P, I, R, and RI forms of this series in Example 10-2 on p. 177. Each series-form begins with a different interval:

*P begins with interval 11*

*I begins with interval 1*

*R begins with interval 7*

*RI begins with interval 5*

So if you identify an ascending semitone, say B–C, as a possible beginning of a series-form in the piece, you know that that series-form must be an I form. The I form beginning with B is I9. Locate I9 on the matrix or on your staff paper. Then check to see if the following pitches in the score agree with that series-form.

If you have trouble deciding where in the score a series-form might begin, find any three consecutive pitches—say, B–C♯–C, interval 2 followed by interval 11. Study the structure of the series-forms to find that interval-pattern. Interval 2 followed by interval 11 occurs in this series only between order numbers 4, 5, and 6 of an I form. Consult your matrix or staff-paper list of the series-forms. The I form with B–C♯–C as order numbers 4, 5, and 6 is I0. Check your result to see if the preceding and following pitches in the score agree with this series-form.

*Summary.*    You now know what a twelve-tone series is, how to construct, name, and recognize its forms, how to identify the pitch-classes in a series with pitch-class and order numbers, how to differentiate a series or series-form from an aggregate, how to list all the series-forms, and how to locate the series and its series-forms in pieces. This concludes the preliminary material about twelve-tone series. In the next chapter we begin to study how the structure of a twelve-tone series affects a piece.

# Points for Review

**1.** A *twelve-tone series* is an ordering of all pitch-classes with each pitch-class occurring once.

**2.** There are four *series-forms:* the *prime* (P), the *inversion* (I), the *retrograde* (R), and the *retrograde inversion* (RI). A number following the letter-designation indicates the level of transposition. The first note of the first series-form to appear is pitch-class 0. P and I forms are numbered by their first pitch-class, R and RI forms by their last.

**3.** *Order numbers* from 0 to 11 indicate the position of a given pitch-class in a given series-form.

**4.** *Aggregate* refers to any collection of the twelve pitch-classes. The term *series* refers to the ordered series on which a passage or work is built, and the term *aggregate* refers to twelve-tone collections other than those directly derivable from the series of that passage or work.

# Exercises for Chapter 10

**Terms and Concepts**

**1.** Define the following terms:

|  |  |
|---|---|
| *twelve-tone series* | *prime* |
| *series-form* | *retrograde* |

| | |
|---|---|
| *aggregate* | *inversion* |
| *pitch-class number* | *retrograde inversion* |
| *order number* | *P, R, I, RI* |
| | *matrix* |

**2.** Answer true or false:

**a)** Any twelve-tone series is an aggregate.

**b)** Any aggregate is a twelve-tone series.

**c)** Every aggregate in a piece is a statement of the series of that piece.

**d)** All twelve-tone series have forty-eight forms.

**3.** Write out the indicated forms of the given series.

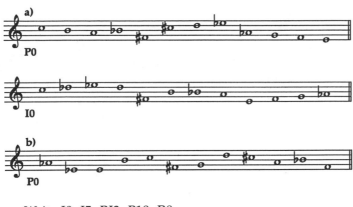

Write I0, I5, RI3, P10, R8.
Write I7, RI4, P8, R5.

**4.** Identify the following forms of the given series.

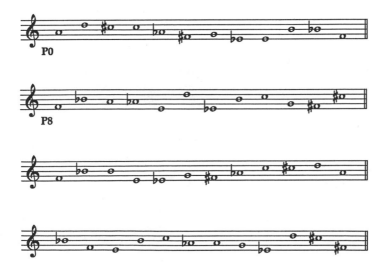

## Analysis

Listen to the following passages. Figure out the P0 form of the series for each. Then identify all pitches by labeling the series-forms and order numbers.

**1.** Schoenberg, *Piano Concerto*, op. 42 (1942), first movement. Don't let some repeated groups of pitch-classes in the melody (D♭/C♯–A–B in mm. 5–6) throw you.

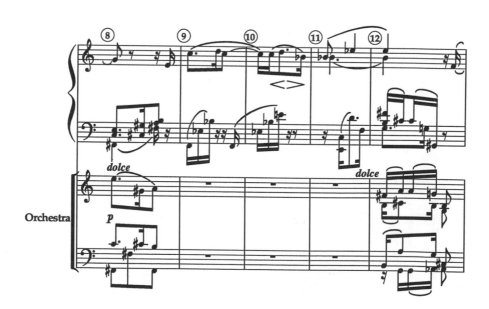

**2.** Webern, *Wie bin ich Froh!*, op. 25 no. 1 (1935)

# 11
# Common Elements

---

common elements          compositional
permutation              precompositional

---

## Hearing Twelve-Tone Series

Though the series may provide much of the structural basis of a twelve-tone piece, you should not assume that hearing the series and all its permutations is necessary to understand or enjoy twelve-tone music. It is difficult enough for a listener to remember a twelve-tone series apart from a composition, even after repeated hearings. And it is certainly impossible for anyone to remember forty-eight forms of that series and recognize them as their pitch-classes appear in melodies and harmonies, and when two or more series-forms may appear simultaneously.

As a matter of fact, labeling series in a score and trying to hear those series in the music (were that possible) is a rather poor way to try to learn about this music. Composers such as Schoenberg, Berg, Webern, and Stravinsky did not compose twelve-tone music to construct unhearable complexities. They adopted this system because it enabled them to control certain aspects of musical structure while it left their creative imaginations free to deal with those aspects they were already exploring in their earlier music.

*Common Elements within Permutations.* As we studied in Unit Two, in all their music, these composers worked in their individual ways with small pitch-class sets as sources for motives within larger pitch-class regions. The twelve-tone system created the pitch-class region for them: the twelve pitch-classes. No matter what series-forms are used, the same pitch-class region is present. Changing series-forms serves only to *permute* (or rearrange) the order of the pitch-classes.

Within this unchanging pitch-class region, *common elements* arise: pitch-class orderings, intervals, and subsets that are common to two or more series or series-forms. These common elements add focus to a passage, bringing a small number of pitch-classes or intervals to the fore, and highlighting them against the background pitches. These highlighted pitch-classes and intervals then form networks with one another, connecting phrases and larger sections to one another.

From this perspective, common elements in twelve-tone music are akin to important harmonic and melodic pitches in tonal music. With non-harmonic tones and passage-work, many tonal excerpts have all the notes of a key in frequent circulation. But these notes are not presented aimlessly. Harmonies group them, focusing on the root of the chord, the bass, or the principal melodic tone. When the harmony changes, the focal harmonic and melodic pitches within one chord change to those of the next. Common elements provide similar types of connections in twelve-tone music, retaining and changing focal pitch-classes while all twelve pitch-classes remain in circulation.

For this reason, studying common elements among series and series-forms opens the door to understanding individual compositions as well as the styles of individual composers. We will discuss separate aspects of the general subject of common elements in Chapters 11, 12, and 13, proceeding from smaller to larger aspects of series. Chapter 11 explores intervals and smaller pitch-class sets in common between series-forms. Chapter 12 surveys combinatoriality, which affects larger groupings of pitch-classes. Chapter 13 covers derived series and other relationships among entire twelve-tone series.

## Common Intervals and Subsets

Intervals and subsets in common between series-forms arise when two or more pitch-classes that are adjacent in one series-form remain adjacent in one or several different series-forms. If, for instance, P0 of a series begins with the pitch-classes B–C, then I1 of that series begins with the pitch-classes C–B. C and B are common elements—adjacent pitch-classes—in the two series-forms.

EXAMPLE 11-1

P0    I1

***Compositional and Precompositional Relationships.*** Numerous factors determine the kind of series and the relationships between series-forms under which intervals and subsets in common will arise. Study of these factors teaches us the possible relationships among series and series-forms.

The difference between possible relationships and those that are used in a given piece is the difference between *precompositional* and *compositional* factors. *Precompositional factors* are those that exist whether or not they are used. For example, B–C are adjacent pitch-classes in P0 and I1 of the series in Example 11-1. This relationship between P0 and I1 will always hold, even if I1 never appears in the piece at all. But for this relationship to be an important factor in the piece under consideration, these pitch-classes must occur in prominent positions. If, for instance, two consecutive phrases begin with P0 and I1, and B–C occurs in the same register and in the same rhythm at the beginning of each phrase, then this precompositional relationship becomes an important *compositional factor* in the piece.

Rather than study the myriad precompositional relationships that can relate different series-forms, we will concern ourselves mostly with those factors that turn up in prominent positions in the pieces studied. After familiarizing ourselves with prominent features in each piece, we will then study the series-form relationships that give rise to those features.

## Model Analysis: Motive, Phrasing, and Continuity at the Opening of Schoenberg's String Quartet No. 4

*Model Analysis: Motive, Phrasing, and Continuity at the Opening of Schoenberg's String Quartet No. 4.* The roots of Schoenberg's musical style lie in the late nineteenth century, in the music of Wagner and Brahms. Schoenberg's early music, written around 1900, is in the intensely Romantic, chromatic tonal language of the time. The string sextet *Verklärte Nacht*, op. 4 (1899), is Schoenberg's best-known tonal composition. Although the direction of his artistic development took him first to writing nontonal music (after 1908) and later to the development of the twelve-tone system (in the early 1920s), his music always retained the sense of phrasing and gesture that grows out of the musical world of the late nineteenth-century. Review our discussions of the *Chamber Symphony*, op. 9 (1906), in Chapter 9 and the variations theme from his *Serenade*, op. 24 (1924) in Chapter 5 for these features in one of Schoenberg's last tonal compositions and one of his last pre-twelve-tone works.

The *Fourth String Quartet* was composed in 1937, over a decade after Schoenberg began composing twelve-tone music. We have already noted in Unit One how the opening of the first movement announces a texture similar to tonal music, featuring melodies and accompaniments.

EXAMPLE 11-2: Schoenberg, String Quartet No. 4, op. 37, first movement

This opening section is organized as an ABA[1] form in three phrases. The A and A[1] sections are related by their similar rhythms and similar accompaniments, while the much shorter B section features different melodic rhythms and a different accompaniment pattern.

| A | mm. 1–6 | first-violin melody |
|---|---------|---------------------|
| B | mm. 7–9 | second-violin melody |
| A$^1$ | mm. 10–16 | first-violin melody |

We will study this section in detail. Familiarize yourself with it by listening to it several times. It is important that you listen to the passage repeatedly as you read this discussion. The relationships cited here do not exist only on paper; they are basic to the sound of the piece.

*Melody.* Each section is a single phrase, with the melody expressing a single series-form: P0 for phrase 1, I5 for phrase 2, and R0 for phrase 3:

EXAMPLE 11-3: Schoenberg, String Quartet No. 4, op. 37, first movement

Common elements relate these melodies to each other in different ways. We will begin by discussing the second phrase in relation to the first.

The beginning of the second phrase sounds like it picks up where the first phrase ends. This effect is created by two common elements: the first is the long B that ends the opening phrase and recurs immediately in the same register as a long note on the first downbeat of the second phrase: violin I, mm. 5–6; violin II, m. 7. The second common element is the second-violin upbeat to this B: the trichord G–A♭–C as the upbeat to m. 7. These three notes occur as adjacent notes in the same register near the end of the first phrase: violin I, mm. 3–4.

These common elements create the impression that the second-violin melody begins where the first-violin melody ends. Register, rhythm, and metric position emphasize the common elements. Both B's are in the same register, and are long pitches on downbeats, preceded by a three eighth-note upbeat. And the G–A♭–C trichord is in the same register in both phrases.

*The Common [0,1,5] Trichord.*    How is it that two different series-forms have G–A♭–C as adjacent pitch-classes? The construction of this series makes it possible. As shown in Example 11-4, a [0,1,5] trichord occurs four times in the course of the series. The trichord G–A♭–C occurs as order numbers 7, 8, and 9 in P0. Each one of these [0,1,5] trichords

EXAMPLE 11-4

can be transposed or inverted to appear as G–A♭–C in some series-form. I5 is the series-form in which G–A♭–C appears as order numbers 0, 1, 2. (See Example 11-5.) I5 is the series-form of the second-violin melody. So G–A♭–C can occur as the opening upbeat of the second-violin melody.

EXAMPLE 11-5

*Common Elements That Are Not Stressed.*    The pitch B and the common trichord G–A♭–C are instances of precompositional common elements brought to the fore by register, rhythm, metric position, or placement in the phrase. For an instance of a precompositional feature *not* utilized here, return to Example 11-5. In I5, order numbers 7–8–9 are the pitch-classes A–C♯–D—the opening trichord of P0 (that is, the opening melodic pitches of the movement).

Yet the return of this common trichord in m. 8 during the second-violin melody is not given any special prominence. See Example 11-3. In m. 8, A–C♯–D does occur. But it is not stressed as a return to the opening trichord of the piece. Instead, it is part of a longer eighth-note passage. The register of the A and C♯ differs from their first appearance in mm. 1–2. And the D is slurred to another pitch, weakening its bond with A and C♯.

Why is it that some common elements are stressed and others ignored? The reason that the common trichord G–A♭–C *is* emphasized in m. 5 and the common trichord A–C♯–D is *not* emphasized in m. 8 has to do with the location of these trichords in the phrase and within the section. The common elements at the *beginning* of the second phrase are stressed so that it grows out of the end of the first phrase. If the return of A–C♯–D in m. 8 had been strongly set off, this beginning trichord might have indicated a conclusion to the phrase or section. But m. 8 is not a conclusion of a phrase or a section. It is part of the contrasting phrase in an ABA¹ form.

*The Third Phrase.*    It is the end of the third phrase that should bring the section to a close. And indeed, the third phrase concludes with A–C♯–D as the last three pitch-classes in R0. Rhythm, register, dynamics, and the reversal in the order of the trichord all emphasize the return to the opening that helps to round off and close out the phrase-group.

*Style.*    Schoenberg's use of the series-forms helps to create these effects. In terms of phrasing, texture, motives, and form, this section is much like a nineteenth-century tonal composition. The way the second phrase picks up from where the first phrase ends, and the way R0 brings the end of the third phrase back to the beginning pitch-classes is similar to tonal harmonic plans of an ABA¹ section. Think of a phrase-group where the first phrase ends on the dominant, where the second continues in the dominant key, and where the third phrase returns at its end to the tonic that began the phrase-group, for instance.

All this is possible because of the traditional textures and the way each phrase is based on a single series-form. Each melodic phrase is set off from its neighbors by changes in the solo instrument and the accompanimental texture. The common elements then work within this phrase structure.

*Other Common Elements.*    Because each phrase in this section is based on a separate series-form, the beginning and concluding notes of the series-forms used are prominent pitch-classes at the beginnings and endings of phrases. The crucial pitch-classes that are emphasized are D–C♯ at the beginning of P0 and the end of R0, and G–A♭ at the beginning of I5. These pairs of pitch-classes are also adjacent within each of these series-forms. (See the series-forms below Example 11-3.)

These pitch-classes participate in the G–A♭–C trichord that is a common element between the first two phrases. But G and A♭ are emphasized even during the first phrase. The opening phrase subdivides into two parts. The half notes that open the phrase are D–C♯; A♭ and G as long notes begin the second half of the phrase in mm. 3–4. Note the marks above the A♭ and G in the score in Example 11-2: they are Schoenberg's indication that the A♭ should be played like a downbeat and the G like a weak beat—creating a parallel to the opening D–C♯.

A♭ and G are further emphasized in the accompaniment at the beginning of the second-violin phrase. The A♭ and G exchange places between first-violin and cello in m. 7, with the G–A♭ of the first violin especially prominent because it is higher than the second-violin melody. Such close motivic and pitch relationships between melody and accompaniment is characteristic of Schoenberg's music from his earliest tonal compositions to his last works.

Another particularly prominent motivic relation between harmony and melody in the opening sixteen measures occurs in the bass. The first two measures in the cello contain a semitone and interval 5 or 7. Both measures state a form of [0,1,6], a trichord that shares two of its three intervals with the [0,1,5] trichord so prominent in the melody. It is these two interval-classes—1,11 and 5,7—that are present in the cello part. The same pattern recurs at the beginning of the $A^1$ section in m. 10.

These and other more large-scale common elements (to be discussed in Chapter 12) help unify the opening portion of the movement even beyond m. 16. This opening portion of the movement features only the series-forms P0, I5, and their retrogrades. Later, as other series-forms occur, new combinations of common intervals and subsets arise, replacing those of the first section of the movement. Thus, although all twelve pitch-classes are in circulation throughout the movement, the networks of emphasized pitch-classes change. Schoenberg uses these to create the equivalent of key changes in tonal music. Since the movement is in sonata form, the changes in these pitch networks coordinates with and helps project the changes in sections as the movement unfolds.

*Model Analysis: Webern,* **Variations for Piano,** *op. 27, Second Movement.* Webern, like Schoenberg, grew up in the musical world of the late nineteenth century. But whereas many of Schoenberg's compositions continue to reflect the gestures, the phrasing, and the forms of late-Romantic music, Webern's music strikes out in new directions.

In earlier chapters we have noted the concision of compositions by Webern that arises from the extremely concentrated use of a small number of pitch-class sets. Review the discussion of his *Movement for String Quartet,* op. 5 no. 4, and the *Concerto for Nine Instruments,* op. 20, in Unit Two.

In his twelve-tone compositions, Webern constructed series and used them so as to bring out a small number of common elements that then pervade every aspect of the music. One such piece is the *Variations for Piano,* a three-movement work. Like all of Webern's music, the three movements are brief and concentrated. The middle movement, a fast, scherzo-like structure, is the briefest of the three.

Listen to this movement without following a score a sufficient number of times to become fully acquainted with the sounds. The movement is quite short, well under a minute in length. When you have a good idea of how it sounds, listen to it with the analytic score in Example 11-6, which omits rhythms and presents only the pitch-pairs that occur throughout the piece.

EXAMPLE 11-6: Webern, *Variations for Piano,* op. 27, second movement

Even on first hearing, the consistent pairing of notes throughout the movement is obvious. Sometimes the pairs of notes are separated from one another by rests (as at the very opening), sometimes the pairs follow one another without pause. Four times, we hear pairs of trichords instead of individual notes.

Also obvious on first hearing are the pairs of A's that recur four times. Subsequently, you probably become aware of additional recurring pairs of pitches. The B♭–G♯ of the very opening recurs twice in the course of the movement and again at the very end. Indeed, every pair of pitches recurs, often in the same register, sometimes with changed registers. For instance, the pairs of A's and the B♭–G♯ pair always are in the same register. The D–E pairs, however, recur sometimes in the same register and sometimes in different registers.

*The Series.* With this orientation, we can now study the series and the process by which these pitch-pairs recur. The first member of each pitch-pair expresses one series-form; the second member of each pitch-pair expresses another series-form. If we name the first series-form P0, the other one is I10.[1]

EXAMPLE 11-7: Webern, *Variations for Piano,* op. 27, second movement

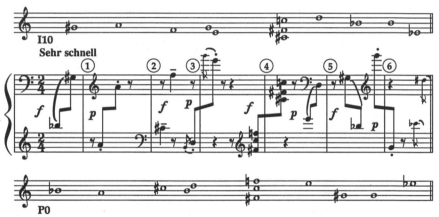

Webern, *Variationen für Klavier,* Op. 27. Copyright 1937 by Universal Edition. Copyright renewed. All Rights Reserved. Used by permission of European American Music Distributors Corporation, sole U.S. and Canadian agent for Universal Edition.

Since order numbers 5, 6, and 7 of both series-forms occur only as a chord throughout the entire movement, we cannot determine the ordering among these three pitch-classes during this movement.[2]

*Why Do These Pitch-Pairs Recur Throughout the Movement?* Example 11-8 begins to shed light on the many recurring pairs of pitches in the movement.

1. Locating the series in this piece is a bit tricky until you realize that the opening is based on two series-forms running simultaneously. If you try to find a single series by following the pitches from the beginning, you will find that there are no E♭'s or D♯'s until after twenty-one pitches have occurred, and that many pitch-classes occur twice before that point. That is the clue that the pitches of each pair do not come from a single series-form, but rather from two series-forms running simultaneously. As Example 11-7 demonstrates, the first pitches in each pair and the second pitches in each pair present two forms of the same series.

2. The same series is the basis of the first and third movements. In those movements there is a clear ordering of these pitch-classes. But since that ordering is not relevant to the second movement, we need not make use of it in this discussion.

EXAMPLE 11-8

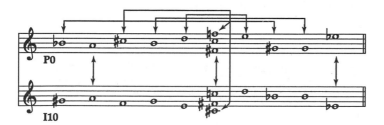

PO

I10

When a pitch-class appears in P0 (say, B♭, order number 0), it occurs along with a pitch-class in I10 (G♯, order number 0). When that same pitch-class appears in I10 (B♭ as order number 9), it is paired with the same pitch-class in P0 (G♯ as order number 9). This holds true for all pitch-classes. Follow the arrows in Example 11-8 to locate each of these recurring pairs.

This is a precompositional feature that always arises when *any* form of *any* series and its inversion occur note-for-note against each other— that is, between any P and I forms of any series, and between any R and RI forms of any series. Some characteristics of this property merit discussion before we return to Webern's *Variations*.

We can study the origin of these recurring pitch-pairs via another series: the chromatic scale.

EXAMPLE 11-9

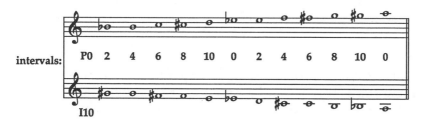

intervals:

| P0 | 2 | 4 | 6 | 8 | 10 | 0 | 2 | 4 | 6 | 8 | 10 | 0 |

I10

When the interval of transposition between P and I is an even number (that is, when it is 0, 2, 4, 6, 8, or 10) as in Example 11-9, all intervals between pairs of pitch-classes are even. Every interval occurs twice, with the second instance being a tritone transposition of the first. Thus, interval 0 occurs in Example 11-9 with pitch-classes A and E♭; interval 2 occurs with pitch-classes G♯–B♭ and D–E (G♯–D and B♭–E are tritones); interval 4 occurs with G–B and C♯–F; interval 6 with F♯–C and C–F♯. Both intervals in the same interval-class recur with the same pitch-classes. Thus, interval 2 occurs with G♯–B♭ and D–E and interval 10 occurs with G♯–B♭ and D–E.

In all these recurrences, the *sum* of all pairs of pitch-class numbers between P0 and I10 pitch-classes add up to 10.

EXAMPLE 11-10

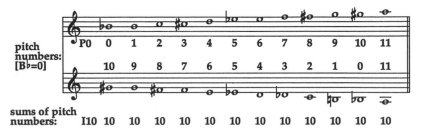

pitch numbers: [B♭=0]

| P0 | 0 | 1 | 2 | 3 | 4 | 5 | 6 | 7 | 8 | 9 | 10 | 11 |
|----|---|---|---|---|---|---|---|---|---|---|----|----|
|    | 10 | 9 | 8 | 7 | 6 | 5 | 4 | 3 | 2 | 1 | 0 | 11 |

sums of pitch numbers: I10  10  10  10  10  10  10  10  10  10  10  10  10

Ordering within the series does not affect any of these pitch-class pairings. So long as the unisons are between A's and Eb's, the same pitch-class pairings remain between P and I forms whose transposition numbers add up to an even number. Example 11-11 reorders these pitch-class pairings to agree with Webern's series in the second movement of the *Variations*.

EXAMPLE 11-11

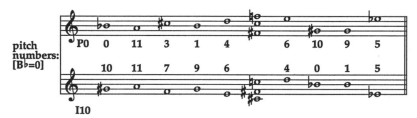

pitch numbers: [B♭=0]

| P0 | 0 | 11 | 3 | 1 | 4 |  | 6 | 10 | 9 | 5 |
|----|---|----|---|---|---|--|---|----|---|---|
|    | 10 | 11 | 7 | 9 | 6 |  | 4 | 0 | 1 | 5 |

I10

Any pair of P and I (or R and RI) series-forms whose transposition numbers add up to 10 will retain the same pitch-class pairings; for instance, P1 and I9, P9 and I1, and so forth. Webern uses four pairs of series-forms in the movement:

    P0–I10    in mm. 1–6
    P5–I5     in mm. 6–11
    P10–I0    in mm. 11–17
    P7–I3     in mm. 17–22

Each pair of series-forms begins with the last notes of the previous pair. Since Bb–G# occurs at the beginning, the end, and the midpoint of the piece, Webern's repeats become possible. See Example 11-12, which presents the beginnings and endings of each pair of series-forms. Compare this to the analytic score of the piece in Example 11-6 (p. 197).

EXAMPLE 11-12

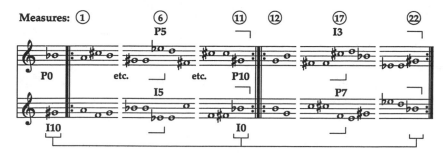

*Form.* In earlier chapters we have had occasion to note Webern's propensity for reducing musical structure to its most essential elements. This movement reduces the entire pitch vocabulary to twelve intervals—or six pitch-class pairs, each of which occurs twice in each series-form. Indeed, we can say that the vocabulary is reduced to four interval-classes (0; 2,10; 4,8; and 6), each of which occurs in two pitch-pairs separated by a tritone.

And yet, within the strict limits imposed by these restrictions on intervals, and by the series-forms themselves, the piece unfolds in the same manner that we expect in more traditional music. The opening measures are an expository section, laying out the basic materials that are then worked with for the remainder of the piece. In this initial section, all the pitch material is stated without repetitions: the P0–I10 pair of series that begins the piece states the maximum possible number of different pitch-pairs before any are repeated. Only when the chords appear do interval duplications arise.

These opening measures are expository not only in terms of pitch, but also in dynamics, rhythm, and articulation. The three dynamic markings of the movement, the various forms of rhythmic interaction, and the different articulations (Example 11-13) make their first appearance during this first pair of series-forms.

EXAMPLE 11-13

Contrast this with the developmental section after the double bar: the B–G pitch-pair occurs twice back to back, as do other intervals, articulations, and dynamics.

Finally, each pitch-pair in mm. 1–3 is separated from the next by an eighth-note rest, giving the impression of a $\frac{3}{8}$ meter. Nowhere else in the movement do four groups occur with such rhythmic regularity.[3]

*The Repeated A's.*    Let us now turn our attention to the repeated A's that stand out even on first hearing of the piece. As we saw in Example 11-9, there are two unisons between series-forms in this piece: A and E♭. As Webern projects the series, however, E♭ is placed in the least prominent positions—as grace notes, or part of chords.

A, however, is the focal pitch of the movement. It is not only present as a literal unison, but is also the registral midpoint of every pitch-pair in the movement. It is the axis around which all other pitch-pairs are displayed.

EXAMPLE 11-14

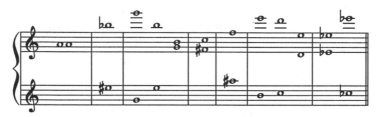

The movement may not begin or end with A, and unlike a tonal tonic, A is not the point of phrase initiations and goals or voice-leading motions. But like a nontonal focal pitch, it is at the center of attention throughout.

*Style.*    Webern composed his *Variations for Piano*, op. 27, in 1936. In this and other late works he further reduced musical elements to their bare essentials. The second movement is essentially an exploration of the four even interval-classes. The intervals are displayed in pairs of notes. The very notions of harmony and melody, or phrasing and form have to be reassessed for this music.

In contrast to Schoenberg, who in his String Quartet No. 4 as well as in many other pieces written throughout his career retained the rhetoric of the late nineteenth century, Webern explored new aspects of musical continuity. One can imagine the opening oi Schoenberg's *Fourth Quartet* as a Brahmsian composition in a new pitch language. But what are the precedents in an earlier era for the second movement of Webern's *Vari-*

---

3. The meaning of Webern's meter signatures has been a matter of some debate. Some musicians believe that the regular meter signatures in movements such as this one are notational conveniences, and that the real meter changes frequently. Others believe that the notated meter does represent the metric organization. For an argument in favor of the notated meter as heard in this movement, see Peter Westergaard's "Webern and 'Total Organization': an Analysis of the Second Movement of the Piano Variations, op. 27," in *Perspectives of New Music* 1 / 2 (1963): 107–120.

*ations?* In large part because they broke such new grounds in musical rhetoric and style, Webern's late works were quite influential on many post–World War II composers.

## Uncovering Common Elements

The two passages analyzed in this chapter illustrate different types and usages of common elements. In Schoenberg's String Quartet No. 4, we traced two crucial pairs of pitch-classes (D–C♯ and G–A♭) and a trichord (G–A♭–C) that remain as adjacent pitch-classes in two series-forms (P0 and I5) and their retrogrades. These are focal pitch-classes in a fairly traditional setting featuring a melody with accompaniment, and balanced phrases—the first theme-group of a movement modeled on sonata form. Webern's *Variations* presents a different kind of music altogether. Series-forms are chosen and presented to project a small number of intervals in different permutations. Pitches, registers, dynamics, and articulations are in a strict canon throughout, with the second voice of the canon following the first by an eighth note. Yet as different as these two twelve-tone pieces are, the key to understanding the pitch structure lies in uncovering crucial common elements.

This is true of most twelve-tone music. As you become acquainted with the sounds of a new piece, you will become aware of prominent pitch-classes and groups of pitch-classes. Uncovering the way these common elements arise helps you to understand the composers's choices of series-forms and his or her motivations for many different aspects of structure.

In your study of a new piece, begin by listening for prominent pitches and repeated pitch-classes, intervals, and pitch-class sets. As you discover a common element in the piece, try to figure out how it works by finding that common element in a very simple series such as a chromatic scale. This will help increase your understanding of the piece, of the composer's choices among the many precompositional possibilities, of the composer's style, and, finally, of the twelve-tone system itself.

## Points for Review

**1.** *Precompositional factors* are those that are always true based on the construction of a series and relationships between series-forms. When placed in prominent positions, precompositional relations become factors in a composition.

**2.** *Common elements*, the intervals or subsets in common between different series-forms, are often essential in the structure of a musical passage.

**3.** When an interval or pitch-class series occurs more than once in a given series-form, there is at least one other series-form that will retain that interval or pitch-class series as a common element.

**4.** When inversionally related series-forms are stated simultaneously, note-for-note, recurring pairs of pitch-classes arise.

# Exercises for Chapter 11

### Terms and Concepts

**1.** Define the following terms:

> *common element*        *precompositional*

**2.** Examples 11-8 through 11-11 discuss the interval relationships that arise when a P form and an I form at an *even* level of transposition are placed note against note. Figure out what types of intervals arise when the sum of a P form and an I form is *odd*. Use the chromatic scale as a model.

### Analysis

Familiarize yourself with these excerpts. Then identify the series in each and answer the questions.

**1.** Schoenberg, String Quartet No. 3, op. 30, second movement (1927). The intervals between first and second violin are pairs of pitch-classes from P0. The viola part gives the complete ordering of this series-form. How are the intervals between first and second violin related? Write out series-forms P0, P6, I3, and I9. What happens to the intervals in P0 in these series-forms? What is there in the construction of the series that allows these relationships to arise?

Now listen to the passage from later in the movement. How are these common intervals used?

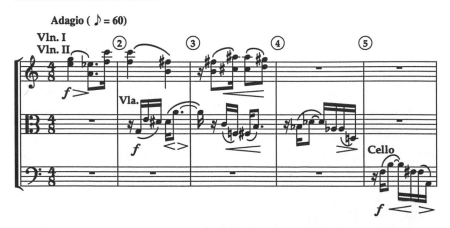

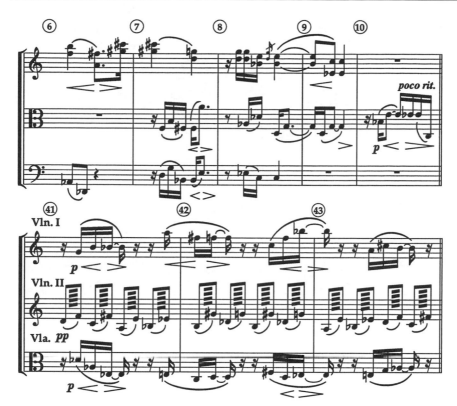

**2.** Webern, String Quartet, op. 28 (1938), first movement. Figure out what series-forms are used here. Two hints: a) P0 is the first twelve pitches. Follow the instrumental lines to determine order among simultaneous pitches. b) The second and succeeding series-forms overlap by two or four pitches with the previous series.

What aspect in the construction of the series gives rise to the common intervals so prominent in the score? What other forms of the series would also give rise to these intervals?

These fifteen measures serve as the theme for a series of variations. When you are familiar with these measures, listen to and study the remainder of the movement.

## Composition

**1.** Using the following series as the source for both melody and accompaniment, compose two phrases for a melodic instrument and piano. Use P0 for the first phrase and I5 for the second. Explore different types of textures, different ways of connecting the phrases, different ways of using the series in melody and accompaniment, and different ways of using common elements.

P0

**2.** Using the same series, write an imitative section in two voices using a prime series-form for one voice and an inverted series-form for the other. Avoid a strict meter. Write for two instruments available in your class.

# Suggestions for Further Study

**1.** Schoenberg, String Quartet No. 4, op. 37, first movement. Continue with a study of the opening section of the movement. Within mm. 1–16, identify the series-forms in the accompaniment. What is the origin of the three chords from the end of m. 15 through m. 16? How do these three chords help to round out the ABA[1] section?

Continue by identifying the series-forms in mm. 17–31.

You will now be quite familiar with the sound of the opening section of the movement. Listen to the remainder of the movement. As you get to know it, concentrate on the groups of emphasized pitch-classes that accompany the changes from one section to another. The following formal outline will help orient you in the sonata-form structure:

Exposition, mm. 1–94
>   first theme group begins in m. 1
>   second theme group begins in m. 66
Development, mm. 95–164
Recapitulation, mm. 165–238
>   first theme group begins in m. 165
>   second theme group begins in m. 188
Coda, mm. 239–84.

A point of particular interest is the beginning of the recapitulation. P6, not P0, is the series-form for the opening of the melody in the recapitulation. What do P6 and its fellow I11 series-forms have in common with the P0–I5 group of series of the opening of the exposition?

**2.** Schoenberg, String Quartet No. 4, op. 37, third movement. Pursue the use of common elements at the beginning of the slow movement, and compare this section with the return to the opening texture in mm. 664 and following. This movement uses the same series as the first movement. But the first series-form to appear in the movement is the prime form beginning on C. Call this P0 for this movement.

**3.** Webern, *Wie bin ich froh!*, op. 25 no. 1 (1935). A score to this song appears on pp. 187–88. Study how Webern isolates common elements or similar figures by means of rhythm, contour, and dynamics. What is the relationship between the voice part and the accompaniment?

**4.** Schoenberg, *Tot*, op. 48 no. 2. Begin your study with the vocal part. What series-forms are used? How do the different tetrachords relate to one another and reflect the laconic nature of the text? (Review Example 8-29 on p. 132.) Then study the piano part.

# 12
# Hexachordal Combinatoriality

---

*combinatoriality*          *hexachordal combinatoriality*

---

The preceding chapter discusses common elements of two and three pitch-classes as they create the sound of two different passages. In addition to these small-scale relations among pitch-classes, many twelve-tone compositions feature larger groupings wherein six pitch-classes (hexachords) are held in common between two series-forms. In the works of Schoenberg in particular these common hexachords provide the pitch-fields that underlie phrase structures.

For an instance of such common hexachords, let us turn once again to the two opening melodic phrases from Schoenberg's String Quartet No. 4.

EXAMPLE 12-1: Schoenberg, String Quartet No. 4, op. 37, first movement

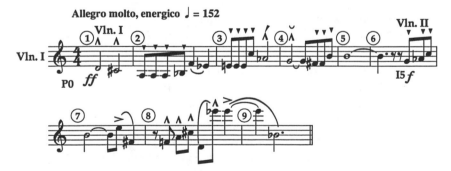

We have already studied several of the factors that contribute to the sense of continuity between these two phrases, noting that the trichord G–A♭–C and the B that begin the second-violin phrase in mm. 7–9 are common elements with the end of the first-violin phrase. (Review the discussions in Chapter 11.)

These common elements between the end of the first phrase and the beginning of the second are only part of a broader relationship between P0 and I5. As demonstrated in Example 12-2, the second hexachord of P0 contains the same pitch-classes as the first hexachord of I5.

EXAMPLE 12-2

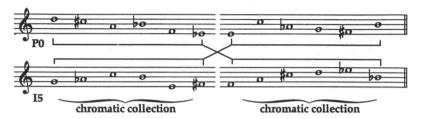

*Hexachordal Combinatoriality.*    This relationship between two series-forms is known as *hexachordal combinatoriality.* Two series-forms are hexachordally combinatorial if the contents of their hexachords are the same. This means that two pairings of hexachords between the two series-forms share all pitch-classes and the other two pairings have no pitch-classes in common. The term *combinatorial* refers to the fact that one hexachord of one series-form and one hexachord of the other series-form *combine* to form an aggregate.

Example 12-2 illustrates this. The first hexachord of P0 has the same content as the second hexachord of I5, and the second hexachord of P0 has the same content as the first hexachord of I5. The first hexachords of each series-form have no pitch-classes in common, and the second hexachords of each series-form have no pitch-classes in common.

*Between What Series-Forms Can Hexachordal Combinatoriality Occur?*    Hexachordal combinatoriality is, of course, a property of any series-form paired with its own retrograde (any P of any twelve-tone series with the R of the same number, any R with the P of the same number, any I with the RI of the same number, and any RI with the I of the same number). But only some series can have hexachordal combinatoriality between a P form and an I form, between a P and an RI form, or between two P forms.

When you analyze a piece, it is unnecessary for you to figure out whether or not a series is combinatorial and with which P, I, or RI forms it may have this relationship. After all, if you recognize two adjacent series-forms in a piece and recognize that one hexachord from one of them forms an aggregate with one hexachord from the other, you know that those series-forms are combinatorial. That is sufficient for you to proceed with your analysis.

But if you wish to study which choices a composer made in his pieces, or if you wish to construct a series that is combinatorial between a P and an I form, a P and an RI form, or two P forms, it is necessary to figure out which series are combinatorial and with which forms that series may have this relationship. The Appendix, which is optional reading, discusses how to do this.

# Combinatoriality in the Works of Schoenberg

*Model Analysis: String Quartet No. 4.*    Not long after Schoenberg began composing twelve-tone music, he discovered that some series were combinatorial with an inverted form. After that point, most of his works employ such series, usually in the P0–I5 relationship. His use of combinatorial series affects such diverse aspects of his music as harmony, texture, the relation of melody and accompaniment, phrasing, and musical form.

We will examine many of these features in our final extended discussion of the first movement of the String Quartet No. 4. A score to the opening of the first movement appears on p. 192. This work is one that uses a series that is inversionally combinatorial. As demonstrated in Example 12-2, P0 of the series in this work is combinatorial with I5.

Combinatoriality affects the following aspects of the work:

*Phrase Connections.*    When combinatorial series-forms are the basis of consecutive phrases, two types of connections are possible: either the second phrase begins with the same hexachord content as the ending of the previous phrase or the second phrase begins with entirely different pitch-class series as the end of the first phrase. Both types of connections occur at the very opening of the first movement and throughout the quartet.

In Chapter 11 we saw how the second phrase of the movement (mm. 7–9) begins as if picking up from the end of the first phrase (mm. 1–6). This is possible because each phrase is a complete series-form (P0 for the first phrase, I5 for the second) and the second hexachord of P0 contains the same pitch-classes as the first hexachord of I5.

The next phrasing connection is of the opposite kind. After the second violin's I5 (mm. 7–9), the first violin enters with R0 (mm. 10–15). In this case, there are no common pitches between the end of one phrase and the beginning of the next. The increased pitch-class circulation here helps make the end of R0, where the opening pitch-classes of the movement return, sound like a return to the very opening to conclude the section. A gradual return to the opening melodic register reinforces this effect.

Throughout this and many other Schoenberg twelve-tone works, the use of combinatorial series give rise to these types of phrasing continuities.

*Octaves, Melody, Accompaniment, and Texture.* Soon after he began writing nontonal music, Schoenberg became wary of using harmonies that were reminiscent of tonal music. He believed that such harmonies would give rise to all sorts of unwarranted tonal implications that would distract the listener.

Along with his avoidance of tonally reminiscent harmonies came a near-total avoidance of simultaneous octaves. Schoenberg believed that octaves would provide too strong an emphasis on the doubled note, possibly imparting to it the aura of a root or a tonic. In many of his pre-twelve-tone and twelve-tone nontonal works, there are no octave doublings. Even in orchestral works, there are few or no doublings except in the extreme upper and lower registers where Schoenberg felt that the sonority absolutely demanded it (such as basses doubling the cellos or piccolo doubling the flute). Indeed, the lack of octave doublings in many of Schoenberg's orchestral works, among them the *Variations*, op. 31, gives his orchestrations a distinctive sound.

Schoenberg found in combinatorial series a practical way to avoid octave doublings between melody and accompaniment. With a combinatorial series, two series-forms can run simultaneously with no possibility of octave doublings between the parts, so long as notes from different hexachords do not overlap. The passage in Example 12-3 illustrates such a use of combinatorial series-forms.

Simultaneous use of combinatorial series-forms is not the only way that Schoenberg avoids octave doublings. Review the very beginning of

EXAMPLE 12-3: Schoenberg, String Quartet No. 4, op. 37, first movement

the movement, where each three pitches of the melody are accompanied by the remaining nine pitch-classes in the series, creating aggregates. The use of combinatorial series opens up additional resources for combining pitch-classes.

A complex interaction of combinatorial series-forms is the source for the beginning of the recapitulation. This recapitulation is not a literal restatement of the opening of the exposition. In register, dynamics, tempo (tempo primo following an accelerando and rit.), and other aspects of gesture, it is a thoroughly recomposed thematic return. (See Ex. 12-4 on p. 214.)

The series-forms are not P0 and I5, as they are at the opening of the exposition. The melody in the first violin uses P6, a series-form that reverses the location within the series of the crucial pitch-pairs A♭–G and D–C♯ in relation to P0. In P0, D–C♯ begins the series, while in P6 it is A♭–G that opens the series. (Since D–C♯ is a tritone transposition of A♭–G, transposing the series by a tritone simply reverses the position of these dyads.) The cello, also using P6, is in a pitch canon with the first violin. The inner voices use the combinatorial series-form I11.[1] As a result, the A♭–G and D–C♯ interactions of the very opening occur in new positions in the phrases. The effect of the entire return is akin to transformed beginnings of recapitulations in many Romantic sonata-form movements (the first movements of Beethoven's *Ninth Symphony*, Schumann's "*Rhenish*" *Symphony*, and Brahms' *Fourth Symphony* come to mind).

*Groups of Series-Forms.* A further consequence of combinatorial series is the association of groups of series-forms. The opening 31 mea-

---

1. In the second-violin part in m. 167 order numbers 9, 10, and 11 occur out of order. Such rearrangements occur occasionally in Schoenberg's twelve-tone music, usually in developmental sections.

EXAMPLE 12-4: Schoenberg, String Quartet No. 4, op. 37, first movement

sures of the *Fourth Quartet*, for instance, use P0, R0, I5, and RI5—a pair of combinatorial series-forms and their retrogrades.

Thereafter, each time a new series-form is introduced, its combinatorial pairing also occurs. Thus, mm. 31–41 use P5, I10, and their retrogrades; mm. 42–50 use P2, I7, and their retrogrades; and so forth throughout the movement.

Since each grouping of series-forms brings with it new associations of common elements, the combinatorial pairs are important in determining the large-scale changes of focal pitch-classes throughout the movement.

## Hexachordal Compositions

Because of the special relationship between combinatorial hexachords, much of Schoenberg's twelve-tone music is based as much on hexachordal relationships as on twelve-tone series. In some of his later compositions, he even uses more than one ordering of the hexachords of the series. This is possible because combinatoriality is dependent on

the total pitch-class content of hexachords, not on the ordering of the pitch-classes. Thus, in his *String Trio*, op. 45 (1946), Schoenberg uses different orderings of each hexachord in a combinatorial series.

In Schoenberg's *Phantasy for Violin with Piano Accompaniment*, op. 47 (1949), there is a single, combinatorial series. But at the opening of the piece only one hexachord from the series (at P0 and I5) serves as the basis for all pitch-classes. The second hexachord in the series does not enter until several phrases into the piece. Also in this piece, hexachords do not always add up to entire series. For instance, at the beginning the violin presents a complete series and then the first hexachord in retrograde order and repeats the procedure:

> *Hexachord A, Hexachord B, Hexachord A; then*
>
> *Hexachord A, Hexachord B, Hexachord A.*

This has led some theorists to cite an eighteen-note series here. However it is described, this is another sign of the primacy of hexachordal units in this piece.

# Points for Review

**1.** *Hexachordal combinatoriality* occurs when two series-forms have the same hexachordal content.

**2.** All series are hexachordally combinatorial with their retrogrades (P0 with R0, P1 with R1, I2 with RI2, and so forth).

**3.** Only some series are hexachordally combinatorial between two P forms, between a P form and an I form, or between a P form and an RI form. The Appendix lists all the hexachords of all such series.

**4.** Much of Schoenberg's twelve-tone music uses inversionally combinatorial hexachords. This allows many possibilities of series-form combinations without encountering the octave doublings that Schoenberg avoided in many works.

# Exercises for Chapter 12

**Terms and Concepts**

Define combinatoriality.

## Analysis

Schoenberg, *Orchestral Variations,* op. 31 (1930), Theme. Listen to this theme until you are familiar with it. Identify all the series-forms. Are these series-forms combinatorial?

What common elements are brought out between phrases, and between melody and accompaniment? What is the link between the melody and the series-form of the countermelody during the final phrase?

What is the form of this theme? How is this form projected? How many measures are there in the different sections and phrases?

When you have completed studying the Theme, you may wish to turn to a score of the piece and listen to the introduction. Schoenberg virtually teaches the listener the principle of combinatoriality at the very opening. How? Are complete series-forms used in the introduction? What sonorities are stressed?

These studies will prepare you for a survey of the series of variations.

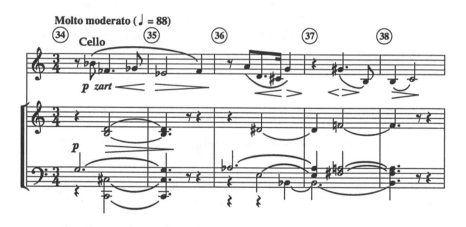

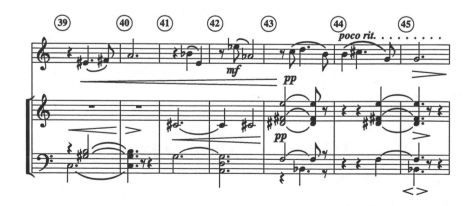

## Composition

Select one of the two series listed below and use it as the basis for two different phrases. Use the combinatorial series-forms in different parts of the texture: in melody versus accompaniment, or in two contrapuntal parts.

Write for instruments that are available in your class.

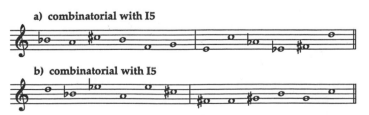

a) combinatorial with I5

b) combinatorial with I5

# Suggestions for Further Study

**1.** Schoenberg, *Klavierstück,* op. 33a. The opening of this piece was discussed in Chapter 10. The piece uses combinatorial pairs of series-forms throughout. See George Perle, *Serial Composition and Atonality,* for a detailed analysis of the form and motivic elements in this piece.

**2.** Schoenberg, *Phantasy for Violin with Piano Accompaniment,* op. 47. The violin part alone presents complete series-forms throughout the piece. The piano accompaniment adds combinatorial series-forms for much of the piece.

Analyze the opening thirty-three measures. What is the relationship between hexachords, series-forms, and phrasing in this section? The opening phrase (mm. 1–2) begins and ends with a short-long rhythm. The middle of the phrase is more active rhythmically. Where else does this phrase shape occur? What role does the piano part play in these shapes?

Study the transformed return of the opening material in mm. 153 to the end.

**3.** Read Schoenberg's essay "Composition with Twelve Tones," in *Style and Idea . . . ,* edited by Leonard Stein (New York: St. Martins Press, 1975): 214–245.

**4.** The interval-content of any hexachord is identical with the interval-content of a second hexachord formed from the six pitch-classes not members of the first hexachord. Demonstrate this by figuring out the interval-content of any hexachord, and then figuring out the interval-content of the hexachord formed by the remaining six pitch-classes.

Consider that Schoenberg's twelve-tone music, especially his twelve-tone music that uses combinatorial hexachords, often features simultaneously two hexachords that add up to an aggregate. How does this property of the interval-content of hexachords that add up to an aggregate relate to Schoenberg's music?

# 13

# Derived Series

---

*derived series*        *palindrome*

---

## Derived Series

A *derived series* is a twelve-tone series composed of several forms of a single trichord or tetrachord. The trichords or tetrachords may be transpositions, inversions, or retrograde inversions of one another.

Example 13-1 illustrates a derived series using four forms of a single trichord. The trichord appears in its prime, retrograde, inversion, and retrograde inversion, as noted by the lower-case letters below the example.

EXAMPLE 13-1

p0        ri7        r6        i1

This is the series used in Webern's *Concerto for Nine Instruments*, op. 24 (1934). In mm. 1–3 of the first movement, shown on p. 223, each trichord cell appears in a separate instrument.

Example 13-2 illustrates a derived series made up from three forms of a single tetrachord.

EXAMPLE 13-2

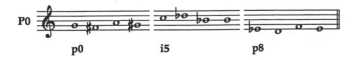

p0        i5        p8

This is the series used in Webern's *String Quartet,* op. 28 (1938). In a later section of this chapter, we will study the use of this series during the first movement.

*Trichordal and Tetrachordal Combinatoriality.* Derived series are possible because trichords and tetrachords can be combinatorial just like hexachords. Just as two forms of a combinatorial hexachord can join to create an aggregate, three forms of many tetrachords and four forms of most trichords can create an aggregate. Such tetrachords and trichords are combinatorial.

*Which Trichords Are Combinatorial?* Of the twelve different types of trichords, all are combinatorial except [0,3,6] (the diminished triad). Therefore, it is possible to compose a derived series from four forms of all trichords except that one.

*Which Tetrachords Are Combinatorial?* Only seven out of the twenty-nine possible tetrachords are combinatorial:

EXAMPLE 13-3

**a)** tetrachord combinatorial with *one* pair of forms:

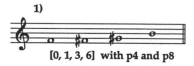

[0, 1, 3, 6]  with p4 and p8

**b)** tetrachords combinatorial with *four* pairs of forms:

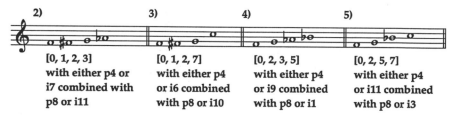

| [0, 1, 2, 3] | [0, 1, 2, 7] | [0, 2, 3, 5] | [0, 2, 5, 7] |
|---|---|---|---|
| with either p4 or i7 combined with p8 or i11 | with either p4 or i6 combined with p8 or i10 | with either p4 or i9 combined with p8 or i1 | with either p4 or i11 combined with p8 or i3 |

**c)** tetrachord combinatorial with *sixteen* pairs of forms:

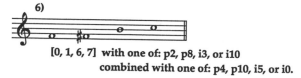

[0, 1, 6, 7]  with one of: p2, p8, i3, or i10
combined with one of: p4, p10, i5, or i0.

**d)** tetrachord combinatorial with *sixty-four* pairs of forms:

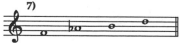

[0, 3, 6, 9]  with one of: p4, p7, p10, i1, i4, i7, or i10
combined with one of: p5, p8, p11, i2, i5, i8, i11.

The tetrachordally derived series in Example 13-2 is based on tetrachord 2 in Example 13-3.

# Derived Series and Webern's Music

We have noted in several earlier discussions that Webern often reduces the structural material of a movement to a minimum and then derives a maximum of music from that material. For him, derived series were another way of doing this. The recurring trichords or tetrachords of a derived series place the emphasis on these three-note or four-note groupings. At the same time, the fact that these recurring trichords or tetrachords are part of a twelve-tone series ensures the continuous circulation of all the pitch-classes.

A number of Webern's twelve-tone compositions use derived series. In this section we will discuss two of these works: the *Concerto for Nine Instruments*, op. 24, first movement, which features a trichordal derived series, and the *String Quartet*, op. 28, first movement, which contains a tetrachordal derived series.

### Concerto for Nine Instruments, *op. 24, first movement*

*The Series and Interval-Classes 1,11 and 4,8.*   The derived series in Example 13-1 is the basis of the *Concerto*. This series contains four forms of the [0,1,4] trichord, each statement of which presents interval-classes 1,11 and 4,8. Scores to the opening of the first movement may be found on p. 223 and to the opening of the second movement on p. 95 (discussed on pp. 103–4 in Chapter 7). Here and throughout the *Concerto*, interval-classes 1,11 and 4,8 are the predominant melodic and harmonic interval-classes.

But the reduction of structural material in the *Concerto* to a minimum goes beyond the concentration on just two interval-classes and a single melodic motive. The series is constructed so that several series-forms retain identical trichords as common elements.

*Trichords as Common Elements.*   The trichords within the series occur in two tritone-related pairs: p0–r6, and i1–ri7. When the series is transposed by a tritone, these trichords remain as common elements between the series-forms.

Similarly, when the series is inverted at the proper transposition, the very same trichords still remain as common elements. Example 13-4 illustrates the eight series-forms that retain the trichords in P0. As a result, instead of forty-eight different series-forms, there are only *six groups* of series-forms that have different trichords (forty-eight forms divided by eight forms in each group).

EXAMPLE 13-4

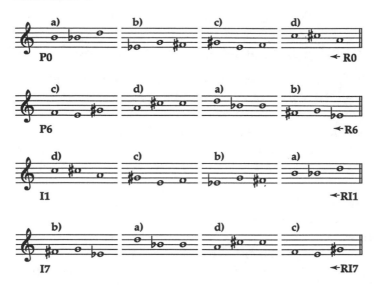

This reduction in structural material is similar to what we found in another twelve-tone work of Webern's, the second movement of the *Piano Variations*, op. 27 (review pp. 196–202 in Chapter 11). That composition features recurring pairs of pitches throughout the movement. By using P and I forms that add up to 10 throughout the movement, Webern reduces these recurring intervals to only four interval-classes, each occurring in two tritone-related forms. That movement is under a minute in length, so the limited group of intervals provides what was for Webern sufficient material. In the *Concerto*, a considerably longer composition, Webern restricts the structural material to the six groups of series-forms that provide different trichords.

***Use of the Common Trichords.*** Example 13-5 presents the opening two phrases (mm. 1–3, mm. 4–5) in the first movement.

Each trichord is separated from the others by instrumentation within the first phrase, and by rhythm and articulation within the two phrases. RI1, the series-form in the second phrase, presents each trichord in the same order as in P0. But within each trichord, the pitches occur in reverse order. Webern keeps the original registers for each pitch and reverses the rhythms.

***Palindrome.*** The rhythm of these two phrases is a *palindrome:* a structure that is the same as its retrograde. Palindromes occur in many Webern compositions. Sometimes only one aspect is palindromic, such as rhythm at the opening of the *Concerto*. Other excerpts, such as the second movement of Webern's *Symphony*, op. 21, feature phrases or sec-

EXAMPLE 13-5: Webern, *Concerto for Nine Instruments,* op. 24, first movement

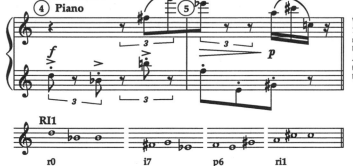

tions in which all aspects, including pitch, rhythm, dynamics, and even tempo fluctuations (ritards and accelerandos), are palindromic.

At the opening of the *Concerto,* the palindrome emphasizes the unity of the section. The opening five measures are an exposition of the structural materials that are used throughout the first movement: the motive, the interval-classes, the rhythms, the articulations, and the texture all appear. (Review the same sort of exposition at the opening of the *Piano Variations* second movement, discussed on pp. 201–2). The intense concentration with which this occurs is characteristic of Webern's music.

### String Quartet, *op. 28, first movement*

*Linking Series-Forms by Common Tetrachords.* The tetrachordally derived series of the *String Quartet* appears in Example 13-2.[1] In this work, as in other works of Webern's that use derived series, consecutive

---

1. P0 of this series is identical to RI9. As a result, every RI form is equivalent to a P form, and every R form is equivalent to an I form. This reduces the number of different series-forms to twenty-four.

series-forms are linked to one another by having the last segment of one series-form serve also as the segment of the next series-form. This technique creates continuities that exceed the length of the series itself.

In Example 13-6, the third tetrachord of the series is p8 of the first tetrachord. So the third tetrachord of P0 can also serve as the first tetrachord of P8. Black noteheads show the common pitch-classes.

EXAMPLE 13-6

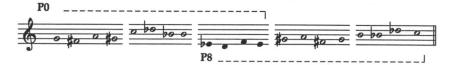

***Linking Series-Forms by Common Dyads.*** In this set, series-forms can also be linked by the last dyad of the series, which is p10 of the first dyad. In Example 13-7, P0 and P10 are linked by a common dyad. Once again, black noteheads show the common pitch-classes.

EXAMPLE 13-7

Webern uses these common dyads and tetrachords to link various series-forms in the first movement of the *String Quartet,* as shown in Example 13-8.

EXAMPLE 13-8

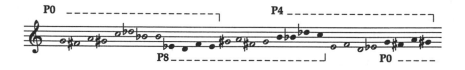

*Common Semitones.* Note that within all these series-forms, each pair of consecutive order numbers (0–1, 2–3, 4–5, 6–7, 8–9, 10–11) presents a melodic semitone, either ascending or descending. The same semitones keep recurring: F♯–G, G♯–A, B♭–B, C–C♯, D–E♭, and E–F. Other possible semitones, G–G♯, A–B♭, B–C, C♯–D, E♭–E, and F–F♯, do not appear.

How is it that only six semitones keep recurring, and the other six semitones never appear? As we have found elsewhere with Webern, the clue to the procedures he uses are found in the structure of the series itself. Each semitone that does appear is an even-numbered transposition of all the others that appear: if F♯ is pitch-class 0, then the semitones that appear are built on pitch-classes 2 (G♯–A), 4 (B♭–B), 6 (C–C♯), 8 (D–E♭), and 10 (E–F). The semitones built on odd-numbered pitch-classes do not occur.

So long as the series is transposed only by even numbers, the adjacent semitones will recur. The same semitones will also recur in odd-numbered I forms. Conversely, all odd-numbered P forms and even-numbered I forms present the other semitones as adjacent pairs of pitch-classes.

*Common Elements in the Music.* See pp. 205–6 for a score to the opening of the first movement. Since the sequence of series in Example 13-8 is the basis for the passage, only one grouping of semitones occurs here throughout this opening passage. Most pairs of semitonally related pitch-classes remain in the same register and instrument throughout the section. Like other Webern pieces, this exposition of structural materials is quite concentrated.

*Form and Style.* The first movement of the *String Quartet* is a Theme and Variations. But the theme and variations are not quite the same as eighteenth- and nineteenth-century variation forms. The score on pp. 205–6 is the Theme for the movement. Each variation that follows is a two-voiced canon. In the first variation, one voice of the canon presents the sequence of linked series-forms P0–P8–P4–P0 at some level of transposition. The other voice in the canon uses the same sequence of series-forms at an odd-numbered level of transposition. Since the level of transposition between the two voices of the canon is odd in each case, these canons always feature both families of semitones simultaneously.

Ex. 13-9 on p. 226 is the first variation. The canon is strict in pitch and rhythm at six beats during mm. 16–25 and at two beats for mm. 26–32. But because of the changes of register and instrumentation every few notes, and because contour, instrumentation, and mode of attack (arco versus pizzicato, slurs versus separate notes) are not canonic, the pitch-

EXAMPLE 13-9: Webern, *String Quartet*, op. 28, first movement

class canon is difficult if not impossible to hear as an imitation in the traditional sense. Rather, it provides the structural framework within which the families of semitones and tetrachords operate. This is much like Webern's presentation of series-forms, which are not set off from one another in phrases, as Schoenberg's often are, but provide the basis for the projection of intervals and smaller pitch-class sets.

Although the structure of the series seems to stress tetrachords or dyads, many of the instrumental or articulative segments during this variation stress trichords. In fact, if the series is divided into its trichords (order numbers 0–1–2, 3–4–5, 6–7–8, and 9–10–11), only two types arise. The first and last trichords of the series are [0,1,3]; the two middle ones are [0,1,5].

As in other Webern compositions we have studied, the structural materials in this piece are quite limited: two groupings of all the semitones in an octave, and two types of trichords. Many pitch-classes are fixed in register during the Theme, and strict canons underlie the variations. The resulting musical continuities, however, are anything but abstract—an intense and dazzling array of notes and small groupings of notes, timbres, registers, rhythm, and articulations that follow one another in unique ways.

*Webern's Influence.*    With overlapping series-forms, groups of series-forms with identical contents, series constructed so as to project only a few intervals or a few small pitch-class sets, strict canons that are more a matter of underlying structure than audible imitation, and palindromic phrases and sections, the style of Webern is far removed from that of Schoenberg. In the years following World War II, many younger composers viewed Webern's music as the way to a new rhetoric more suited to twelve-tone music, as opposed to the more traditional and tonally reminiscent interaction of melody and harmony, of texture, of musical phrasing and form, and of motivic development found in the music of Schoenberg and Berg. The last section of this chapter and Chapter 16 in Unit Four survey some of these developments in music after World War II.

*Pictorial Aspects.*    Perhaps the most intriguing characteristic of Webern's music is not its use of structural devices, its compression, or its intensity, but its pictorial programs. Following the often flamboyant personal expression that seemed a part of so much nineteenth-century music, twentieth-century composers from many different schools adopted a more reserved stance. Stravinsky, for instance, even questioned music's ability to express any emotions at all. (This is not to say that Stravinsky's music is unexpressive, but merely to record his sentiments on this matter.)

Webern's music has often been cited as the very model of abstract constructionism. Yet the recent biography of Webern by Hans and Rosaleen Moldenhauer[2] mentions numerous works of Webern's that were motivated by pictorial programs as literal and extramusical as those of any nineteenth-century tone poem. In the *Concerto for Nine Instruments*, for instance, Webern began the work with a program referring to Schwabegg and Annabichl, the sites of his parents' graves, to Einersdorf and Koralpe, his favorite outing spots near Vienna, and to his wife and son. A later series of sketches associates these localities with specific movements, and associates his family members' names with specific sections of the finale. When he completed the second movement, he wrote to his friend Hildegard Jone, whose poems he had set, that the movement "expresses something similar to your picture with the harvest wagon." The initial sketches to the *String Quartet*, op. 28, refer to the same places, to various members of his immediate family, and to such aspects of nature as seeds, life, water, and the forest.

These programs were never published, and their relation to the finished work is a matter for debate. But they do raise important questions about the meaning of Webern's music and his place in the history of twentieth-century music. What is certain is Webern's thoroughly negative attitude toward performances of his own music that merely rendered the notes on the page. His own performances were extremely expressive, treating each individual note or gesture as a major expressive event.

## Multiple Derived Series in a Single Composition

Some post–World War II composers have used families of derived series as a way of gaining greater variety from a single series. Milton Babbitt's *Composition for Four Instruments* (1948) is one such work. It is based on the series in Example 13-10.

EXAMPLE 13-10

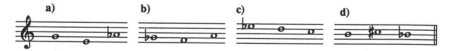

Except for the very last twelve pitches in the piece, this series does not occur as such during the composition. In its place, we have in the remainder of the work derived series based on each of the trichords.

---

2. (New York: Alfred A. Knopf, 1979), pp. 431–436, 486.

During the flute-violin duo (mm. 89–118), for instance, a derived series built on trichord *c* in Example 13-10 serves as the basis of the flute part.

EXAMPLE 13-11

This series appears in two forms, each of which occupies its own register in the flute part. These series-forms are hexachordally combinatorial (P0 with I11), so each half of each series presents an aggregate with the corresponding half of the other. Listen to Example 13-12.

EXAMPLE 13-12: Babbitt, *Composition for Four Instruments*

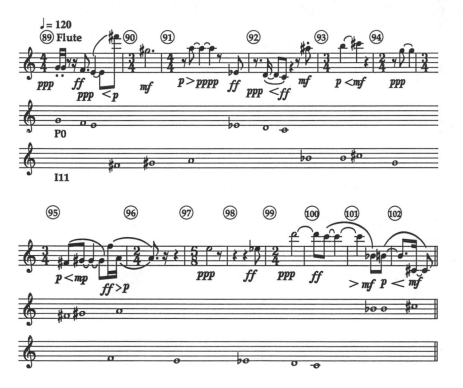

The derived series on which the violin part is based include both trichords *c* and *d*. As in the flute part, each of the two series in the violin part occupies its own register. These series are also hexachordally combinatorial.

EXAMPLE 13-13: Babbitt, *Composition for Four Instruments*

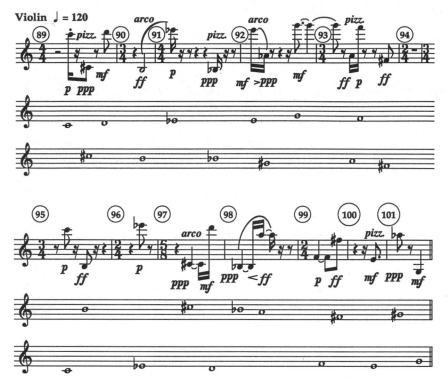

Trichords *c* and *d* are forms of the same pitch-class set: [0,1,3]. The trichord, like all trichords but one, is combinatorial. The ordering of trichords among these four series (two in the flute; two in the violin) is so arranged that each of the trichords forms an aggregate with the three corresponding trichords with which it occurs:

EXAMPLE 13-14

Similar processes occur throughout the piece. Four series or series-forms are continually present, forming hexachordally combinatorial pairs, and trichordally combinatorial foursomes. The piece in effect features four series or series-forms continually running against one another. But as we found with Webern's use of canons, this four-voice structural polyphony is not reflected in a four-voice polyphony at the compositional surface. In fact, the four-voice structural polyphony occurs whether one, two, three, or four instruments play in a section.

Although the series ordering the flute-violin duet is as we have discussed, other aspects of ordering in this section introduce trichords not part of these series. For instance, listen to the violin part in Example 13-13 by itself. Consecutive pitches are from alternate series-forms. As a result, even though the registrally separate series are based on trichords *c* and *d*, the immediate ordering after a while is based on trichord *b*. (The trichord names are listed in Example 13-10.) The alternation of arco and pizzicato reinforces this. See Example 13-15 (in which pitch-classes from the different series-forms are written in white or black noteheads) and listen again to Example 13-13.

Example 13-15

As a result, the piece features continuous permutations of aggregates in each derived series, in pairs of series, and in foursomes of series. The basic trichords appear in different guises throughout, leading from one section to another, and referring within one section to other sections. Rhythm and dynamics are closely related to series structure, as we will see in Chapter 15.

Even the form of the work is permutational. Every possible combination of four instruments serves as the basis of a section. There are four solos, one for each instrument, the six possible duet combinations, the four possible trios, and a single quartet section. These fifteen sections fall into pairs with each instrument playing once. Review p. 62 in Chapter 4 for a listing of the sections.

*Style.*    Babbitt's music, like the Webern compositions discussed earlier in this chapter, does not present melodies and accompaniments or phrasings or textures like those found in works of Schoenberg. The *Composition for Four Instruments*, like much of Babbitt's music, uses common elements in series-forms as the structural basis for a musical surface that is athematic. The combinations of derived series and of series-forms continuously creates aggregates in several ways, keeping the twelve pitch-classes in constant circulation, and providing a unity of conception for the arrays of musical ideas that populate the surface of his music.

# Points for Review

**1.** A *derived series* is a twelve-tone series composed of several forms of a single combinatorial trichord or tetrachord. With the sole exception of [0,3,6], all trichords are combinatorial. The seven combinatorial tetrachords appear in Example 13-3.

**2.** Derived series are the basis of many of Webern's compositions.

**3.** Derived series are used by some composers to relate different twelve-tone series to a common series.

**4.** A *palindrome* is a pattern identical in prime and retrograde.

# Exercises for Chapter 13

**Terms and Concepts**

**1.** Define the following terms:

*derived series*          *palindrome*

**2.** Compose a derived twelve-tone series based on each of the following trichords or tetrachords. The first has been completed for you.

**Analysis**

Babbitt, *Composition for Four Instruments*, clarinet solo (mm. 1–35). The derived series on which the clarinet solo is based is built on trichord *a* in Example 13-10. Four different series-forms are maintained throughout the section, each in its own register. The opening three pitches (B–E♭–C) are the first trichord of one series-form. Other forms of this trichord in mm. 1–6 are D♭–B♭–D, G♭–A–F, and A♭–E–G. Each of these trichords begins a series-form. Trace the continuations of these four series-forms for the remainder of the solo.

Each trichord creates an aggregate with the corresponding trichord in the other three series-forms. In mm. 1–6, this gives rise to an *all-interval series* (a twelve-tone series with one instance of each interval). Where else does this series occur? What other series arise from these aggregates? Four major or minor triads are spelled out by successive notes at two points in this passage. Where? By what series-forms?

# Suggestions for Further Study

**1.** Webern, *Concerto*, op. 24. Continue the analysis begun in this chapter. Study the derived series in all three movements. A detailed analysis by Robert Gauldin of the second and third movements appears in *In Theory Only*, journal of the Michigan Music Theory Society: vol. 2 no. 10, and vol. 2 nos. 11–12 (1977).

*String Quartet*, op. 28. Continue the analysis begun in this chapter. Study the variations in the first movement, concentrating on the different relationships within the series that are brought to the fore.

The second movement contains many palindromic features. How are these constructed?

*Symphony*, op. 21. The two movements of the *Symphony* feature many characteristic aspects of Webern's twelve-tone music: strict canons, palindromes, *Klangfarbenmelodie*, and the exploration of intervallic properties. See George Perle, *Serial Composition and Atonality*, for a survey of many crucial aspects of the structure.

**2.** Babbitt, *Composition for Four Instruments*. Explore the use of derived series in other sections of the work. Study the harmonic intervals that appear in each section. How many occur in each section? What types?

*Semi-Simple Variations* (1956). Two articles offer analyses of this two-page composition for piano: "A Simple Approach to Milton Babbitt's *Semi-Simple Variations*" by Elaine Barkin, in *The Music Review*, vol. 28 (1967), pp. 316ff.; and "Milton Babbitt's *Semi-Simple Variations*" by Christopher Wintle, in *Perspectives of New Music*, vols. 14/1 and 15/2, pp. 111ff.

# 14
# Multiple Orderings of Twelve-Tone Series

---

---

Schoenberg originally conceived of the twelve-tone method as one based on a single ordering of all twelve pitch-classes. This master-motive would be in some sense the basis for ordering of pitch-classes throughout an entire composition. For much of Schoenberg's twelve-tone music, and for all of Webern's, the ordering of the original series does indeed fulfill this role.

But strict adherence to a single series is not characteristic of all twelve-tone music. Occasionally in Schoenberg's twelve-tone music, often in Berg's, and frequently in Stravinsky's, orderings arise that cannot be directly derived from a single series. Sometimes these multiple orderings result from the use of two or more series. In other cases reorderings arise because of the way segments of different series-forms appear. This chapter surveys some characteristics of reorderings and some compositions that use more than one ordering of a series.

## In Schoenberg's Music

Orderings not directly derivable from the series are found in Schoenberg's twelve-tone music under the following circumstances:

1. When aggregates are created by combining segments of the series.

2. From developmental rearrangements of the series.

3. From the systematic use of more than one ordering of a hexachord.

*Combinations of Segments.* In Chapter 10 we discussed the creation of aggregates between melody and accompaniment in the opening phrase of Schoenberg's *Fourth Quartet.* (Review Example 10-4 on p. 179.) For each trichord in the melody of this phrase, the accompanying chords add the remaining nine pitch-classes of the series. The principle by which the accompanimental chords arise is based on the ordering of the series, and each segment (the melody, and the accompanying chords) is ordered. But the entire texture does not follow the ordering of the series-form that is the basis of the passage. Similar situations are quite common in Schoenberg's twelve-tone music.

*Developmental Rearrangements.* Schoenberg viewed a twelve-tone series in part as a motivic construction. He believed that once the series had been established in a composition, minor adjustments in ordering might be made, just as one might develop a motive. We have already noted one such reordering in the first-movement recapitulation from the *Fourth Quartet.* (Review the footnote to the discussion of Example 12-4 on p. 213.) There are occasional instances of such reorderings throughout Schoenberg's twelve-tone music.

*Different Hexachord Orderings.* Several late twelve-tone compositions of Schoenberg's use more than one ordering in a more systematic manner than what has just been described. One such work is the *Phantasy for Violin with Piano Accompaniment,* op. 47 (1948). The basic series is:

EXAMPLE 14-1

EXAMPLE 14-2

This series-form is hexachordally combinatorial with I5. At the very beginning of the piece, instead of using complete series-forms as the basis of the melody, P0 and I5 forms of the first hexachord by itself are used to form aggregates in consecutive phrases. This gives rise to two independent orderings of the second hexachord from the basic series of the piece. Compare the second hexachord in Example 14-1 to that in Example 14-2.

More extensive use of reorderings occurs in the *String Trio,* op. 45 (1946) and the *Ode to Napoleon,* op. 41 (1942). The *String Trio* uses one series, but employs three different orderings within the hexachords in different sections of the one-movement piece. And the *Ode* is unique among Schoenberg's twelve-tone music in that it uses unordered hexachords.[1] The *Ode* also introduces numerous octave doublings and prominent triads throughout. The end of the work focuses on E♭-major triads. This is a clear reference to Beethoven's "Eroica" Symphony in that key—a work that at least in its original conception also refers to Napoleon.

These types of reorderings of a series are not necessarily contradictory to Schoenberg's twelve-tone method because of those series properties that are determined by content and not by ordering. Hexachordal combinatoriality, for instance, depends on the content of a hexachord, not its ordering (see the Appendix). And as we pointed out in Chapter 12, one of the reasons for using series that are combinatorial is to gain different orderings of the same hexachord. In any event, despite the presence of the various types of reorderings discussed here, the vast majority of Schoenberg's twelve-tone music is based on a single ordering of a single series.

# In Berg's Music

In many respects, Berg's twelve-tone music is freer in conception than Schoenberg's or Webern's. Berg never adopted the ban on octaves that Schoenberg did in many works. Nor did he avoid tonal elements in his twelve-tone works, as Schoenberg usually did, and Webern always did. Berg's *Violin Concerto,* for instance, uses the series in Example 14-3, a series that presents four triads in a row. These four triads, whose roots are fifth-related (G–D–A–E—the four open strings of the violin) appear as unadorned harmonies at many points in the course of the work. Other tonal references in the *Concerto* include an entire Bach chorale in the last

EXAMPLE 14-3

1. The only other passage from a completed Schoenberg work that uses an unordered series is a portion of the *Tanzscene* (Dance Scene) from Schoenberg's *Serenade,* op. 24 (1920-23), Schoenberg's last composition before he began writing works that were entirely twelve-tone in structure. Mm. 33–35, 49–111, 128–133, 177–184, and 199–200 of the Tanzscene use an unordered combinatorial hexachord to form aggregates.

movement, scored for winds one phrase at a time with no other music sounding against it.

In addition, many of Berg's twelve-tone pieces use several different series or several orderings within parts of one series. Among these compositions is his string quartet entitled the *Lyric Suite*.

*The* **Lyric Suite** *(1926).*    This piece includes twelve-tone movements as well as movements and sections of movements that are not twelve-tone in structure. The first movement is a twelve-tone movement, but instead of a single ordering of a single series, it uses three different orderings of the same hexachords. Example 14-4 illustrates all three.

EXAMPLE 14-4

Series A

Series B

Series C

Both the structure of the series and its uses in the piece relate to both tonal and twelve-tone music. Let us first consider the structure of the series. The lowest ordering of the hexachords is that in ordering B: [0,2,4,5,7,9]. The hexachord is a six-note segment of a major scale. As the interval content of this hexachord shows, each interval-class occurs a different number of times.[2]

| Interval-class: | 1,11 | 2,10 | 3,9 | 4,8 | 5,7 | 6 |
|---|---|---|---|---|---|---|
| Number of Instances | 1 | 4 | 3 | 2 | 5 | 0 |

Each of the three orderings of the hexachords profiles a different aspect of the series. Ordering A is a complete circle of fifths, emphasizing both

---

2. The interval content of only one other hexachord (a semitone scale [0,1,2,3,4,5]) has a different number of each interval-class. And only two heptachords have interval contents with a different number of each interval-class: the diatonic heptachord [0,1,3,5,6,8,10] (a major scale) and [0,1,2,3,4,5,6] (a semitone scale).

that the ordering within each hexachord is a fifth-series and that intervals 5 and 7 predominate in the interval content of these diatonic hexachords. Ordering B reflects the diatonic and scalar possibilities of a series with so many steps. In contrast to orderings A and B, each of which stresses only one or two intervals, ordering C is an *all-interval series*; it contains one instance of every possible interval from 1 to 11.

For two reasons, each hexachord presents a clearly defined pitch-class region. One reason for this is the hexachord's similarity to a major scale. Our tonal background has accustomed us to hearing a diatonic structure as a unified pitch-class region or key area. Further, there are no tritone-related pitch-classes within either hexachord of this series. Each pitch in each hexachord is tritone-related to a pitch in the other hexachord. As in tonal music, the tritone relation between scales or pitch-class regions here effects a marked shift in harmonic focus.[3]

The effects of these series properties resonate throughout the first movement of the *Lyric Suite*.

EXAMPLE 14-5: Berg, *Lyric Suite*, first movement

---

3. Compare to a similar effect discussed in connection with Bartók's *Diminished Fifth*. Review the discussion of Example 8-6 on p. 112.

The hexachords are not the focus at first. Rather, the opening measure begins with tetrachords: series A appears as three four-note chords. Each chord is the [0,2,5,7] tetrachord, a segment of the fifth-series, which contains only the three most common interval-classes in the hexachord of this series. The voicing of each tetrachord emphasizes the predominant interval-class 5,7.

| Interval-class: | 1,11 | 2,10 | 3,9 | 4,8 | 5,7 | 6 |
|---|---|---|---|---|---|---|
| Number of Instances | 0 | 2 | 1 | 0 | 3 | 0 |

The last chord in m. 1 contains the first hexachord of series-form P7. Like the tetrachords that precede it, it is voiced to emphasize interval 7. Since each hexachord of the series contains five instances of interval-class 5,7, transposition to P7 maintains five pitch-classes in common with P0. As a result, the effect of the opening measure is to establish the predominant harmonic sounds and basic harmonic regions.

The first-violin upbeat in m. 2 initiates the first thematic material of the movement. The melody is based on series C. The slurring and registration exploit the single appearances of each interval in the hexachord to support the upward sweep of the phrase. Each slurred interval increases in size during the measure (F–E is a semitone, C–A contains three semitones, G–D contains five semitones). And each unslurred interval increases in size during the measure (E–C, then A–G). But this new series-ordering (series C after series A in m. 1) does not abandon the perfect-fifth sound of the opening measure. The successive notes on each eighth (the first notes of each slur) are interval 7 above one another, giving the measure the sense of growing out of the preceding chords.

The tritone leap to the A♭ in m. 2 announces the shift to the new harmonic region of the second hexachord. The accompaniment completes P7, again retaining five pitch-classes in common with the second hexachord of P0, and thereby changing the harmonic region of the accompaniment in support of the change of harmonic region in the melody.

The melody in m. 3 reverses the order of interval-classes from m. 2 and replaces each interval by its complement. Listen to Example 14-6. Once again, the primary notes of the melodic descent stresses interval 7: A♭, D♭, G♭, and B.

The result of these structurings is the measured rise and fall of the overall line in mm. 2–3, announcing the sensuous sweep so typical of the *Lyric Suite.* These structures and pitch-class regions continue

EXAMPLE 14-6: Berg, *Lyric Suite,* first movement

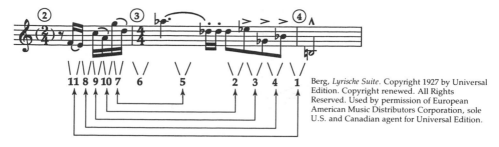

throughout the movement. The music gives the impression of great freedom in construction and expression. Yet as we have seen here in the opening measures, every detail is worked out with the utmost care.

***Third Movement.*** The third movement of the *Lyric Suite* is in ternary form. The middle section of the movement is not twelve-tone in structure, but the outer sections, which we will discuss here, are. These outer sections use a series different from those in the first movement.[4]

EXAMPLE 14-7

It is of special significance to this movement that the series contains the three instances of the tetrachord [0,1,2,6] noted in Example 14-7.

At the opening of the third movement, each series-form is transposed so that [0,1,2,6] always occurs with some ordering of the pitch-classes F–A–B♭–B. The series are then *rotated;* that is, shifted around in a loop so that a note other than order number 0 is in first position. Each rotation is so arranged that some form of F–A–B♭–B occurs at the beginning of the series-form. (See Ex. 14–8 on p. 242.)

The remaining eight pitch-classes, which are reorderings of one another, then function as a separate eight-note series. The tetrachord F–A–B♭–B remains a motto throughout this section. Since the last portion of the movement is a literal retrograde of the first portion, this section and these isolated pitch-classes also end the movement.

---

4. This is series C of the first movement, with order numbers 3 and 9 reversed.

EXAMPLE 14-8

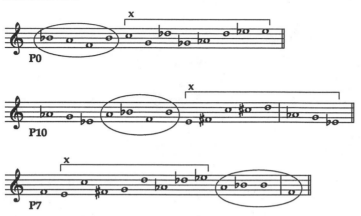

The choice of the four pitch-classes F–A–B♭–B for emphasis is not an arbitrary one, for these notes carry extramusical significance. Berg secretly dedicated the work to an intimate friend, and the four pitches A–B♭–B–F spell out the first letters of his and her names: A̲lban B̲erg and H̲anna F̲uchs-Robettin. (In German usage, the letter B̲ stands for the note B♭, and the letter H̲ stands for the note B.) Indeed, the *Lyric Suite* is replete with such encodings and also with various types of numerological symbolism.[5]

## Stravinsky's Twelve-Tone Music

In the 1950s and 1960s, Stravinsky turned to writing music based on series with fewer than twelve tones, and then to writing twelve-tone music. This was a fairly dramatic turn of events in the history of twentieth-century music. For several decades before that time, Stravinsky's neo-Classic style had been viewed by many musicians as the irreconcilable antithesis to the serial music of Schoenberg, Berg, and Webern.

What was perhaps most remarkable about Stravinsky's adoption of a new system of pitch organization is that it in no way made his music sound like that of Schoenberg, Berg, Webern, or any of the other composers who had adopted twelve-tone music in the interim. Stravinsky's music remained Stravinskian, despite the change in the underlying pitch organization. His timbral combinations, both striking contrasts and unprecedented blends, his clear textures, his own brand of phrasing and formal continuities, as well as other features of his style, remained *sui generis*.

---

5. See George Perle, "The Secret Program of the Lyric Suite," in three issues of *The Musical Times:* vol. 118 (August, September, and October, 1977).

True, there were changes in many aspects of his music. But as with all the other changes Stravinsky's style underwent during his long and productive creative life, certain underlying aspects of his style were retained in these late works. His fascination with textures and timbres, for instance, is reflected in most of these late pieces of his with sparser textures than those found in his earlier music. In terms of musical form and phrasing, too, there were changes. We have noted earlier in this book Stravinsky's use of layered textures and repetitious melodic parts or ostinatos in creating sections and larger forms. In the serial works, layered textures give way to sparser textures. And ostinatos and even motives sometimes give way to phrase-length units with virtually no literal repetitions, sequences, or even recurring motives. Larger forms also feature few thematic or sectional returns.

In terms of pitch, however, Stravinsky found ways to use twelve-tone techniques to give him the carefully controlled pitch-class regions that we have observed in his earlier works. He did this by the extensive use of a number of serial techniques, including rotation.

**Canticum Sacrum,** *second movement.* Consider, for instance, the tenor solo in the second movement of his *Canticum Sacrum* (1956). The movement is based on the twelve-tone series in Example 14-9.

EXAMPLE 14-9

Throughout the movement, the tenor solo sings pitches in order from series-forms (that is, it does not share pitches from a series-form with any of the accompanimental parts). But by the use of three serial techniques, the pitches are selected so that instead of twelve circulating pitch-classes, there are a small number of pitch-classes that are the basis of most of the melody. The three techniques are:

**1.** The series-forms used retain five or six pitch-classes between hexachords.

**2.** Occasionally, single hexachords appear independently of the remainder of the series.

**3.** The series-forms in the accompaniment line up so that many pitch-classes in the accompaniment occur along with or close to the same pitch-classes in the melody.

Let us now study how each of these techniques affects the music:

***Series-Forms with Maximum Common Pitch-Classes; Hexachords Independent of the Series.*** Note in Example 14-9 that P0 of this series is combinatorial with I11. In addition, P0 and I6 share five of the six pitch-classes in each hexachord. Using the proper combinations of these series-forms following one another allows Stravinsky to retain five or six pitch-classes between melodic segments. And that is exactly what the tenor part does. The series-forms of the opening of the tenor part are those in Example 14-10.

EXAMPLE 14-10: Stravinsky, *Canticum Sacrum*, second movement

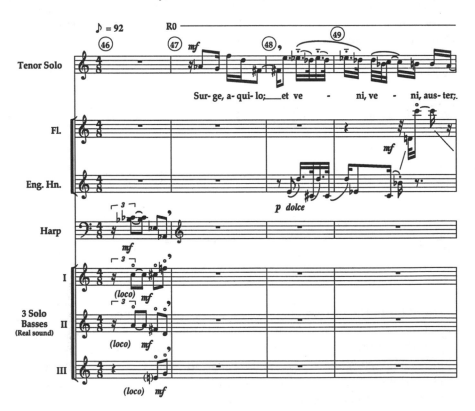

These series-forms appear after a one-measure introduction in which the harp and three solo basses playing harmonics (note the timbral combination!) present P0 in three chords. The tenor begins with R0, as shown in Example 14-10. The first hexachord only of P0 follows; this hexachord reverses the pitches of the second hexachord of R0 (of course, since P0 is the retrograde of R0). Then only the first hexachord of I6 appears; as shown in Example 14-9, this hexachord pretty much reverses the order of pitches in the preceding first hexachord of P0. Then the entirety of P0 appears; once again the first hexachord pretty much reverses the order of pitches in the preceding hexachord. Of the six hexachords that appear during this melody, all except the first and last share five of their six pitches.

Since the melody keeps most pitch-classes in the same register throughout, the ultimate effect is almost that of an underlying ostinato (compare with melodies from the *Rite of Spring*, *Petrushka*, the *Concerto for Piano and Winds,* and the *Symphony of Psalms* that we studied in earlier chapters). Another technique that adds to the sense of an ostinato here is that some pairs of notes are repeated two or more times. Often these repeated notes emphasize some of the common pitches between series-forms. For instance, in the very first R0 form, the E♭–D♭ dyad is repeated three times; in the following first hexachord of P0, the D♭–E♭ dyad also occurs three times; this time it is the last dyad of this hexachord and overlaps into the E♭–D♭ that begins the first hexachord of I6.

Similar processes continue for the entire movement. The series-forms used throughout in the tenor solo are P0, R0, I6, I11, the first hexachord only of P0, and the first hexachord only of I6.

*The Accompaniment.*    The orchestra supports this solo tenor melody with a texture consisting mostly of single lines sparsely orchestrated. The instruments used are solo flute, solo English horn, harp, and three solo basses. Coming after the more fully orchestrated first movement featuring the full chorus, this change to a chamberlike setting along with the single texture for fairly long stretches of music imparts a neo-Baroque aspect. In this movement, the pitches of the chamber accompaniment come from the series-forms in the tenor solo as well as from others.

*The Use of Rotation.*    In later works, Stravinsky used rotation of the series or of individual hexachords extensively, often gaining in the process the types of pitch continuity we have just seen in the *Canticum sacrum,* as well as focus on specific pitch-classes. We will take note of the use of rotation in two late works: *Abraham and Isaac* (1963) and *Variations: Aldous Huxley in Memoriam* (1964).

**Abraham and Isaac.**    The textures throughout *Abraham and Isaac* are similar to those of the second movement of the *Canticum Sacrum:* a baritone solo for much of the piece, with much of the sparse orchestral accompaniment consisting of one or a few lines. Those lines often feature frequent changes of instrumentation. In both the voice part and the accompaniment, the pitches arise from hexachords and series-forms in order.

But in this piece, the complete series is stated in order only once, at the very beginning of the work. All later series-forms are single hexachords or rotations of single hexachords. Example 14-11 presents the series at P0 as well as six rotations of each hexachord. The numbers below each hexachord are the order numbers of the pitches in P0.

EXAMPLE 14-11

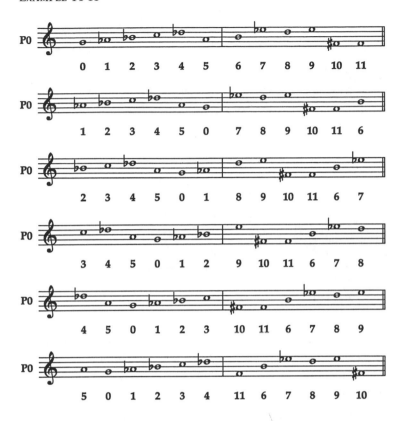

The instrumental section that opens the piece begins to use some of these rotations, as shown in Example 14-12.

EXAMPLE 14-12: Stravinsky, *Abraham and Isaac*

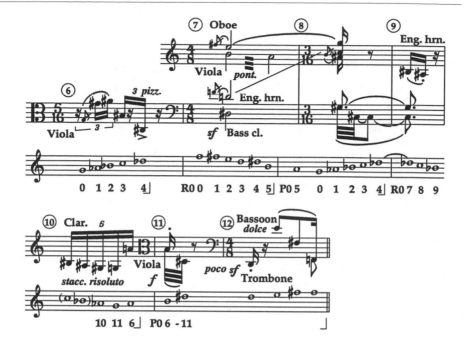

In later sections in the piece, rotations and series-forms are often arranged so that the series-forms or hexachords consistently begin or end on C♯ or F. These two pitch-classes are prominent as focal pitches throughout much of the work.

**Variations.**     Similar rotations, but this time of entire series-forms, not just hexachords, abound in the *Variations*. Example 14-13 illustrates the series of the piece, and the series-forms used in a monophonic passage in mm. 6–22. At two strategic points between series-forms, there are repeated dyads emphasizing specific pitch-classes, much as we found in the *Canticum sacrum* in Example 14-10. These repeating dyads, as well as many other pitch changes, occur along with changes of instrumentation or back-and-forth exchanges of instruments, giving rise to a novel texture reminiscent of both twentieth-century *Klangfarbenmelodie* and fourteenth-century hocket. As in the *Canticum Sacrum, Abraham and Isaac*, and the earlier Stravinsky pieces we studied in previous chapters, these techniques give rise to ostinato-like melodic fragments and the sound of a limited pitch region, even in the presence of a wide circulation of pitch-classes in complete twelve-tone series-forms.[6]

---

6. In this and some other late works, Stravinsky abandoned the use of flats in music notation, using only naturals and sharps for all notes. To facilitate the reading of intervals, some of Stravinsky's sharps have been changed to flats in Examples 14-13 through 14-15.

EXAMPLE 14-13: Stravinsky, *Variations: Aldous Huxley in Memoriam*

The *Variations* are not directly related to traditional series of theme-and-variations. Instead, they feature a number of widely divergent textures that contrast with each other during the piece. These textural contrasts include among others the monophonic texture we have just studied (mm. 6–22) and a recurring twelve-part polyphony. In the twelve-part polyphony each part has its own series-form rotations and its own rhythmic structure. And each time the polyphony recurs it has a different orchestration: in mm. 23–33 it is scored for twelve solo violins, all playing pianissimo ponticello; in mm. 47–57 for ten solo violas and two solo basses, again all playing pianissimo ponticello; and on its final appearance in mm. 118–128, for woodwinds, once again pianissimo. With twelve different soft parts, many sharing the same register in each of these sections, and with each part having its own pitch and rhythmic structure, the texture and sonority is unique.

Also occurring in the piece are totally chordal textures, mostly in the opening and closing passages. The chords that appear in these passages arise from a special use of rotation. Example 14-14 illustrates the chords and the solo bass-clarinet G♯ that end the *Variations*.

EXAMPLE 14-14

These chords derive from the series in the following manner: the underlying series-form is the second hexachord of I0. Example 14-15 illustrates this hexachord and all of its rotations transposed to begin on the note G♯.

EXAMPLE 14-15

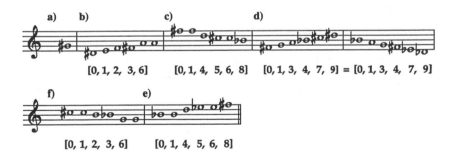

[0, 1, 2, 3, 6]      [0, 1, 4, 5, 6, 8]      [0, 1, 3, 4, 7, 9] = [0, 1, 3, 4, 7, 9]

[0, 1, 2, 3, 6]      [0, 1, 4, 5, 6, 8]

If the rotated series-forms are lined up vertically, they will form the six six-note chords shown in Example 14-15. The first chord (labeled *a*) is a unison (of course, because we transposed all the rotations to begin on the same pitch). Of the remaining chords, *b* and *f* are inversions of one another, *c* and *e* are inversions of one another, and *d* is its own inversion. Since the six rotations were all transposed to begin with G♯, G♯ does not appear in any chord except *a*.

The inversional and other relationships among these chords arise if any hexachord is manipulated in this way. Stravinsky used such chords in two passages in *Abraham and Isaac* as well as in several passages from the *Variations*. In the closing measures of the *Variations* illustrated in Example 14-14, the series of chords begins with *b* and continues through *f*. The solo G♯, a focal pitch at several points earlier in the *Variations* as well, is the missing pitch-class that completes the rotations as well as the composition.

Note that some of these chords contain pitch doublings: two A's in chord *b* and two G's in chord *f*. These doublings arise because of repeated melodic intervals in the hexachord: the two semitones.

Stravinsky's adoption of twelve-tone techniques while retaining his own personal musical style in these twelve-tone works was one of the factors that led other composers in the 1950s and 1960s to adopt serial techniques in their own music. Stravinsky's approach demonstrated that the twelve-tone method need not be associated solely with the aesthetic of Schoenberg and his associates. In addition, by exploring rotation and other methods of controlling pitch regions within twelve-tone music, Stravinsky indicated a path toward a whole new range of musical possibilities within the world of serial music. These possibilities, including but not limited to rotation of series segments of different sizes, have been explored by a number of composers in recent years.

*Summary.* This brings to an end our formal discussion of twelve-tone serial music. We will touch on a few additional aspects in Chapter 16. It is clear that twelve-tone music carries with it no single specific musical style or aesthetic. And it is also clear that twelve-tone music extends far beyond the use of an ordering of twelve pitch-classes in a series and the orderings derivable from the forty-eight transpositions, inversions, retrogrades, and retrograde-inversions of that series. Twelve-tone music is by no means the only music written since the 1920s, nor is it the only music being written today, but it continues to be an important part of the world of twentieth-century composition.

# Points for Review

**1.** Different orderings of the series arise in Schoenberg's twelve-tone music from the combination of series segments to form aggregates, from developmental rearrangements, and from the use of more than one ordering of a hexachord.

**2.** Berg's twelve-tone compositions often use several orderings of a series or several series.

**3.** *Rotation* and other serial techniques that help establish pitch regions within twelve-tone series occur in much of Stravinsky's twelve-tone music.

# Exercises for Chapter 14

## Terms and Concepts

**1.** Define the following terms:

*rotation*          *all-interval series*

**2.** Identify the following rotated forms of the given series. Use the notation in Example 14-11, using order numbers to show the rotations. All are rotations of prime forms, but not necessarily of P0.

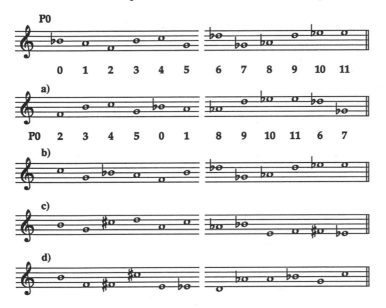

## Composition

Using the series in Terms and Concepts Exercise 2, compose a lyrical piece. Use the rotations given in that exercise, or others. P0 of this series is hexachordally combinatorial with I5.

# Suggestions for Further Study

**1.** Berg, *Lyric Suite*, first movement. The series orderings used in the first movement appear in Example 14-4. Study this movement. Concentrate on the types of harmonic structures we discussed at the opening of the movement (review Examples 14-5 and 14-6).

Elements reminiscent of tonality are common in this movement, especially as triads and diminished seventh chords. How do these tonal elements function in the piece?

What is the form of the movement?

**2.** Schoenberg, *Ode to Napoleon,* op. 41. This piece uses many orderings of the hexachord [0,1,4,5,8,9]. P0, P4, P8, I1, I5, and I9 all give rise to the same pitch-classes in each hexachord. As a result, there are only four transpositions or inversions of this hexachord that differ in pitch content (twenty-four possible transpositions and inversions divided by six equivalent forms). Only eight pitch-class regions can be outlined by the two hexachords of this twelve-tone series.

Each hexachord of the series can be divided into six pairs of triads. These triads appear for much of the piece in the piano part. The prominence of E♭-major triads, especially in the later portions of the piece, is a reference to Beethoven's Symphony No. 3 in E♭-major (the *"Eroica"*), which also has associations with Napoleon.

**3.** Stravinsky, *Abraham and Isaac.* Review the opening passage in Example 14-12 and the series-forms in Example 14-11. Study the use of instrumentation and rhythm in this passage. For instance, the pitch-classes in the bassoon in m. 5 form the chord in m. 7, and five of the six pitch-classes in the clarinet in mm. 10–11 form the chord on the downbeat of m. 8. The septuplet and quintuplet help to call attention to these instrumental solos. Study these types of relationships in the remainder of the piece. Study the emergence of C♯ and F as focal pitches.

*Canticum Sacrum.* Review the discussion of the second movement in Examples 14-9 and 14-10. Complete an analysis of this movement by identifying all the series-forms and studying their interactions.

Study also the third movement. The series for this movement appears at the very opening. This series is used, usually in slower rhythmic values, as a bass line for much of the movement.

*Variations: Aldous Huxley in Memoriam.* Review the discussion of this piece in Examples 14-13 through 14-15. Study the twelve-part polyphony in mm. 23–33, 47–57, and 118–128. What series-forms are used? How are these three sections related? Then turn your attention to the contrapuntal sections in mm. 34–46, 59–71, 74–82, 86–95, and 104–117. How do the chordal passages in the piece relate to the chords that arise from rotation at the end (review Examples 14-14 and 14-15)?

Claudio Spies discusses serial techniques and other aspects of all these Stravinsky pieces in a number of articles reprinted in *Perspectives on*

*Schoenberg and Stravinsky*, edited by Benjamin Boretz and Edward T. Cone (New York: W. W. Norton & Co., 1972).

4. A number of articles and books explore additional aspects of twelve-tone music and the nature of the twelve-tone system. Among these are:

Milton Babbitt, "Some Aspects of Twelve-Tone Composition," in *The Score* (1955): 53–61; reprinted in *Twentieth Century Views of Music History* (New York: Scribner's, 1972), pp. 362–371.

——— "Series Structure as a Compositional Determinant," in *Journal of Music Theory* 5 (1961): 72–94; reprinted in *Perspectives on Contemporary Music Theory*, edited by Benjamin Boretz and Edward T. Cone (New York: W. W. Norton, 1972), pp. 129–147.

——— "Twelve-Tone Invariants as Compositional Determinants," in *Musical Quarterly* 46 (1960): 246–259; reprinted in *Problems of Modern Music* (New York: W. W. Norton, 1960), pp. 108–121.

Douglas Jarman, *The Music of Alban Berg* (Berkeley: University of California Press, 1978).

George Perle, *Serial Composition and Atonality* (Berkeley: University of California Press, in five editions since 1963).

Charles Wuorinen, *Simple Composition* (New York: Longman, 1979).

# 15
# Other Aspects of Serialism

---

*time-point system*          *rhythm series*
*nonretrogradable rhythm*    *dynamic series*

---

The preceding chapters in Unit Three deal with only one facet of serialism: pitch structure in twelve-tone music. Composers have also used serialism in other ways: series with fewer than twelve pitch-classes, and orderings of musical elements other than pitch, such as rhythm, dynamics, register, timbre, and articulation.

## Series with Fewer than Twelve Pitch-Classes

*In Schoenberg's Music.*    Schoenberg's first opus entirely twelve-tone in structure is the *Suite*, op. 25, completed in 1923. In the years immediately preceding completion of this work, Schoenberg composed a number of compositions using series with fewer than twelve pitch-classes. In some of these compositions, these serial elements combine with nonserial techniques, while other works are entirely serial.

A variety of compositional techniques may be found in the *Serenade*, op. 24, composed between 1920 and 1923. In its seven movements, this piece contains nonserial music, serial writing using a twelve-tone series, and serial writing with fewer than twelve pitch-classes. Many serial techniques that became important in later twelve-tone music by Schoenberg and others, such as hexachordal combinatoriality, rotation, and emphasizing common elements, appear here for the first time.

The third movement, for instance, is a set of variations, with the Theme based on a fourteen-note series containing only eleven pitch-classes. See Example 15-1, and review Example 5-8 (p. 73) for the unaccompanied

256

EXAMPLE 15-1

PO

I0

statement of this theme. The only series-forms that appear during the movement are P0, R0, I0, and RI0. P0 and R0 omit the pitch-class B, while I0 and RI0 omit the pitch-class A.

These four series-forms and the missing pitch-classes B and A account for all the pitches in the entire movement. The missing pitches arise repeatedly as pedal points on either B or A.

In our discussion of the opening theme of the variations (see pp. 73–76), we noted the prominence of B♭ as a focal pitch in the passage and the use of registral symmetry around B♭ in this theme. Such registral symmetries around a central pitch, either the B♭ that opens P0 and I0, or the missing B or A, are prominent throughout the movement.

The climax of these symmetries and emphases on B♭, B, and A occurs

EXAMPLE 15-2: Schoenberg, *Serenade*, op. 24, third movement

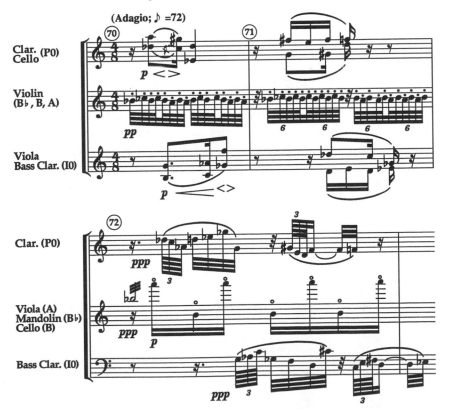

in the coda of the movement, a portion of which appears in Example 15-2. In mm. 70–71, the violin pattern combines B♭ with A and B in semitone alternations. Meanwhile, the cello / clarinet pairing presents P0 (without the opening B♭ that is already in the violin) and the viola / bass-clarinet pairing presents I0 (again without B♭). The violin's B♭ is the focal pitch for the measures.

In m. 72, B♭ appears in the mandolin tremolo, equidistant from the alternating A and B in harmonics. The clarinet and bass-clarinet state P0 and I0, this time without the first *two* pitch-classes that are in the tremolo or harmonics (B♭–A or B♭–B).

The magical result here and throughout the coda is a sense of fleeting activity around the shimmering pedal pitches, an effect enhanced by the special timbral blends (the rapid violin figure in mm. 70–71, the mandolin tremolo in m. 72, the antiphony betweeen viola and cello harmonics in m. 72) and the extremely soft dynamics.[1]

According to sketches for the *Serenade*, Schoenberg originally planned to use the fourteen-note series of the variations movement as the basis for all seven movements of the composition, but he never put this plan into effect. The first movement, a march, is based on an eight-measure phrase that recurs entirely inverted and, later, developed. As in the variations movement, registral symmetries around a central pitch are important in this movement.[2] The second movement, a minuet and trio, uses several different ordered segments along with nonserial elements.

The fourth movement, a setting of *Sonnet No. 217* by Petrarch in a German translation, is based on a twelve-tone series used only in its P0 form. The vocal part follows the ordering of the series strictly. Since there are only eleven syllables per line of verse, and the vocal setting is entirely syllabic, the result is a rotation of the series in each vocal phrase, as shown in Example 15-3. The instrumental parts also derive from the series in its P0 form, but with more freedom of ordering than in the vocal part. With only one series-form present in the entire movement, there are no elements in common between different series-forms to emphasize as in Schoenberg's later twelve-tone works. Instead, the presence of the series is treated as the cohesive element, and there is considerable variety in the way each series statement appears.

---

1. For an extensive discussion of this movement, see Joel Lester, "Pitch Structure Articulation in the Variations of Schoenberg's *Serenade*," in *Perspectives of New Music* 6 (1968): 22–34.

2. See David Lewin, "Inversional Balance as an Organizing Force in Schoenberg's Music and Thought," in *Perspectives of New Music* 6 (1968): 1–21, for a discussion of the symmetries in this movement.

EXAMPLE 15-3: Schoenberg, *Serenade*, op. 24, fourth movement

O könnt' ich je der Rach' an ihr ge-ne - sen, die mich durch

Blick und Re - de gleich zer-stö-ret, und dann zu

The fifth movement, a dance scene, alternates nonserial sections with sections built on unordered aggregates arising from a combinatorial hexachord. (See footnote 1 in Chapter 14 on p. 237.) The sixth movement, a song without words, is nonserial except for some rhythmically condensed reminiscences of earlier melodies.

The seventh movement is largely a literal return of the opening march, but the opening passage unites the entire *Serenade* by restating themes from the march, minuet, trio, and dance scene, many now based on the series from the variations movement. See Example 15-4 for both the original forms of these themes and their reappearance in the opening of the seventh movement, recast in the series of the variations movement.

EXAMPLE 15-4: Schoenberg, Themes from *Serenade*, op. 24

A similar combination of serial and nonserial techniques characterizes Schoenberg's preceding opus, the *Fünf Klavierstücke*, op. 23. The fifth piece, a waltz, is entirely twelve-tone, using P0 and R0. The other movements use a variety of ordered series, unordered series, and freer material. The first piece, for instance, uses three series: a twenty-one note series containing ten pitch-classes, a twenty-note series containing ten pitch-classes, and a thirteen-note series containing eight pitch-classes. These three series, which share a number of trichords among their adjacent pitches, participate in a contrapuntal texture at the beginning. In later sections of the piece these series combine with nonserial elements.

After he began composing twelve-tone music, Schoenberg occasionally returned to tonal music, completing some earlier compositions that had been abandoned, as well as new ones. But he did not again pursue nontonal composition with series of fewer than twelve pitch-classes.

*In Stravinsky's Music.* While Schoenberg and Stravinsky were both alive, many people believed the new-music world was divided into two antagonistic camps, the twelve-tone school and the neo-Classic school. But soon after Schoenberg's death in 1951, Stravinsky began writing serial compositions, and by the late 1950s was writing twelve-tone music. We have already discussed Stravinsky's individual manner of using twelve-tone series in Chapter 14. Here we will survey some of his pre-twelve-tone music that uses series with fewer than twelve pitch-classes.

These serial compositions of Stravinsky's retain many of the features of his neo-Classical music. The three-movement *Septet* (1953), for instance, is similar to a miniature Baroque suite: the second movement is a passacaglia, and the finale is a fugal gigue. All three movements center around the focal pitch-class A and share thematic materials.

The first movement is not serial. Like the nonserial Stravinsky works studied in Unit Two, it uses pitch-class sets in clearly defined pitch regions. The passacaglia, by contrast, is nearly entirely serial, based on a sixteen-note series using eight pitch-classes. It relates closely to the first movement because the first six notes of the series are identical with the important motive that opens the work (see Example 15-5). The third movement,

EXAMPLE 15-5: Stravinsky, Themes from *Septet*

**First movement:**

**Second movement:**

**Third movement:**

like many a Baroque gigue, offers a series of fugatos. The fugue subject itself is based on the series of the passacaglia.

Because the octachord that provides the pitch-classes for this series contains six instances of interval-class 5,7, transposition of the series by interval 5 or 7 maintains six pitch-classes as common elements:

EXAMPLE 15-6

solid noteheads indicate common pitch-classes

This allows the fugue-subject entries to be a fifth apart from one another, imparting a tonal aura to the fugatos, all the while maintaining a clear sense of pitch-class region because of the network of common pitch-classes. Example 15-7 illustrates the opening three statements of the fugue

EXAMPLE 15-7: Stravinsky, *Septet*, third movement

subject. Note that each part (first the viola, then the violin) continues to use the eight pitch-classes of its series-form in its countersubject. (Stravinsky himself notates the sets in the score, with each instrument's set appearing as a scale in the clef used in the score.)

As in many Baroque gigues, the second half of the movement (beginning at study number 40) uses the inversion of the fugue subject. It turns out that inversionally related series-forms can share up to seven of their eight pitch-classes, so similar pitch-class regions are outlined in the opening fugue and the inverted fugue.

EXAMPLE 15-8: Stravinsky, *Septet*

*In Messiaen's Music.* Some composers who have never written twelve-tone music have incorporated non-twelve-tone series into their compositions. One such composer is Messiaen, whose extensions of serialism into rhythm (to be discussed later in this chapter) were an important influence on many European composers after World War II.

In the middle section of the sixth movement of the *Quartet for the End of Time*, a sixteen-note series recurs numerous times through changing rhythmic patterns. See Example 15-9 for the pitch series in its first few presentations. The brackets below the music indicate the pitch series.

EXAMPLE 15-9: Messiaen, *Quartet for the End of Time*, sixth movement

In the first movement of the *Quartet,* he treats a series of twenty-nine chords in the piano part as an ordered series. This chord sequence recurs throughout the movement in changing rhythms. Meanwhile, the cello part repeats a series of five pitches, also in changing rhythms.

In contrast to other serial composers we have studied, Messiaen does not use series as a way of developing or relating groups of pitch-classes to one another. The recurrence of series with no changes in register over ever-changing rhythms reduces pitch action to a minimum and creates a static area or a static background within which there is only limited motion. These techniques help produce the hypnotic effect of the long expanses of time so characteristic of his music.

## Serialization of Rhythm

Several composers since the 1940s have serialized rhythm along the lines of serialized pitches, though in quite different ways. Some have used series of durations in music that is not twelve-tone and some have serialized durations in twelve-tone music, using series with twelve durations or with fewer or more durations. In the remainder of this section, we will discuss some principles of each of these approaches and some representative excerpts.

*Series of Durations in Messiaen's Music.* Messiaen transferred many pitch concepts to the rhythmic aspect of music. Much as he used recurring series of pitches, he used recurring rhythmic patterns, treating them as rhythmic ostinatos or pedals. In the first movement of his *Quartet,* for instance, the cello part uses a recurring series of fifteen durations. This pattern interacts with the five pitches in the repeating pitch series. Since three statements of the five-pitch series occur within each statement of the rhythm series, the original pitch-rhythm alignment begins anew every fifteen notes.

EXAMPLE 15-10

The piano part in this first movement features a series of seventeen durations to present its pitch series of twenty-nine chords:

EXAMPLE 15-11

With twenty-nine chords in the pitch-series and seventeen durations in the rhythm series, it would take 493 chords ($29 \times 17 = 493$) before the original alignment of pitch and rhythm patterns would recur. Since there are not that many chords in the movement, the combination of pitch and rhythm is ever-changing. The manner of construction is similar to isorhythm in fourteenth-century music, where a rhythmic series (called the *talea*) and a melody (called the *color*), each of different length, recur, giving rise to ever-changing interactions of pitches and rhythms.

The interaction in these situations gives rise to what might be described as the aural equivalent of a kaleidoscope. A number of pitch and rhythm elements continually recur, but only occasionally, if ever, in their original patterning. Limited pitch resources and a small number of durations in each series reinforce this effect. The cello part uses five pitches of a whole-tone scale. And most of the twenty-nine chords in the piano part belong to a small number of pitch-class sets. The series of fifteen durations in the cello contains only three different rhythmic values (eighth notes, dotted quarters, and half notes). Similarly, the series of seventeen durations in the piano part contains only five rhythmic values.

Larger aspects of structure in the first movement of the *Quartet* reinforce the kaleidoscopic quality of changing patterns within a larger static section. The violin part features irregularly spaced recurrences of two birdcall-like patterns and occasional other patterns. Only the clarinet melody is not based on changing patterns; yet it too contains only a limited number of recurring and only minimally developed motives.

The use of these rhythmic series in the first movement is closely related to the role of this movement in the entire *Quartet for the End of Time*. The *Quartet* is a long piece, running over fifty minutes for its eight movements. Several of the movements are extremely slow: the tempo of the fifth movement cello solo, for instance, is ♪ $= 44$, with the cello part containing many quarters and half notes; the tempo of the eighth movement violin solo is ♪ $= 36$, also with many long rhythmic values. Part of the function of the first movement is to slow down the listener's expectation of the rate at which change takes place in preparation for these and other slow sections. Messiaen accomplishes this via these patternings in the first movement. You might begin by hearing each chord change in the piano as a harmonic event, the cello line as an unfolding melody, or the violin entries as new events. But the recurring patterns soon cause you to realize that no new events are occurring. And you become attuned to the larger static aspects of the movement in preparation for the longer and slower music that follows.

*Nonretrogradable Rhythms.* Another type of rhythm common in Messiaen's music is what he calls nonretrogradable rhythms—rhythmic palindromes that are the same forwards and backwards and hence cannot produce a new rhythm in their retrograde form. In the sixth movement of the *Quartet*, you will find a series of rhythmic palindromes, each of different length because of added values. (See the brackets above the music in Example 15-9.)

*Rhythmic Series.* Some post–World War II composers extended to rhythm the serial principles underlying pitch structure in their works. One way they did this was by creating a rhythmic series in which the durations range in length from one to twelve units. (The unit may be of any duration.) Durations are counted from the attack of one note to the attack of the next. This series can then be treated like a twelve-tone series. For example, to "transpose" a rhythm series, add the number of transposition, subtracting twelve from any number over twelve. Consider a series in which the sixteenth note is one unit:

EXAMPLE 15-12

Transposition to P10 results in:

EXAMPLE 15-13

As in the case of pitch series, the result is a reordering or permutation of the elements of the series.

To invert a series, replace each number by its complement, and then transpose as necessary. I5 of the series given in Example 15-12 is:

EXAMPLE 15-14

Once again, a permutation of the original ordering is the result.

Pierre Boulez (born 1925), Karlheinz Stockhausen (born 1928), and others have used such rhythmic series in compositions written in the early 1950s. When the series-forms for the rhythm series differ from the series-forms of the pitch series, the result is an ever-changing interaction of pitch and rhythm.

Other composers have used rhythmic series with fewer than twelve durations in their twelve-tone music. At the beginning of Babbitt's *Composition for Four Instruments*, the durations are based on the four-unit series 1,4,3,2. The ordering of the series is the basis for the note-to-note durations: one unit, four units, three units, two units. And the series is the basis for choosing the unit of counting itself: the unit of counting at the beginning is a sixteenth note (*1*), then a quarter note (4 times a sixteenth), then a dotted eighth (3 times a sixteenth), and finally an eighth (2 times a sixteenth). See Example 15-15. (See the score to this passage on p. 233.) Later sections of the piece use different orderings of this rhythm series, subdivisions of units, and different units of counting.

EXAMPLE 15-15

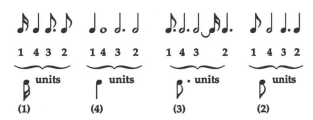

Other works of Babbitt's treat rhythmic series in a different way. In the *Semi-Simple Variations* (1956), for instance, the rhythmic series derives from the sixteen different ways that a quarter note can be filled by sixteenths:

| | |
|---|---|
| no sixteenth notes | 1 possibility |
| a single sixteenth on beat-subdivisions | |
|     1, 2, 3, or 4 | 4 possibilities |
| two sixteenths on beat-subdivisions 1–2, | |
|     1–3, 1–4, 2–3, 2–4, or 3–4 | 6 possibilities |
| three sixteenths on beat-subdivisions 1–2–3, | |
|     1–2–4, 1–3–4, or 2–3–4 | 4 possibilities |
| all four sixteenths | 1 possibility |
|         TOTAL . . . . . . . . . . . . . . . . . . . . . . . . . . . | 16 possibilities |

Babbitt combines these sixteen possibilities into the following rhythm series:

EXAMPLE 15-16

This series determines the *attack point* of all notes—exactly when they begin. But the actual length of notes varies from a single sixteenth to sustained values.

The Theme, which is sixteen beats long, presents this series. In Variation 1 the durational pattern of the Theme is reversed. In Variation 2, the rhythmic series appears *inverted*, which Babbitt defines to mean the replacement of the attack of a note by a rest. Thus the first beat, which has four sixteenths in the prime form of the series, has none in the inverted form. The second beat of the prime has attacks on subdivisions 1 and 2; so in the inversion it has rests on 1 and 2 and attacks on 3 and 4, and so forth.[3]

The result is a diversity of rhythm within a clear set of options. Since the entire set of variations uses only sixteenth-note divisions of a quarter-note beat, the same sixteen beat-possibilities keep recurring in ever-changing orderings. This is analogous to the pitch structuring of Babbitt's music, with its ever-changing pitch patternings forming aggregates.

***The Time-Point System.*** A different manner of working with a rhythmic series, called the *time-point system*, was devised by Milton Babbitt and first described in print in 1962. Instead of measuring durations, the rhythmic series determines the placement of the beginnings of notes in recurring series of twelve units. Thus, the time-point system attempts an approximation of meter and metric placement. If the sixteenth note is the unit of counting in a $\frac{3}{4}$ measure, time points in the measure are those shown in Example 15-17.

EXAMPLE 15-17

The series from Example 15-12 results in the following durations in the time-point system:

EXAMPLE 15-18

---

3. See "Milton Babbitt's *Semi-Simple Variations*," by Christopher Wintle, in *Perspectives of New Music* 14 / 1 (1976), for a more comprehensive survey of the rhythms and pitches of this piece.

Transpositions and inversions are arranged as explained above. Possible modifications during the course of a piece include changes in the unit of counting in addition to straightforward serial procedures.

As is obvious from a comparison of the same rhythmic series in Examples 15-12 and 15-18, use of the time-point system results in a very different structuring of rhythm than that which arises from use of a series of durations. "Interval" sizes (the difference between time-point numbers) are retained in the time-point system as equal durations between pitches; not so with series of durations. Review the instances of "interval 1" between successive numbers of the series in Example 15-12, 15-13, 15-17, and 15-18. In the time-point system, "interval 1" always results in attacks separated by one unit of counting. The size of identical "intervals" also remains the same even in different series-forms. Thus, common elements between series-forms arise, just as they do in pitch series. By contrast, in the series of durations, instances of "interval 1" result in different durational patterns.[4]

## Serialization of Other Aspects

A number of European composers, including Stockhausen and Boulez in the 1950s, extended serialization to other aspects of music, creating series of twelve durations, twelve articulations, twelve instrumental combinations, twelve dynamics, and so forth. Music created by these means contains combinations of pitch, rhythm, articulation, register, and instrumentation in which recurrences of any easily audible pattern rarely if ever occur. Themes, motives, and musical forms in the traditional sense happen by coincidence, if at all. To many listeners, this music sounds indistinguishable from music produced by chance means. Indeed, some composers writing this type of music later turned to writing pieces in which chance plays a major role in the creation and/or performance of the composition.

Of a different nature is the use of articulation, timbre, instrumentation, and dynamics by composers such as Babbitt to help articulate aspects of the pitch structure. Listen again to the flute-violin duet from his *Composition for Four Instruments* on pp. 229 and 230, and review the discussion there.

The basic dynamics in the flute and violin are *ppp, p, mf* (occasionally *mp*), and *ff*. In every case, the dynamics are coordinated with the hexachordal and trichordal structures. One hexachord from each series-form

---

4. See Charles Wuorinen, *Simple Composition* (New York: Longman, 1979), Chapter 10, for a thorough discussion of the time-point system.

in each instrument uses the dynamics *ff* and *ppp*; the other hexachords use *p* and *mf* (or *mp*). Within each hexachord the dynamics alternate according to the [0,1,3] trichords. The flute's dynamics alternate with each note, as follows:

EXAMPLE 15-19

In the violin part, the dynamics alternate with each note when [0,1,3] occurs in scalar order. But when the ordering within the trichords changes, the dynamics proceed as if the original ordering were used: Within each aggregate formed by pairs of trichords in each instrument, notes with the same dynamics are tritone related, or, if they occur in two pairs of notes, they always form a [0,3,6,9] tetrachord (the diminished seventh chord).

EXAMPLE 15-20

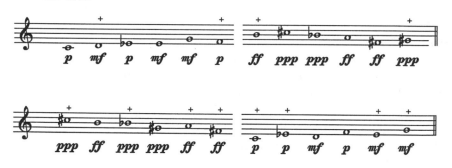

+ indicates violin pitches played pizzicato

The alternation of arco and pizzicato in the violin follows a pattern similar to that of the dynamics. As already discussed in Chapter 13, the arco and pizzicato notes bring out a different group of trichords than those on which this section is built (review Example 13-14 on p. 230).

These dynamics and articulations join the four pitch-series and the rhythmic structures to project the intricate four-part polyphony of this piece. Despite its formidable appearance, the music consists of simple and easily heard elements. The aggregates formed by so many combinations of elements gives a harmonic consistency to the whole and to its parts. Within these aggregates only two trichords, each in two orderings, provide the melodic connections on the local level. Rhythm, dynamics, articulation, timbre, and register support these pitch structures. This is music without melodic or harmonic patterns, phrases, and forms as they exist in earlier music. But it is music with its own coherence and creativity.

# Points for Review

**1.** Several composers, among them Messiaen, Schoenberg, and Stravinsky, have used ordered series with fewer than twelve pitch-classes.

**2.** There are different types of serialization of rhythm, including the use of series of durations in non-twelve-tone music, series of durations associated with twelve-tone series, and the *time-point system.*

**3.** Additional musical aspects, including dynamics, articulation, register, and instrumentation have been serialized in some compositions.

# Exercises for Chapter 15

**Terms and Concepts**

**1.** Define the following terms:

> *time-point system*        *rhythm series*
> *nonretrogradable rhythm*      *dynamic series*

**2.** Label each pitch in the following series. Then translate the pitch series into a rhythm series both as durations and in the time-point system, using a sixteenth-note as the unit of counting and $\frac{3}{4}$ as the notated meter. Write out the following forms of the series in both systems: P0, P6, I0, RI5. A preliminary exercise is completed for you.

**Duration set:**

P0: 12 11 7 8 3 1 2 10 6 5 4 9

P6: 6 5 1 2 9 7 8 4 12 11 10 3

I0: 12 1 5 4 9 11 10 2 6 7 8 3

RI5: 8 1 12 11 7 3 4 2 9 10 6 5

**Time-point system:**

P0: 0 11 7 8 3 1 2 10 6 5 4 9

P6: 6 5 1 2 9 7 8 4 0 11 10 3

I0: 0 1 5 4 9 11 10 2 6 7 8 3

RI5: 8 1 0 11 7 3 4 2 9 10 6 5

## Composition

Use the following ordered series as the basis for a short polyphonic composition. Use P, I, R, and/or RI forms.

# Suggestions for Further Study

**1.** Stravinsky, *Greeting Prelude* (1955). Stravinsky based this brief piece on *Happy Birthday*. Study the various uses of the phrases and the complete melody as a series. How do serial usages and other elements expand the pitch-field as the piece progresses?

*Septet* (1953). Review the discussion of this piece in the first section of this chapter. Study the different ways the series appears in the passacaglia movement. Study the third movement fugue, and the manner in which the pitch-class regions are defined by the uses of the series as an ordered entity and as a pitch-class set.

*In Memoriam Dylan Thomas* (1954). The five-pitch series given in the composition exercise is the basis of this piece. Study how series-forms are chosen so as to give rise to harmonies at the beginnings and endings of phrases.

**2.** Schoenberg, *Fünf Klavierstücke*, op. 23. In the first piece, study the three voices in the opening measures. What is the relationship between melodic and harmonic structures here? Then study the recurrence of these lines in later sections of the piece. What elements are serial, what elements are not? See George Perle, *Serial Composition and Atonality*, for a discussion of the opening passage. For a discussion of the use of these series later in this movement and in other movements of this opus, see John Graziano, "Serial Procedures in Schoenberg's Opus 23," in *Current Musicology* 13 (1972): 58–63.

*Serenade*, op. 24. Review the discussion earlier in this chapter concerning the first movement, the variations movement, the sonnet, and the dance scene. Study these movements.

**3.** For Milton Babbitt's own presentation of the time-point system, see his article, "Twelve-Tone Rhythmic Structure and the Electronic Medium," in *Perspectives of New Music* 1 (1962): 49–79, reprinted in *Perspectives on Contemporary Music Theory*, edited by Benjamin Boretz and Edward T. Cone (New York: W. W. Norton, 1972), pp. 148–179.

# Unit Four

---

# Since World War II

# 16
## More Recent Developments

*aleatory*          *minimalism*
*prepared piano*     *musique concrète*

## A Century of Change

Throughout the recorded history of Western music, musical styles and techniques have been changing continuously. When we survey these changes from a long-range perspective, it seems that changes in style and techniques in some historical periods have been gradual, while in other periods the pace of change has been more rapid and the extent greater. Thus we commonly divide the past into eras of relative stylistic stability and other periods of greater stylistic change.

But some of this attitude toward history is the result of taking a long-range view of musical styles. For musicians living in almost any historical period have viewed present and recent past as periods of flux. Musicians of, say, 1740, 1760, 1780, 1800, 1820, 1840, 1860, or 1880 would have had little trouble differentiating the music produced in their cultural milieu from that written twenty years earlier. And that musician would have recognized a considerable variety of styles in "contemporary music" composition, ranging from music written in older styles to the "newer" music, some evolving gradually from the music of the recent past, and some seeming to veer off in new and foreign directions. Only as an historical era fades into the past, as the full range of musical activity is forgotten, and as only the "historically significant" works of that era remain in the general consciousness—only then do we begin to formulate our conceptions of the musical activity of that era.

With this in mind, it is altogether understandable that twentieth-century musicians have viewed this century as a period of great changes in musical styles and techniques, and as a period in which entirely antithetical types of music coexist. For our century, and especially the recent decades, is an era in which the changes seem more extreme and the types of new music that coexist seem to differ more from one another than those of any other historical period. Nowadays, we can listen to performances of music from all recorded historical eras, and from many different cultures. Composers are writing music that is traditionally tonal, that is tonal in new senses of the term, that is freely nontonal, that is serial, or that falls into none of these categories. They are composing music in which traditional pitch differentiations may or may not be a significant aspect of structure, that uses traditional instruments in traditional ways or in new ways, or uses entirely new physical or electronic sound sources, and that is largely determined by the composer or in which significant compositional decisions about the piece are left to the performer.

In Units One, Two, and Three of this text we have introduced a number of analytic approaches designed to aid understanding, performing, and listening to music of the twentieth century. Most but not all of the musical excerpts studied were composed during the first half of the twentieth century. But the analytic approaches are equally applicable to more recent music. This chapter, the only one in this unit, surveys some representative compositions and musical styles of the past generation. The intent, as in Units One, Two, and Three, is neither to provide a complete historical survey nor to catalog all music composed during this period. Rather, it is to offer representative excerpts from a variety of types of recent music in order to explain the extent to which the analytic approaches introduced in this text are applicable to this music.

# Serial Music

*The Spread of Serial Music.*     Prior to World War II, twelve-tone music was associated almost exclusively with Schoenberg, Berg, Webern, and their circle. But during the two decades following the war, this method was adopted or adapted, at least temporarily, by composers as diverse as Babbitt, Boulez, Copland, George Rochberg (born 1918), Roger Sessions (1896–1985), Stockhausen, and Stravinsky.

Several factors contributed to this situation. The dispersal of the members of the Viennese School, especially the emigration of Schoenberg and several disciples to the United States in the 1930s, spread his influence in a personal way. In addition, the end of World War II lifted the ban on the performance of all twelve-tone music in much of Europe. Especially important was the discovery of much of Webern's late music after its unavailability and suppression for several years prior to Webern's death in 1945. Another factor contributing to the spread of serial music was Stravinsky's adoption of serial techniques after 1953, thereby undercutting the consensus that his music and twelve-tone music were irreconcilable. That Stravinsky's serial music was still "Stravinskian" demonstrated to many other composers that writing serial music did not necessarily mean writing music like Schoenberg's, Berg's, or Webern's. In addition to these purely musical reasons, there may also have been the sense that World War II had marked the end of an historical, geopolitical, and technological era. A new musical language may have been seen as the new expression of that era.

*Schoenberg's and Webern's Influences.*   To serial composers immediately after World War II, there seemed to be a polarity between the twelve-tone music of Schoenberg and Berg, as opposed to the later works of Webern. Schoenberg had continued to write in traditional genres and forms. He wrote string quartets, concertos, themes and variations, suites, and so forth, using traditional notions of phrasing, and formal layouts such as binary and sonata form. Traditional textures (melody with accompaniment, imitative counterpoint, and so forth) and traditional conceptions of musical continuity (antecedent and consequent phrases, the differentiation of exposition and development of musical material) underlie his music. Review, for instance, our discussions of his String Quartet No. 4, op. 37, on pp. 191–96 and 211–14. Some composers, the American Roger Sessions among them, adopted this conception of serial music in their own twelve-tone music.

Others rejected this marriage of serial techniques to nonpitch aspects of tonal music. They viewed Webern's late works as pointing the way toward a new musical rhetoric more in line with the nature of twelve-tone technique.[1] Some aspects of Messiaen's music of the late 1940s, especially the use of series of durations and dynamics in *Mode de valeurs et d'intensités* (1949), were also a strong influence on many younger European composers, among them Boulez and Stockhausen.

In the 1950s, these composers extended serial procedures to several nonpitch aspects (such as duration, dynamics, mode of attacking a note, register, instrumentation, and tempo changes, as described in Chapter 15). The resulting musical surface in these compositions is often complex

---

1. For an historically influential presentation of this position, read Pierre Boulez's article, "Schönberg is Dead," in *The Score* 6 (May, 1952) pp. 18–22; reprinted in a slightly different form in Boulez's *Notes of an Apprenticeship* (New York: Knopf, 1968), pp. 268–276.

and rapidly changing with little sense of continuous texture, melodic continuity, or motivic statements and development as understood in earlier music. Stockhausen's *Kontra-Punkte* (1952–53) and Boulez's *Structures I* (1952) are representative compositions.[2]

Arriving at serialization of nonpitch aspects from a different direction, but around the same time, was Milton Babbitt. We have already discussed serialization of pitch and rhythm in his *Composition for Four Instruments* (1948) in Chapters 14 and 15, and surveyed the differences between his approaches to the serialization of rhythm and those of Boulez and Stockhausen.

*Serialism in Non-Twelve-Tone Music.* Other composers incorporated serial procedures in music that is not twelve-tone in structure. In Chapter 15, we discussed non-twelve-tone serial music by Schoenberg, Messiaen, and Stravinsky. In the case of Schoenberg and Stravinsky, their non-twelve-tone serial music was a stepping stone toward their adoption of twelve-tone music. But other composers have adopted serial techniques without ever turning to twelve-tone music.

*Peter Maxwell Davies,* **Ave maris stella** *(1975).* One such composer is the English Peter Maxwell Davies (born 1934), whose *Ave maris stella* is representative of a number of recent works in its eclectic mixture of strictly serial procedures alongside of nonserial procedures, the comfortable coexistence of tonal and nontonal features, and its evocation of a variety of historical musical influences ranging from the medieval era to different types of music of the twentieth century.

The work is scored for flute (doubling on alto flute), clarinet, viola, cello, piano, and marimba. It is cast in a single continuous movement consisting of nine sections. Indeed, the number nine permeates many structural aspects of the work. The pitches, for instance, arise from the following nine-pitch series:

EXAMPLE 16-1

In the first of the work's nine sections, the cello plays nine phrases. Each phrase is set off from the next by a brief rest, the only rests in the otherwise legato cello part. Each of these phrases presents a different rotation of the pitch series. Example 16-2 lists each rotation at the transpositional level at which it occurs in the cello solo. As shown in the

---

2. For an extensive analysis of Boulez's *Structures I,* see Györgi Ligeti's "Pierre Boulez, Decision and Automatism in *Structures Ia,*" in *Die Reihe* 4, translated by Leo Black (Bryn Mawr: Theodore Presser, 1960) pp. 36–62.

example, the rotations are from right to left: that is, the last pitch of one series-form becomes the first pitch of the next rotated series-form.

EXAMPLE 16-2

Rhythm is also fully serialized in the cello solo. A series of nine durations controls the rhythm of each phrase. Like the pitch series, the duration series also rotates in each of the nine phrases. But this rotation is from left to right, the opposite of the rotation in the pitch series: that is, the first duration of one series-form becomes the last duration in the next rotated series-form. Listen to Example 16-3, which illustrates the pitch and duration rotations during the first three cello phrases.

What is perhaps most remarkable here is how little the sound has in common with music of other composers who also serialize pitch and rhythm. This lyrically evocative music employs all of its serial procedures to create an apparent freedom of melodic invention and expression. In this sense the work is representative not only of Davies's music but also of works of other composers of the 1970s and 1980s who aim for open expression as much as structural cohesion. (Some works of Joseph Schwantner from the 1970s come to mind in this connection.) Much as Stravinsky's adoption of serial techniques demonstrated that serialism is a constructive technique, not a musical style, Davies' adoption of serialized rhythm illustrates the broad range of music that can be composed using this method.

EXAMPLE 16-3: Davies, *Ave Maris Stella*, mm. 1–15, cello part

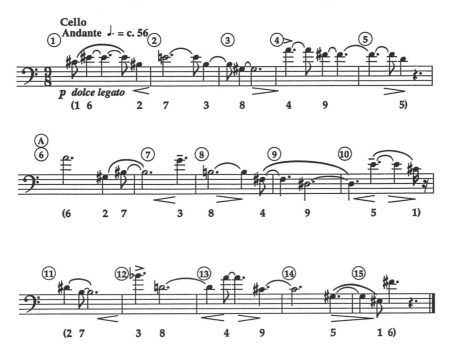

The numbers in parentheses below the staff show the number of eighth notes in each duration. The rests at the end of each phrase are part of the duration from the last note in the phrase to the first note in the next.

In *Ave maris stella*, the serial control of pitch and rhythm affects not only the expression of the opening cello melody but also the evolution during sections 1–5 of the piece from slower music at the opening to progressively faster and more complex music. The first section, of which the cello solo is the leading part, begins this process. The cello opens the piece entirely alone. During the first of the nine phrases, the marimba enters, resonating pitches in the cello solo. The alto flute enters, also during the first phrase, with freely derived fragments of the cello's pitch series. The durations are not strictly notated, left to be improvised by the flutist within an indicated time span.

In the fourth phrase, the viola joins, playing the entire nine-phrase pitch-rhythm complex of the cello part, but in retrograde and at a faster pace than the cello solo so that the end of the viola part coincides with the end of the cello solo. The counting unit of the duration series in the cello is the eighth note. In the viola part it is one quintuplet of a dotted quarter, allowing the faster unfolding of the nine phrases. Finally, the piano enters in the seventh phrase, structured like the viola, but at an even more rapid pace. The counting unit is the thirty-second note.

EXAMPLE 16-4

The result is growth of textural activity, an increase in rhythmic activity, and the accumulation of timbres over the entire section. Those aspects not controlled serially support this growth of activity. Register, for instance, expands throughout the section. In the cello solo, phrases grow from a range of thirteen semitones (barely more than a single octave) in the first mostly unaccompanied cello phrase to thirty-nine semitones (over three octaves) in the ninth phrase. The viola and piano parts, each based on the same pitch and duration series as the cello part, cover a wider range than the cello part in many phrases. And, of course, as new instruments enter, the total register of the ensemble expands. Example 16-4 on the facing page illustrates graphically the registral, rhythmic, and timbral shape of this first section of the composition.

The remaining eight sections of *Ave maris stella* also combine serial and nonserial aspects, always with flexible treatment of serial procedures to fit the needs of the section. The second section, for instance, continues the growth in activity begun in the first. The clarinet, the only instrument absent in section 1, carries the leading part in section 2.

The second section is about as long as the first, but since its tempo gradually speeds up, many more notes are needed to fill in the time. The serial techniques are arranged so as to provide these additional notes. The rhythmic series of the clarinet solo in section 2 is the same as that of the cello solo, and the viola and piano parts in section 1. But each successive duration in the series occurs an increasing number of times: the first duration occurs once, the second duration occurs twice, the third duration three times, the fourth four times, and so forth.

EXAMPLE 16-5

The second half of the clarinet solo repeats the duration series, but with the number of repetitions in reverse order: eight times, seven times, six times, and so forth. During some of the longer rhythmic values, the clarinet often adds short flourishes or rearticulates the pitch, further animating the rhythm.

The resulting repetitions of durations gives rise to easily perceived changes in meter. This is in contrast to the more leisurely $\frac{9}{8}$ measures maintained through section 1 (the cello solo). Increased dynamic levels (fortes and, in general, more rapid changes between dynamic levels), greater densities of texture and rhythmic activity, along with a gradual accelerando, all contribute to the accumulating drive of the section.

Pitches in the clarinet solo are also based on the series of section 1. But consecutive pitches in the clarinet solo derive from more than one series rotation. Example 16-6 illustrates the manner in which the repeated durations shown above complement the pitch structure.

EXAMPLE 16-6: Davies, *Ave Maris Stella*, section II, clarinet part

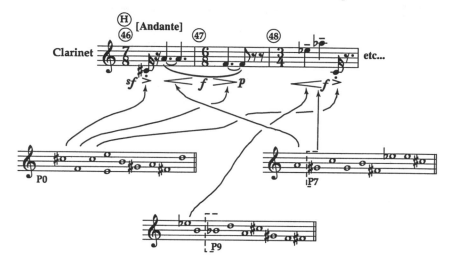

Compare rhythms with Example 16-5. Compare set-forms with Example 16-2.

The first duration (♪) presents the first pitch-class of the first phrase of the cello solo. The second duration (♩.), repeated twice, draws upon the first pitch from the second cello phrase and the second pitch from the first cello phrase. The third duration (♩) draws upon the first pitch of cello phrase 3, the second pitch of cello phrase 2, and the third pitch of cello phrase 1. The same process continues throughout section 2. If a repeated pitch-class would arise from this procedure, the repetition is omitted.

These manipulations are hardly audible as serial procedures. A listener could hardly follow the interaction of the different pitch and rhythm rotations during the cello solo, much less the more complex derivation of pitches during the clarinet solo. But the effects of these serial operations on levels of activity and on the expressive side of the music are clear.

Another feature that also depends on the series structure and its manipulations is the incorporation of tonal reminiscences amid all the nontonal aspects. The pitch series itself spells out two major triads: see the arpeggiation of E-major and D-major triads in mm. 2–5 of Example 16-3. Other triads arise during the later transposed rotations of the series.

Furthermore, the transpositions of the rotations are so arranged that several triads and other diatonic passages arise during the clarinet solo in section 2: for instance, the F-augmented and the A♭-major triad arpeggiations that open the clarinet solo (see Example 16-6).

*Ave maris stella,* then, features an eclectic combination of serial and free techniques, the adaptation of strict serial techniques to the expressive needs of the individual passages, and the free mix of atonal sounds with tonal reminiscences. These features, combined with Davies's strong dramatic sense, are characteristic of a body of music in which he explores new ways of working with elements from our diverse musical heritage.

# Freer Pitch Structures

*Athematic Musical Surfaces.* When we began our study of twelve-tone music in Unit Three, we took note of the way twelve-tone series in the music of Schoenberg, Berg, and Webern often provided a pitch-field within which motives are exposited and built upon in manners not different from the way they function in tonal music. But much of the post–World War II serial music discussed earlier—music by Babbitt, Stravinsky, Boulez, and Stockhausen—avoids such surface motives as prominent features. In this athematic music, musical aspects other than motivic structures are more important to the musical continuity. These aspects include the presentation of complete chromatic collections and of more limited pitch collections, timbre, texture, register, rhythm, and dynamics.

The same athematic surface appears in much nonserial music since the 1950s. Both Boulez and Stockhausen, for instance, ceased writing totally serialized music after the early 1950s. But their freer compositions of the next few years retained a similar athematic surface.

The American composer Elliott Carter has written a large body of music that is not serial in structure, but that often presents this type of athematic surface. In the liner notes to two of his compositions written thirteen years apart, the *Double Concerto for Harpsichord and Piano* (1961) and *Duo for Violin and Piano* (1974), Carter specifically rejects a thematic-motivic conception of music:

> The general form of both works on this record is quite different from that of the music I wrote up to 1950. While this earlier music was based on themes and their development, here the musical ideas are not themes or melodies but rather groupings of sound materials out of which textures, linear patterns, and figurations are invented . . . There is no repetition, but a constant invention of new things—some closely related to each other, others, remotely.[3]

3. Elliott Carter, liner notes from Nonesuch Records H71314 (1975).

Although much of Carter's music since the 1950s features a continual circulation of all twelve pitch-classes, he has not used twelve-tone series. In the absence of recurring themes or motives and the absence of a recurring series of pitches or pitch-classes, the pitch structure of pieces like the *Double Concerto* (1961) may sound somewhat improvisatory, imparting to nonpitch aspects (especially timbre and texture) more crucial roles than is the case in much earlier music.

A series of works entitled *Synchronisms* by the Argentinian-American composer Mario Davidovsky is representative of those works in which free pitch structurings gives rise to an athematic surface. In his music, the levels of activity and dramatic interaction among timbres are generally far more important than the intricacies of pitch interaction. The *Synchronisms* are composed for tape and various combinations of instruments or voices.

The *Synchronisms No. 2* (1964) is scored for flute, clarinet, violin, cello, and tape. We will discuss some of the timbral aspects of this work later in this chapter in connection with new timbres. At this point we will just take note of the freely structured pitch collections that exist within a twelve pitch-class field. During much of the piece, individual parts or entire textures feature collections of ten to twelve pitch-classes. But different patterns of recurring pitch-classes and different orderings of the pitch-classes in each segment create a sense of freedom and improvisation in the pitch domain. Example 16-7 illustrates some of these opening pitch collections. (See Example 16-11 for a score to the passage.) Arrows within some of the collections indicate repeated pitch-classes.

EXAMPLE 16-7

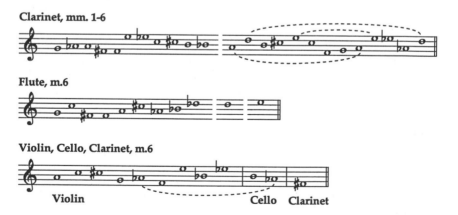

**Clarinet, mm. 1-6**

**Flute, m.6**

**Violin, Cello, Clarinet, m.6**

Violin               Cello   Clarinet

*Pitch Clusters.*     The works of a number of composers, mostly Europeans, from the late 1950s to the 1960s, explore a novel way of using pitches. In these works, clusters or bands of pitches are continually present; every semitone in every octave is played continuously. As a result, the very notion of pitch in these works becomes virtually indistinguishable from texture.

*Györgi Ligeti,* **Atmosphères.** *Atmosphères* (1961) by the Hungarian composer Györgi Ligeti (born 1923) is one such work. This composition was one of the widely varied scores used in Stanley Kubrick's movie *2001: A Space Odyssey.*

For much of the piece, large expanses of the usable pitch field are continually present, with all or virtually all semitones sounding simultaneously. The sustained opening sonority of the piece, for instance, contains every semitone listed between the limits shown in Example 16-8.

EXAMPLE 16-8

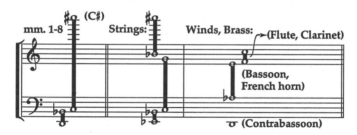

The solid vertical bars connecting pitches indicate clusters with all semitones present between the indicated pitches.

Some contrast and change occurs during the piece by reductions or expansions in the size of the pitch clusters. The pitch fields in mm. 9–13 and 14–18 are as follows:

EXAMPLE 16-9

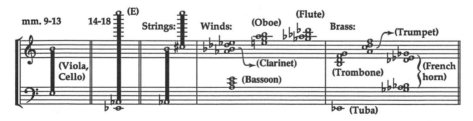

Greater variety and contrast arise from changes in the orchestration of the clusters, in their dynamics, and, later in the piece, by the presence of varying rhythmic patterns within the sustained sonorities. Mm. 9–13, for instance, feature a much smaller band of pitches than mm. 1–8. Only strings play here, in contrast with the mixed strings, woodwinds, and horns of mm. 1–8. Within the sustained pianississimo of these measures, swells to forte isolate groups of pitches in the order indicated below:

EXAMPLE 16-10

The change from each of these dyads to the next creates the impression of ascent and descent within the fixed pitches.

The sonority of mm. 14–18 is similar in scope to that of mm. 1–8 (compare Example 16-8 and 16-9). But the changed orchestration of the second sonority sets it off from the opening one. The various wind and brass choirs contain pitches of either the white notes or black notes on a keyboard. In mm. 17–20 the strings isolate first the seven white pitches, then the five black ones by dynamics (*ff* versus *pppp*), while various of the wind and brass choirs project their content by means of dynamics swells to *ff*. Similar processes operate for much of the piece.

Other compositions utilizing similar techniques contain additional features such as quarter tones, nonpitched sounds, and nontraditional instrumental techniques. One such work is *Threnody for the Victims of Hiroshima* (1960) for fifty-two separate string parts by the Polish composer Krzysztof Penderecki (born 1933).

# Timbre

In Chapter 3, we discussed new timbres as well as the increased role of this element as a determinant of musical structure in the twentieth century. Tone color continues to play an evermore prominent structural role in this music of the past generation. Where there are extremely complex pitch structures (whether the totally serialized music of Boulez and Babbitt or the freer structures of Carter and Davidovsky), timbral changes are more easily heard than pitch-structure nuances. Similarly, in music with little or no pitch structuring in the traditional sense (whether works like Varèse's *Ionisation* for a large percussion ensemble or Ligeti's *Atmosphères* with its persistent clusters filling in large areas of the pitch field) timbre necessarily takes on a prominent role.

*George Crumb,* **Eleven Echoes of Autumn, 1965 *(1966).*** Many compositions by the American George Crumb (born 1929) are innovative in the discovery and imaginative use of new timbral possibilities. His *Eleven Echoes of Autumn, 1965* is scored for alto flute, clarinet, violin, and piano. Each instrumental part includes traditional modes of playing as well as nontraditional performance techniques. The piano part includes harmonics (playing on the keys while placing a finger at a harmonic node on the string inside the piano), stopped notes (playing on the keys while damping strings inside the piano with the fingers), rubbing on the strings with a piece of hard rubber to produce high sustained harmonics, scraping on the strings with fingernails, glissandos over the strings, plucking the strings, and knocking on the soundboard to produce a resonant aftertone of vibrating strings. In addition, the piano strings and soundboard are allowed to resonate sympathetically to clarinet and alto flute sounds in Eco 8 as these two instruments are played directly into the piano while the dampers are raised.

The other instruments use a similar range of effects including toneless breathing sounds on the wind instruments, bowing behind the fingers on the fingerboard of the violin to produce frail sounds, holding the violin like a mandolin and playing tremolos with fingernails to produce a sound like a mandolin, and bowing with the hair on the bow completely loosened to produce a distant colorless tone. Finally, whistling and whispered syllables are part of the palette of colors.

These effects are not used haphazardly, but are carefully integrated into the overall structure of the piece. This is a structure that features an increase in many types of activity from Eco 1 to the climax in Eco 8 and a decrease in activity from Eco 8 through the end of Eco 11. Dynamics increase and decrease. The tempo speeds up and then slows down. Ensemble textures change in density from only one or two instruments at a time in the opening and closing sections to the entire ensemble in the middle sections, with uncoordinated ensemble playing in some interim sections. The pitch structures change from simple dyads and tetrachords at the opening and closing of the piece to increasingly complex and dense structures in the middle sections. The type of continuity changes from hesitant gestures at the beginning and end of the piece, often separated by long rests, to more continuous music in the middle sections of the piece. Finally, the overall registral spans open up from the beginning to the middle and then narrows toward the end. Eco 1 spans only an octave and a semitone and Eco 2 is largely within seven semitones. But the register in Eco 8, the climax of all the factors listed above, spans the entire seven-octave-plus-three-semitone range of the piano.

The special effects in all the instruments support the increase and decrease in activity over the entire piece. The piano, for instance, helps create the mood of the opening (Ecos 1 and 2) by playing only harmonics. The violin enters in Eco 2 playing only harmonics. The first entries of the winds, also in Eco 2 are breath tones, *ppppp*. But by Eco 8 all the stops are out. Winds and violin play high and very loud (*fff*, "shrill, screaming"). The piano begins Eco 8 by hitting *ffffz* an eight-note chord in the very bottom octave and allowing this sonority to resonate with the sustaining pedal depressed for the entire Eco.

Crumb's music is heavily symbolic, with quotations from the poetry of Federico García Lorca, with special notations, and with special programmatic implications for many of the innovative timbres. His frequent annotations suggest effects to the performers through the use of tempo markings and performance directions such as fantastico, languidamente, hauntingly, "wind music," nervously, "a distant mandolin," mournfully, cristallino, fuggevole, quasi meccanico, ghostly, hushed, "like the gentle rustling of wind," frailly, and plaintively. His score notation is highly individualistic, with unusual rhythmic values for beats ($\frac{1}{\flat}\cdot$) as the meter marking in Eco 3), broken staff systems, staffs shaped into circles, spatial notations, and the like. For *Eleven Echoes*, Crumb even suggests possible stage lightings, complementing the piece's sounding structure.

Crumb's works have been regarded by some as mere shows of sound effects. But as the discussion above indicates, the structure of these works is carefully planned. The instrumental effects play their roles, enhancing the overall effectiveness of the music.

***Nontraditional Timbres in the Works of Other Composers.*** Explorations of new timbral possibilities in recent years occur in many different types of composition. John Cage (born 1912), in works for prepared piano (piano with various items inserted on or between the strings to affect the tone) such as *Sonatas and Interludes* (1946–48); Penderecki, in fully notated orchestral works such as *Threnody for the Victims of Hiroshima* (1960); Harvey Sollberger (born 1938), in serial flute works such as *Riding the Wind* (1973–74) which feature a wide range of key clicks, buzz tones, whistle tones, breathing, pedal tones, simultaneous singing and playing, and so forth—all use a wide variety of new timbres.

***Electronic Music.*** Another timbral possibility developed in recent years is the electronic generation or alteration of sounds. By the present time, a large body of electronic music has been produced in a wide range of styles. There is twelve-tone music and totally serialized music that is realized by the composer on tape because of its complexity. There is *musique concrète*, manipulating pre-existent sounds (whether musical sounds or what have been traditionally considered nonmusical sounds), a well-known early example of which is Stockhausen's *Gesang der Jüng-linge* (1956), which utilizes a child's singing as the basis of the musical material. There is electronic music which uses a wide palette of timbres, and electronic music which uses only a limited range.

Since electronic compositions exist on tape, there is no need for scores. Scores, after all, are primarily for communication with performers. To the extent that electronic compositions use the chromatic octave, their pitch structures are analyzable by the techniques introduced in Units Two and Three of this text. To the extent that they use timbres, textures, dynamics, and rhythms, the analytic considerations introduced in Unit One of this text are applicable.

*Mario Davidovsky,* **Synchronisms No. 2.**     Finally, there is the category of compositions that add an electronically generated tape part to instrumental or vocal music. We have already noted a series of such works by Davidovsky entitled *Synchronisms*. These works pair a tape part with various solo instruments, or with an instrumental or vocal ensemble. We have already discussed some aspects of the freely non-tonal pitch structure of the *Synchronisms No. 2* (1964) for flute, clarinet, violin, cello, and tape (review Example 16-7). The instruments in this piece play in some passages without the tape part. Elsewhere, they play along with the tape part. And the tape part itself has occasional solos.

One of the remarkable timbral aspects of the work is the similarity between those passages in which the tape is present and those that are purely instrumental. The writing for instruments combines timbres so that the individual qualities of the instruments are deliberately masked. Listen to Example 16-11 on pp. 292–93.

The opening clarinet solo begins with a unison pizzicato attack on the violin; the resulting sound is that of a "pizzicato clarinet attack." The same timbre, a unison between clarinet and a pizzicato attack beginning a clarinet solo, recurs in mm. 9 (cello and clarinet) and 12 (violin and clarinet).

The end of the opening clarinet phrase (mm. 1–6) dissolves in mm. 5–6 into a rapidly descending passage played with a diminuendo. The flute and then the violin enter with fleeting passages, *ppp*, joined by two cello pizzicatos, all leading to the final clarinet note. It is out of short, extremely soft notes in mixed timbres in m. 7 (including *col legno* for some string notes) that the solo flute emerges to begin the next phrase. The change to clarinet (mm. 8–9) is covered by the violin figure in m. 8, the sudden but brief *ff* flutter in the flute, and the cello-pizzicato/clarinet unison (m. 9). Similarly mixed timbres, and rapid passages cutting across instrument changes appear during much of the opening.

EXAMPLE 16-11: Davidovsky, *Synchronisms No. 2*

= play as fast as possible
+ = key slap
V = short pause

**Pizz** = play behind the bridge
= play as high as possible

Similar timbral interactions occur during the first tape entry (mm. 42–61). Listen to mm. 41–50 in Example 16-12.

EXAMPLE 16-12: Davidovsky, *Synchronisms No. 2*

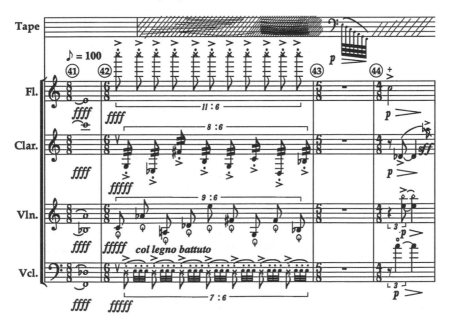

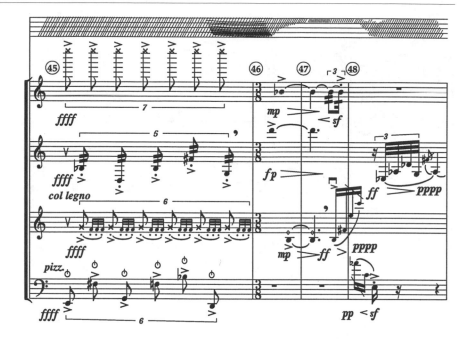

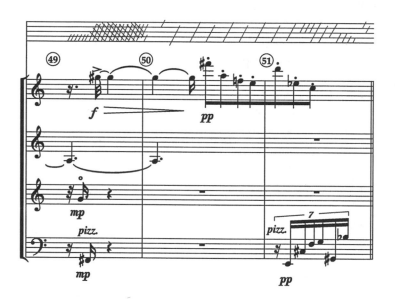

The uncoordinated, repeated loud attacks in the instruments in m. 42 cover the details of the emerging tape sound (much as the beginnings of the clarinet and flute solos at the opening of the piece are masked by other timbres). The tape descends pell-mell into the instrumental entry in m. 44 (much as the clarinet solo in mm. 1–5 ends by descending rapidly into the entry of the other instruments in m. 6).

The mixes of timbres out of which a single pure sound emerges are like the sleights of hand of a fine magician. As the ear is drawn to a prominent timbre (such as the violin pizzicato in m. 1) or to a rapid passage or series of passages (such as the interaction in m. 42, or mm. 47–48), another timbre enters to become the next feature. This imparts a sense of improvisatory freedom to the entire piece—a feature complemented by the free pitch structure discussed earlier. This improvisatory sense is all the more remarkable in that the tape part is, of course, fixed in every performance.

## Improvisatory and Aleatoric Music

The extraordinary complexity, for composers, performers, and listeners, of some post–World War II music led some musicians to conclude that the organized complexity of some pieces sounded as if the works had been created by chance. This awareness led some composers to explore whether they might leave minor or even major performance decisions to the performer. Other composers questioned the notion of only a single version of a musical composition. They pointed to earlier periods in music history in which performers were expected to improvise continuo parts, ornamentation, and cadenzas, and to many types of more popular contemporary music in which improvisation plays a major role.

The result is a wide range of recent music in which the traditional control by the composer over various aspects of the piece is relaxed. At one end of the spectrum are passages in which only a limited flexibility is allowed. Listen again to Davidovsky's *Synchronisms No. 2* (1964), in which a group of notes is to be played "as fast as possible" (see m. 6 in Example 16-11), in which the rhythms within a measure are not specified (see m. 7 in Example 16-11), or in which the coordination of the instruments and tape is specified only in a general way and will differ somewhat from one performance to another (see mm. 42ff in Example 16-12). Similarly, the precise interaction of instruments and the exact rhythms within instrumental parts are not specified in some passages from George Crumb's *Eleven Echoes* (1966). In Eco 5, for instance, the exact rhythms in the flute cadenza are not specified in the score. The violin-piano duet begins at a specific point during the flute cadenza, but the exact correspondence between this duet and the flute part is not specified, save that the duet must be completed by a certain point.

At the other end of the spectrum of improvisatory practices are pieces where the performer is granted great latitude in deciding what to play and when to play it. In Stockhausen's *Klavierstück XI* (1956), for instance, the score contains nineteen sections for piano to be played in any order, in any of six tempos, using any of six dynamics, and using any of six modes of attack for the notes. Whenever any section has been played three times, the piece comes to an end.

But even greater latitude is afforded the performer in those pieces that arose from the desire to eliminate the boundaries between art and non-art and between musical sounds and the sounds that are our everyday environment. The acknowledged father of this movement is John Cage, whose pieces include *4′ 33″* (1952), the title of which denotes the total length of the three movements during which any number of performers are to be silent, and *Imaginary Landscape No. 4* (1951), in which twelve radios are the only instruments. In the latter, the content depends entirely on the available radio programming at the location and time of the performance. In other works by Cage, the events (pitches, rhythms, instructions, and so forth) are determined by chance procedures such as rolls of the dice or are based on the ancient Chinese book of prophecy *I Ching*. The adjective aleatoric (derived from the Latin *alea* meaning dice) refers to such pieces.

***Analysis of Improvisatory or Aleatoric Music.*** To the extent that musical aspects are specified and remain constant from one performance to the next, improvisatory or aleatoric compositions are as analyzable as any fully notated pieces. But to the extent that an improvised or aleatoric piece differs at each performance, those features are beyond analysis as structural features of that piece. A single rendition can, of course, be studied. But that rendition may be no more than a single possibility. Another equally correct rendition might differ in many or virtually all perceptible features.

# Simplification of the Musical Language: Tonality, Minimalism

A trend away from excessive complexity and toward simplification is perceptible in many different musical styles since the 1960s. One manifestation of this trend is the presence of features associated with tonal music: diatonic pitch collections, tonal harmonies, and even the establishment of a tonic by traditional tonal means. Another manifestation of this trend is in so-called minimalist pieces, wherein a small musical fragment is repeated at great length.

***Return to Tonality.*** Some composers, among them the Americans George Rochberg and David Del Tredici (born 1937), have returned to writing in a distinctly tonal style. Others have incorporated tonal elements into their own style of music. Crumb, for instance, often cites passages from tonal pieces (among them quotes from J. S. Bach and

Mahler in *Ancient Voices of Children* [1970]) and composed passages reminiscent of keys (such as the closing pages of *Vox Balaenae* [1971]).

*Minimalism.* Another manifestation of simplification is in the minimalist music of Philip Glass (born 1937), Steve Reich (born 1936), and others. Patterns are repeated numerous times with no change or with only very gradual and slight changes over many repetitions. Building from such small blocks, Glass and Reich have composed pieces of considerable length, some lasting many hours. Prominent in many of Glass's compositions are triads, seventh chords, and other configurations common in tonal music. The patterns used as building blocks are often intricate and constructed so as to allow for different interpretations. Rhythms are generally quite active and reminiscent of rock music in their persistently exaggerated accentuation of every beat. A primary aspect of this music is the creation of hypnotic effects simply by means of multiple repetitions.

Many of Steve Reich's compositions have a fairly large prime number of beats in repeated groups. His *Music for Four Organs* (1970), for instance, has repeated sections of eleven beats at the beginning. The eleven beats are subdivided in several different ways during the opening portions of the piece. Similarly irregular large groupings characterize his *Music for Mallet Instruments, Voices, and Organ* (1973) and *Drumming* (1971). The polarity of the uneven grouping and the persistent texture is part of what creates the hypnotic dynamic of these compositions.

*In Other Styles.* Even in the music of composers who have continued to write serial music or music with few aspects reminiscent of tonality, there has been a marked simplification of style in recent years. More traditionally lyrical lines, more easily perceptible motivic patterns, and simpler rhythmic and metric structures are characteristic of much of this music.

# A Codetta

This completes our brief survey of some of the major stylistic trends in music of the past generation or so. The purpose of this book has been to present analytic approaches useful in studying the construction, aural effects, and expressive designs of many types of music that have been written since the dissolution of tonality in the years around the turn of the twentieth century. In model analyses, some suggestions about the application of these analytic tools have been offered. But the analytic discussions of individual excerpts generally concentrate on one or only a few aspects of a given passage—mostly on the aspects being discussed theoretically at that point in the text. Each of the compositions discussed in this book merits more intensive scrutiny. To study these pieces and the world of twentieth-century repertoire in general is to study the music by which composers of our time have communicated to us. With the analytic tools provided in this text, and with the suggestions for further study appended to many chapters, you can proceed to explore the frontiers of musical creation.

## Points for Review

The past few decades have seen the creation of music in an exceptionally broad range of styles and techniques: serial techniques have been adopted and adapted, at least temporarily, by many composers, freer pitch structures, the use of bands of pitches as textural elements, new dimensions in timbres in music for traditional instruments as well as electronic ones, the incorporation of improvisatory and aleatoric concepts, and new attempts at simplification (via return to tonality, minimalism, and within other techniques) all coexist in the new-music world.

## Exercises for Chapter 16

Since it is hard to predict the availability of scores and recordings of recent music in any given music library, there are no Analysis Exercises for this chapter. Any of the pieces mentioned or discussed here, or any other recent music, can serve as a springboard for the exploration of recent music.

# *Appendix*

## Combinatorial Hexachords

Chapter 12 discusses hexachordal combinatoriality. The focus of the discussion there concerns recognizing combinatorial series in musical passages that you are analyzing, and understanding the effects of combinatoriality on that musical passage.

In Chapter 12, we do not discuss how to recognize whether or not a series is combinatorial and at what transposition(s) and inversion(s) it may be combinatorial. That is the focus of this Appendix.

The factor that determines if a series can be combinatorial with a P or I form is the content of the hexachords in the series. Of the fifty different hexachords that exist, twenty are hexachordally combinatorial with a P or I form. Example A-1 lists these twenty types of hexachords that can be combinatorial with a P or I form. Each hexachord is in its lowest ordering. The series-form(s) listed with each is/are combinatorial. (The transposition number of the P or I form holds only if the hexachord begins with the first pitch of the lowest order. See the discussion below to figure out the transposition number if this is not the case.)

EXAMPLE A-1

*a)* Hexachord that is combinatorial with one P form.

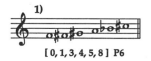

*b)* Hexachords that are combinatorial with an I form at *one* level of transposition.

[ 0,1,4,5,6,8 ] I3    [ 0,1,2,5,7,8 ] I11    [ 0,2,3,4,6,8 ] I1    [ 0,1,2,4,6,8 ] I11

[ 0,1,3,4,6,9 ] I11    [ 0,1,3,5,8,9 ] I7    [ 0,2,3,5,7,9 ] I1    [ 0,1,3,5,7,9 ] I11

*c)* Hexachords that are combinatorial with a P and an I form at *one* level of transposition.

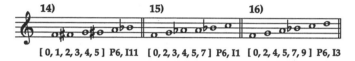

[ 0,1,2,3,4,5 ] P6, I11    [ 0,2,3,4,5,7 ] P6, I1    [ 0,2,4,5,7,9 ] P6, I3

*d)* Hexachord that is combinatorial with an I form at *two* levels of transposition.

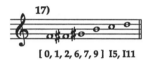

[ 0,1,2,6,7,9 ] I5, I11

*e)* Hexachord that is combinatorial with a P and an I form at *two* levels of transposition each.

[ 0,1,2,6,7,8 ] P3, P9, I5, I11

*f)* Hexachord that is combinatorial with a P form and an I form at *three* levels of transposition each.

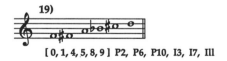

[ 0,1,4,5,8,9 ] P2, P6, P10, I3, I7, I11

*g)* Hexachord that is combinatorial with a P and an I form at *six* levels of transposition each.

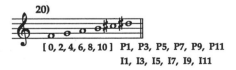

[ 0,2,4,6,8,10 ] P1, P3, P5, P7, P9, P11
I1, I3, I5, I7, I9, I11

***How to Figure Out If a Series Is Combinatorial.*** When you have identified a series or constructed a series, follow these steps to determine if that series is hexachordally combinatorial, and, if so, with what series-form(s).

*Step 1: Write out the first hexachord of the series.*

EXAMPLE A-2

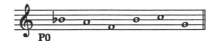

PO

*Step 2: Then rewrite the hexachord in lowest order. But do not invert or transpose it. Mark with an asterisk the note that is the first pitch-class in your original hexachord.*

EXAMPLE A-3

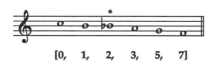

[0,   1,   2,   3,   5,   7]

*Step 3: Check the list of combinatorial hexachords in Example A-1. If the hexachord is not in that example, the series is not combinatorial. If the hexachord is in that example, write out the combinatorial form(s) of the hexachord.* NOTE: *If the result in step 2 is an inversion of the lowest order, the combinatorial form(s) of inversions is/are the complement of the series-form(s) in Example A-1. Since the result in step 2 here is an inversion, the combinatorial hexachord for this series is I1, not I11.*

EXAMPLE A-4

I1

*Step 4: Locate the first pitch from the original hexachord in the lowest order in Step 2. See the asterisk in Example A-3. Calculate the interval from the first pitch in the original hexachord up to the corresponding order number in the combinatorial hexachord. In the series we are using, B♭, the first pitch in the original hexachord, is the third pitch in the lowest order. E♭ is the third pitch in the combinatorial hexachord in Step 3. B♭ up to E♭ is interval 5. Hence, the combinatorial form of this series is I5.*

EXAMPLE A-5

I5

# Glossary of Foreign Terms

All foreign terms occurring in examples and exercises concerning performance directions are included here, except for literal cognates of English words (such as *in* or *tempo*). The abbreviation in the middle column identifies the language: *Fr.* for French, *Ger.* for German, *It.* for Italian.

| | | | | | |
|---|---|---|---|---|---|
| A | *Fr.* | By | Diminuendo, dimin., dim. | *It.* | Getting softer |
| A | *It.* | At | Distinto | *It.* | Distinct |
| Adagio | *It.* | Slow | Dolce | *It.* | Sweet, soft |
| Agitato | *It.* | Agitated | Doucement | *Fr.* | Sweetly |
| Allegretto | *It.* | Slower than allegro | Doux | *Fr.* | Sweet |
| Allegro | *It.* | Fast | Drängend | *Ger.* | Pushing forward |
| Als | *Ger.* | As, than | Du | *Fr.* | Of the |
| Am | *Ger.* | At the | Energico | *It.* | Energetically |
| Andante | *It.* | Moderately slow | Entrée | *Fr.* | Entrance |
| Andantino, And° | *It.* | Faster than andante | Environ, env. | *Fr.* | About |
| Animez | *Fr.* | Speed up | Ergänzend | *Ger.* | Complementing |
| Arco | *It.* | Bowed | Espressivo, espr. | *It.* | Expressive |
| Assai | *It.* | Very | Et | *Fr., It.* | And |
| Au | *Fr.* | At | Etwas | *Ger.* | Somewhat |
| Augmentez | *Fr.* | Slow down | Expressif | *Fr.* | Expressive |
| Äusserst | *Ger.* | Extremely | Extatique | *Fr.* | Ecstatic |
| Battuto | *It.* | Hit | Extrêmement | *Fr.* | Extremely |
| Ben | *It.* | Well | Fliessender | *Ger.* | More flowing |
| Breve | *It.* | Brief | Flüchtig | *Ger.* | Fleeting |
| Brume | *Fr.* | Haze, mist | Ganzen | *Ger.* | Whole, entire |
| Calando | *It.* | Slowing and getting softer | Gioviale | *It.* | Jovial |
| | | | Glissando | *It.* | Sliding |
| Calme | *Fr.* | Calmness | Granitique | *Fr.* | Like granite |
| Cantabile | *It.* | Lyrical, singing | Grazioso | *It.* | Graceful |
| Col | *It.* | With the | H (Haupstimme) | *Ger.* | Principal voice |
| Con | *It.* | With | Immer | *Ger.* | Always |
| Crescendo, cresc. | *It.* | Getting louder | Infiniment | *Fr.* | Infinitely |
| | | | Jusque'à | *Fr.* | Until |
| Dämpfer | *Ger.* | Mute | La | *Fr.* | The |
| Dans | *Fr.* | In | Langsam | *Ger.* | Slow |
| De | *Fr.* | Of | Lebhaft | *Ger.* | Lively |
| Décidé | *Fr.* | Resolute | Legato | *It.* | Smooth |
| Decrescendo, decresc. | *It.* | Getting softer | Legno | *It.* | Wood of the bow |
| | | | Lent | *Fr.* | Slow |
| Den | *Ger.* | The | Lenteur | *Fr.* | Getting slower |
| Détaché | *Fr.* | Detached | Lento | *It.* | Slow |
| Die | *Ger.* | The | Lointain | *Fr.* | Distant |

302

| | | | | | | |
|---|---|---|---|---|---|---|
| Ma | *It.* | But | | Ruhig | *Ger.* | Calm |
| Majestueux | *Fr.* | Majestic | | Sans | *Fr.* | Without |
| Marcato, marc. | *It.* | Marked, separated | | Satz | *Ger.* | Movement |
| Marqué | *Fr.* | Marked, separated | | Schmachtend | *Ger.* | Yearning |
| Mässig | *Ger.* | Moderate in tempo | | Schnell | *Ger.* | Fast |
| Meno | *It.* | Less | | Sehr | *Ger.* | Very |
| Misterioso | *It.* | Mysteriously | | Semplice | *It.* | Simply |
| Mit | *Ger.* | With | | Sempre | *It.* | Always |
| Moderato | *It.* | Moderate in tempo | | Simile | *It.* | Similarly |
| Modéré | *Fr.* | Moderate in tempo | | So | *Ger.* | As |
| Möglich | *Ger.* | Possible | | Sonore | *Fr.* | Resonant |
| Molto | *It.* | Very | | Sortant | *Fr.* | Coming out |
| Moto | *It.* | Motion | | Souple | *Fr.* | Supple |
| Mouvement, mouvᵗ | *Fr.* | Tempo | | Sourdine | *Fr.* | Mute |
| Munter | *Ger.* | Cheerful | | Soutenu | *Fr.* | Sustained |
| N⁻ (Nebenstimme) | *Ger.* | Subsidiary voice | | Steg | *Ger.* | Bridge |
| Non | *It.* | Not | | Straff | *Ger.* | Tense |
| Normale | *It.* | Normally | | Subito, sub. | *It.* | Sudden |
| Paradisiaque | *Fr.* | Resembling paradise | | Sul | *It.* | On the |
| Pesante | *It.* | Heavy | | Tempo giusto | *It.* | Moderate or strict |
| Peu | *Fr.* | Little | | | | |
| Più | *It.* | More | | Tendre | *Fr.* | Tender |
| Pizz. | *It.* | Pizzicato | | Tranquillo | *It.* | Tranquil |
| Poco | *It.* | Little | | Très | *Fr.* | Very |
| Ponticello | *It.* | Bridge | | Troppo | *It.* | Too much |
| Presser | *Fr.* | Speeding up | | Une, un | *Fr.* | One, a |
| Profundément | *Fr.* | Profoundly | | Und | *Ger.* | And |
| Progressivement | *Fr.* | Gradually | | Verklingend | *Ger.* | Fading away |
| Punta | *It.* | Point of the bow | | Vivace | *It.* | Fast |
| Rallentando, rall. | *It.* | Slowing down | | Vif | *Fr.* | Lively |
| Rasch | *Ger.* | Fast | | Vigoureux | *Fr.* | Vigorously |
| Recueilli | *Fr.* | Contemplative | | Wieder | *Ger.* | Again |
| Ritardando, ritard., rit. | *It.* | Slowing down | | Zart | *Ger.* | Tender |
| Rubato | *It.* | Freedom of tempo | | Zögernd | *Ger.* | Hesitant |

# Index

Page numbers in boldface indicate musical examples. Other references to musical compositions indicate discussions of those works apart from the immediate discussion of the indicated examples.

added value   18–21, 31
aggregate   183, 184, 236
  defined   178–80
aleatoric music   295–96
all-interval series   233, 239
all-interval tetrachord   105, 166
ameter   24–27, 31
Antokoletz, Elliott
  *The Music of Béla Bartók*   143, 172
arch form   57–58
athematic music   285–88

Babbitt, Milton
  *Composition for Four Instruments*   **26,**
    32, 54, 62, 63, **79, 228–32, 233,** 234,
    267, 269–71
  and form   62
  *Semi-Simple Variations*   234, 267–68
  and serialized rhythm   267–69
  "Series Structure as a Compositional
    Determinant"   255
  "Some Aspects of Twelve-Tone
    Composition"   255
  style   228–32, 269–71
  "Twelve-Tone Invariants as Composi-
    tional Determinants"   255
  and twelve-tone music   277, 285
  "Twelve-Tone Rhythmic Structure
    and the Electronic Medium"   273
Bach, J. S.
  *Invention in C major*   **3, 8,** 10
Barkin, Elaine
  "A Simple Approach to Babbitt's
    *Semi-Simple Variations*"   234
Bartók, Béla
  *Arabian Dance*   **158**
  *Concerto for Orchestra*   **128–31,** 138, 149
  *Contrasts*   **21,** 24
  *Diminished Fifth*   32, 54, 63, **112, 116,**
    131–32, **136,** 146, 157, 163, 239
  and form   57–59, 127–31
  *Music for Strings, Percussion, and
    Celesta*   **30, 48–50,** 58, 64, **67, 78,** 143
  String Quartet No. 1   14
  String Quartet No. 2   14, **59–60**
  String Quartet No. 3   32, 54, 63, **154–
    56,** 170
  String Quartet No. 4   57–58, 64, 143
  String Quartet No. 5   57–58
Beethoven, Ludwig van
  Piano Sonata, op. 31, no. 1   **18**
  Piano Trio, op. 70, no. 1   **20**

Symphony No. 3, op. 55   **51,** 254
Symphony No. 5, op. 67   **29,** 47
Violin Concerto, op. 61   47
Berg, Alban
  *Lyric Suite*   **30, 238–42,** 253–54
  and twelve-tone music   183, 235,
    237–41
  *Violin Concerto*   237
Berger, Arthur
  "Problems of Pitch Organization in
    Stravinsky"   171
Berry, Wallace
  *Structural Functions in Music*   55
Bogen form   57
Boulez, Pierre
  "*Schönberg is Dead*"   278
  and serialism   266, 269, 277–79, 285,
    288
  *Structures I*   279
Brahms, Johannes
  *Intermezzo*, op. 119, no. 2   **23**
Burkhart, Charles
  "The Symmetrical Source of Webern's
    Opus 5, No. 4"   144

Cage, John
  *Imaginary Landscape No. 4*   296
  *Sonatas and Interludes*   290
Carter, Elliott
  *Double Concerto*   285–86
  *Duo for Violin and Piano*   285–86
  *Sonata for Cello and Piano*   **25**
combinatoriality   209–18
  hexachordal   209–18, 299–301
  tetrachordal   220, 223–24
  trichordal   220–22, 228–31
common elements, defined   189–90,
  203
complement   69, 76
  and set-inversion   83–84
Cone, Edward T.
  "Stravinsky: The Progress of a
    Method"   171
continuous variation   60
Copland, Aaron
  *Appalachian Spring*   **152–53**
  and twelve-tone music   277
Crumb, George
  *Ancient Voices of Children*   51, 297
  *Black Angels*   50, 54
  *Eleven Echoes of Autumn*   51, 145, 289–
    90, 295
  *Vox Balanae*   297

Davidovsky, Mario
  *Synchronisms No. 2* **27,** 286–87, **292–94,** 295
Davies, Peter Maxwell
  *Ave Maris Stella* **279–84**
Debussy, Claude
  and form 61
  *Images* 170
  *Jeux* 14
  *La Mer* 14, **32, 41–42,** 54, 61, 63, **118–21,** 131–32, 147, 148
  *Preludes for Piano* 14, 144
  *Rêverie* 14
  String Quartet 14
  *The Sunken Cathedral* **82, 83,** 104–5, 116–17, 131–32, 145, 148
  *Voiles* 159, 170
del Tredici, David
  and tonality 296
derived series 219–34
diatonic scale
  altered 157–58
  as a region 147–58, 159–61, 164, 166–68, 170
  as a set 116–21, 126
dynamics
  and form 163
  serialized 269–71

Fibonacci series 143
fixed-0 notation 67, 76
form 56–64
  and tonality 34–37
  (see also phrasing, rondo, sonata form, theme and variations)
Forte, Allen
  *The Structure of Atonal Music* 107

Gauldin, Robert
  "Webern's *Concerto,* op. 24" 234
Glass, Philip
  and minimalism 297
Graziano, John
  "Serial Procedures in Schoenberg's Opus 23" 273

heptachord, defined 81
hexachord, defined 81
homophony 33

improvisation 295–96
interval 68–71
  ascending and descending 72–73
  calculating size of 69, 76
  inversion of 69, 76
  number in a set 97–98
  in rhythm series 266–69
  (see also interval-class, interval content, complement)
interval-class 72–73, 76
  (see also interval content)
interval content 97–105
  calculating 97–99

defined 97, 105
  and set inversion 113–14, 134
  and set transposition 110–13, 134
inversion
  and interval content 100–1, 113–14, 134
  of pitch-class sets 83–84, 87, 90, 113–14, 134
  of rhythm series 266–69
  of twelve-tone series 176, 184
Ives, Charles
  *The Unanswered Question* 40, 64, 170

Jarman, Douglas
  *The Music of Alban Berg* 255

Klangfarbenmelodie 53, 104, 234, 248

Lester, Joel
  "Pitch Structure Articulation in . . . Schoenberg's *Serenade*" 258
Lewin, David
  "Inversional Balance . . . in Schoenberg's Musical Thought" 258
Ligeti, Györgi
  *Atmosphères* **287–88**
  "Pierre Boulez . . . *Structures Ia*" 279
lowest ordering
  calculation of 85–87
  defined 84–85, 90

Mahler, Gustav
  *Kindertotenlieder* **45–46**
  Symphony No. 4 **52**
Messiaen, Olivier
  and form 61
  *Quartet for the End of Time* **19,** 20, **22,** 23, 24, 32, 40, 54, 61, 63, **80, 83, 159, 164–65,** 171, **263,** 264–66
  and serialized rhythm 264–66, 278
  *The Technique of My Musical Language* 24, 172
meter 16–32
  irregular 18–22
  in nontonal music 18–29
  and notation 23–24, 202
  in tonal music 16–18
metric modulation 24
minimalism 296–97
Moldenhauer, Hans and Rosaleen
  *Anton Webern* 228
monophony 33
motives
  and form 58–60
  in nontonal music 10–11
  rhythmic 29–31
  in tonal music 7–9
movable-0 notation 67, 76
Mozart, Wolfgang Amadeus
  Symphony No. 40 **35–36,** 51
  Symphony No. 41 **17**

Nancarrow, Conlon
  *Studies for Player Piano* 51

octachord, defined 81
octatonic scale 162–68, 170
order number, defined 178, 184
ostinato 40, 117–21

palindrome 222–23, 232, 234, 266
Penderecki, Krzysztof
    *Threnody for the Victims of
        Hiroshima* 288, 290
pentachord, defined 81
pentatonic scale 104, 116–21, 159
Perle, George
    *Serial Composition and Atonality* 144,
        218, 234, 255, 273
    "Symmetrical Formations in the
        String Quartets of Béla
        Bartók" 143
permutation
    and form 62
    and twelve-tone series 189–90
Persky, Stanley
    "A Discussion of Compositional
        Choices in Webern's op. 5, no.
        1" 144
phrasing
    and nontonal melodies 75, 191–95,
        209–12, 281–85
    and timbre 51–53
    and tonality 34–37
pitch-class 66, 76
pitch-class region 146–70
pitch-class set 81–91
    defined 81
    with identical interval content 133
    and inversion 113–14
    listing 107
    locating in pieces 89–90
    and motive 11, 88
    names 82
    relations among 108–34
    self-inverting 114
    and transposition 82–83, 87, 90, 100,
        110–13
    (see also diatonic scale, pentatonic
        scale, subset)
pitch names and numbers 12–13, 66–
    67, 76
polymeter 21–23, 31
polyphony 33, 42–43
precompositional, defined 191, 203

Rahn, John
    *Basic Atonal Theory* 107
Ravel, Maurice
    *Sonate* for violin and cello 144
register 33, 42–44
    and melodic structure 74
Reich, Steve
    *Drumming* 297
    *Music for Four Organs* 297
    *Music for Mallet Instruments, Voices,
        and Organ* 297
rhythm 15–32

and melodic structure 74–75
rhythmic motives 29–30, 32
serialized 26–69, 278–79, 280–85
Rochberg, George
    and tonality 296
    and twelve-tone music 277
rondo 163
rotation 241, 246, 252, 279–85

Schenker, Heinrich
    on Stravinsky's *Concerto for Piano and
        Winds* 151
Schoenberg, Arnold
    *Chamber Symphony*, op. 9 14, 46,
        **160–61**
    "Composition with Twelve
        Tones" 218
    *Erwartung*, op. 17 62
    *Five Pieces for Orchestra*, op. 16 53
    and form 62, 207
    *Fünf Klavierstücke*, op. 23 260, 273
    *Harmonielehre* 14
    *Ich darf nicht dankend*, op. 14, no.
        1 144
    *Klavierstück*, op. 33a 3, **10, 182–83,** 218
    *Ode to Napoleon*, op. 41 237, 254
    *Orchestral Variations*, op. 31 **216–17**
    *Phantasy*, op. 47 215, 218, 237
    *Piano Concerto*, op. 42 **186–87**
    *Pierrot lunaire*, op. 12 14, 46, 144
    "Problems of Harmony" 14
    *Serenade*, op. 24 **73,** 237, **257–60,**
        273
    *String Quartet No. 1*, op. 7 14
    *String Quartet No. 2*, op. 10 14
    *String Quartet No. 3*, op. 30 **86,
        204–5**
    *String Quartet No. 4*, op. 37 32, **37–
        39,** 54, 63, **68, 79, 176, 179,** 182,
        **192–93,** 207, **209–14,** 236
    *String Trio*, op. 45 215, 237
    style 195, 211–14
    *Three Pieces for Piano*, op. 11 14, 144
    *Tot*, op. 48 **132,** 208
    and twelve-tone music 173–74, 183,
        235–37, 277–79
    *Verklärte Nacht*, op. 4 14
Schwantner, Joseph 280
series of fifths 238
    and diatonic sets 147–49
series-form, defined 178, 184
Sessions, Roger
    and twelve-tone music 277–78
Sibelius, Jean
    *Symphony No. 2* 14
    *Symphony No. 4* 14
Skryabin, Alexander
    *Étude*, op. 65, no. 3 **94**
    *Poem of Ecstasy* 14
    *Preludes* 14
    *Prometheus* 14
Sollberger, Harvey
    *Riding the Wind* 290

sonata form 39, 57–60, 64, 127–31, 207
spacing 33
Spies, Claudio
  "On Stravinsky's *Abraham and Isaac*,"
    and "On Stravinsky's
    *Variations*" 254
Sprechstimme 46
Stockhausen, Karlheinz
  *Gesang der Jünglinge* 291
  *Klavierstücke XI* 295
  *Kontra-Punkte* 279
  and serialism 266, 269, 277, 285
Straus, Joseph
  "Recompositions by Schoenberg,
    Stravinsky, and Webern" 107
Stravinsky, Igor
  *Abraham and Isaac* **247–48,** 254
  *Canticum sacrum* **243–45,** 248, 254
  *Concerto for Piano and Winds* **150–
    51,** 245
  *The Fire Bird* 14
  and form 62
  *Greeting Prelude* **44,** 273
  *L'Histoire du Soldat* **19,** 20, **21,** 24, 40,
    46
  *In Memoriam Dylan Thomas* 273
  *Petrushka* 14, 20, 32, 46, 54, 64, **93,**
    101–2, **110, 125–27,** 131–32, 147,
    148, 245
  *The Rite of Spring* 14, 20, **26,** 40, 46,
    47, 54, 64, **78,** 171, 245
  *Septet,* 64, **261–63,** 273
  style, 126–27
  *Symphony of Psalms* 32, 54, 64, **166–
    67,** 171, 246
  *Three Pieces for String Quartet* 144
  and twelve-tone music 235, 242–51,
    277–78, 285
  *Variations: Aldous Huxley in
    Memoriam* **249–51,** 254
subset 114–21, 134

Taruskin, Richard
  "Chernomor to Kashchei . . . Stravin-
    sky's 'Angle'" 172
Tchaikovsky, Peter
  *Romeo and Juliet* **28,** 46
tempo 28–29, 31
tetrachord, defined 81
texture 33–43, 53, 166–68
  layered 23, 40–42, 53, 61–62, 243
  and pitch-bands 286–88
theme and variations 225–27, 250,
    256–58
timbre 33, 44–53, 288–95
time-point system 268–69, 271, 273
tonality
  dissolution of 6–7, 13–14, 159–61
  and form 34–37, 56
  functional 4–7, 296–97

  and motives 7–9
  and meter 16–18
  and nontonal melody 75
  and nontonal sets 116–21, 126–27,
    144, 150–53, 165–68, 237–38, 254
  and pitch-names 12
  and texture 34–37
transposition
  of pitch-class sets 82–83, 87, 90, 100,
    110–13, 134
  of rhythm series 266–69
  of twelve-tone series 177–78
Treitler, Leo
  "Harmonic Procedure in the *Fourth
    Quartet* of Béla Bartók" 143
trichord, defined 81
twelve-tone music 68
twelve-tone series, defined 175, 184

van den Toorn, Pieter
  *The Music of Igor Stravinsky* 172
Varèse, Edgard
  *Ionisation* 47, 64, 288
  *Octandre* **138–42,** 168

Wagner, Richard
  and orchestration 51
  *Das Rheingold* 47
  *Tristan und Isolde* **95**
Webern, Anton
  *Concerto for Nine Instruments,* op.
    24 **53, 95,** 103–4, 132, 219, **223,**
    228, 234
  and form 60–61
  *Movement for String Quartet,* op. 5, no.
    1 144
  *Movement for String Quartet,* op. 5, no.
    4 32, 48, 54, 61, 64, **89,** 102–3,
    **122–24,** 132, **137,** 144, 168
  orchestration of Bach's **Ricercare** 53,
    107
  *String Quartet,* op. 28 **43, 205–6,**
    **224–26,** 234
  style 122–24, 202, 221–28
  *Symphony,* op. 21 **80,** 234
  and twelve-tone music 183, 235,
    278
  *Variations for Piano,* op. 27 32, 54, 61,
    64, **198–202**
  *Wie bin ich froh!,* op. 25, no. 1 **187–
    88,** 207
Westergaard, Peter
  "Webern and Total
    Organization" 202
whole-tone scale 158–61, 170, 265
Wintle, Christopher
  "Babbitt's *Semi-Simple
    Variations*" 234, 268
Wuorinen, Charles
  *Simple Composition* 255

# DATE DUE

|  |  |  |  |
|--|--|--|--|
|  |  |  |  |
|  |  |  |  |
|  |  |  |  |
|  |  |  |  |
|  |  |  |  |
|  |  |  |  |
|  |  |  |  |
|  |  |  |  |
|  |  |  |  |
|  |  |  |  |
|  |  |  |  |
|  |  |  |  |
|  |  |  |  |
|  |  |  |  |
|  |  |  |  |
|  |  |  |  |
|  |  |  |  |